*The Pastoral Son and
the Spirit of Patriarchy*

NEW DIRECTIONS IN
ANTHROPOLOGICAL WRITING

History, Poetics, Cultural Criticism

GEORGE E. MARCUS
Rice University

JAMES CLIFFORD
University of California, Santa Cruz

EDITORS

Nationalism and the Politics of Culture
in Quebec
Richard Handler

The Pastoral Son and the Spirit
of Patriarchy: Religion, Society, and Person
among East African Stock Keepers
Michael E. Meeker

Belonging in America: Reading
Between the Lines
Constance Perin

The Pastoral Son and the Spirit of Patriarchy

Religion, Society, and Person among East African Stock Keepers

MICHAEL E. MEEKER

THE UNIVERSITY OF WISCONSIN PRESS

The University of Wisconsin Press
114 North Murray Street
Madison, Wisconsin 53715

The University of Wisconsin Press, Ltd.
1 Gower Street
London WC1E 6HA, England

Copyright © 1989
The Board of Regents of the University of Wisconsin System
All rights reserved

5 4 3 2 1

Printed in the United States of America

Meeker, Michael E.
 The pastoral son and the spirit of patriarchy: religion, society, and person among east African stock keepers / Michael E. Meeker.
  216 p.   cm. — (New directions in anthropological writing)
  Bibliography: pp. 185–190.
  Includes index.
  1. Ethnology—Africa, East. 2. Herders—Africa, East. 3. Cattle breeders—Africa, East. 4. Patriarchy—Africa, East. 5. Africa, East—Social life and customs. I. Title. II. Series.
GN658.M44   1989
306.3'49'09676—dc20   88-40438
ISBN 0-299-11740-5
ISBN 0-299-11744-8 (pbk.)

To my father and my mother

Contents

Figures and Maps   ix

Preface   xi

Acknowledgments   xvii

Note to the Reader   xix

1. Youths, Songs, and Personality Oxen   3

2. Elders, Creation Myths, and the Cosmic Patriarchal Spirit   29

3. The Multiplicity of Patriarchal Spirits and the Power of Cattle-Owning Fathers   49

4. The Nuer Warrior Identity and the Segmentary Principle   68

5. The Compromise of Patriarchal Authority and Nuer "Monotheism"   92

6. Authority and Individuality among Bantu-Speaking Cattle Herders   107

7. The Northern Somali Pastoralists: Cosmic Patriarchal Spirit, Segmentary Society, Poetry of Self and Other   131

8. Early Indo-Europeans: Socio-Cosmic Patriarchal Spirits, Community of Production, Divided Self   155

Notes   165

References   185

Index   191

Figures and Maps

FIGURES

1.1 The Genres of Dinka Songs as Self-Representations   27
4.1 An Idealized Genealogy of an Aristocratic Clan   81
4.2 Evans-Pritchard's Diagram of the Segmentary Principle   82
8.1 The Three Functions in Indo-Iranian Mythology   159

MAPS

4.1 The Spatial Relationships of Nuer and Dinka   69
6.1 Kingdoms of the Interlacustrine Region   108
7.1 East Cushitic Speakers in the Horn of Africa   132

Preface

This study is based on a reading of ethnographies, some of them classics, which describe traditions and institutions of African peoples who practiced an archaic mode of stock keeping. Together with the specific goals of my project explained below, I would also like to demonstrate that good ethnographies are valuable research documents, not only as assemblages of observed fact, but as interpretations of cultural forms and social meanings. In working on this project over the years, I have had in mind the criticism that cultural anthropologists are interested only in particulars and unwilling or unable to consider the significance of cross-cultural similarities and differences. I hope to have shown that the comparison of cultural forms, such as religious beliefs, social representations, and poetry composition, is not only possible, but especially suitable as an approach to certain aspects of social history.

There is a large ethnographic literature which describes the place of cattle in the traditions and institutions of the precolonial peoples and kingdoms of East Africa.[1] Addressing this impressive body of evidence, anthropologists have considered whether it might be possible to arrive at general conclusions about the social correlates of stock keeping among peoples who practice archaic modes of food production. While there have been many separate insights into different sides of this problem, no global picture which would indicate major types or processes has yet been achieved.

The present study does move toward such a global picture, but from a somewhat different perspective from that of comparative social anthropology. The study isolates the effects of stock keeping on masculine identity by a comparative method. It does not provide a systematic account of the similarities and differences in patterns of social life among East African stock keeping peoples. In this respect, the stance of the study is necessarily analytical rather than oriented toward categorizing and classifying social institutions.

The analytical stance of the study explains why most of the chapters are devoted to a comparison of small differences between two similar pastoral peoples, the Dinka and the Nuer. This procedure was necessary because slight differences between similar peoples can be more reliably attributed to specific causes. After arriving at an interactive model of masculine identity and pastoral experience in the initial chapters, a variety of stock-keeping peoples are considered, all of them very different from the Dinka and Nuer. Here again, the objective is to test and to extend the analysis of the effect of pastoralism on masculine identity and experience, not to arrive at a theory of the organization of stock-keeping societies. Accordingly, the examples of pastoral traditions and institutions that are examined in the final chapters have been selected to serve this analytical purpose, not because they are necessarily representative of major types of pastoral social organization.

The specific thesis of the study is that stock keeping is associated with an underlying psychological and institutional tension which is not typical of other forms of early food acquisition or production. This tension issues from a conflict which is built into a pastoral ecology: As an important food resource, stock keeping requires a high degree of cooperation and reciprocity. But as a form of wealth, stock serves as a vehicle for articulating individual autonomy and independence. Because of this conflict, pastoral traditions, which are otherwise variable, all feature strong concepts of authority at one level which are contradicted by strong concepts of individualism at another level. Tracing this effect of a pastoral ecology, I show how religion, society, and personal identity among stock keepers can be understood in terms of how this contradiction is resolved in a particular historical and environmental setting. In the study two basically different patterns are considered.

Among most East African cattle-herding peoples, the resolution of the contradiction between authority and individualism takes the form of reinforcing the position and authority of fathers and elders, if not chiefs and kings, while projecting contests and conflicts from inside to outside society. Where this pattern holds, religion is concerned with a multiplicity of patriarchal spirits and ghosts, patriarchal authority is a prominent feature of social organization, and personal identity is divided between dependency on intimate others and antagonism toward anonymous others.

In other instances, which are the exception rather than the rule among East African cattle herders, there is a very different pattern. This is where historical and ecological factors prevent the reinforcement of authority. In such a setting, religion is focused and centered on a monotheistic concept of God and man, social organization features a segmentary principle of solidarity and opposition, and the self is conceived as problematically related to both intimate and anonymous others. At the same time there is a fall in stature of beneficent and punitive patriarchal spirits and ghosts.

The first three chapters analyze Dinka traditions and institutions from the perspective of tension between patriarchal authority and filial individualism.

In chapter 1, the way in which the personal identity of the Dinka son is shaped by his relationship with his father is considered. The Dinka father is an impressive figure of authority who controls the fate and fortunes of his son, but the son, as he comes of age, would assert his autonomy and independence. In most contexts, the son acts only hesitantly, but in others, which are narrowly delimited, he acts more defiantly. After showing how this feature of the son-father relationship is a direct consequence of Dinka pastoral ecology, the songs composed and performed by Dinka youths are examined. Both the content and form of these songs, which can be described as *self-representations*, reflect the various dimensions of tension between patriarchal authority and filial individualism in Dinka experience. The principal ethnographic sources are the various studies of Dinka society and songs by F. M. Deng.

In chapter 2, the representations of Dinka fathers and elders are compared to the songs of Dinka sons. These representations are myths and hymns in which the "oneness" of a cosmic patriarchal spirit figures prominently. In these myths and hymns, a cosmic patriarchal spirit stands opposed to the very form of "self" that appears in the songs of the Dinka son. The conclusion is that tension in the son-father relationship, as it is affected by Dinka pastoral ecology, lies behind religious representations of a cosmic patriarchal spirit just as it lies behind the secular representations of individuality.

In chapter 3, another side of Dinka religion is considered, one that is not altogether compatible with belief in the oneness of a cosmic patriarchal spirit. This second side of Dinka religion is linked with the considerable spiritual and material power of cattle-owning patriarchs, rather than with tension in the son-father relationship. Among the Dinka, most individuals are not the masters of their own fates, but are in various ways subject to the favor of a cattle-owning patriarch for most of their lives. As a consequence of this, sentiments about personal or collective welfare tend to be symbolized by a multiplicity of patriarchal spirits, which are associated with different social contexts and respected in various ways. Since this second side of Dinka religion is the more usual form of religiosity among East African cattle herders, the conclusion is that Dinka religion is a "mixed case" which has been partly, but not decisively, influenced by tension in the son-father relationship. The principal ethnographic sources for chapters 2 and 3 are Godfrey Lienhardt's ethnography of Dinka religion.

The next two chapters consist of a controlled comparison of the pastoral traditions and institutions of the Nuer and Dinka, two neighboring cattle-herding peoples who are very similar to one another, save in certain narrow respects.

In chapter 4, the differences between Nuer and Dinka traditions and institutions are analyzed in terms of the different emphasis on cattle raiding.

Among the Nuer, cattle raiding is correlated with the compromise of patriarchal authority. This is because access to cattle through stealth and force diminishes the importance of the father's herds as bridewealth and inheritance. The compromise of patriarchal authority among the Nuer is shown to be correlated with the prominence of an antagonistic and oppositional concept of person and collectivity. However, this prominence does not diminish, but rather enhances, the necessity for cooperation and reciprocity among the Nuer. As a consequence, the principle of sociability is just as important a feature of Nuer social relations as the principle of antagonism and opposition. The result is that Nuer representations of their social organization tend to feature a *segmentary principle* whereby groups and individuals alternately join with and divide against one another. In effect, tension between father and son among the Dinka has taken the form of a problematical relationship of self and other in Nuer thinking and experience.

In chapter 5, Nuer religion is compared with Dinka religion. The differences between the two are shown to be closely correlated with the compromise of patriarchal authority which follows from the greater emphasis on cattle raiding among the Nuer. Because of the prominence of antagonism and opposition among a people for whom cooperation and reciprocity are a necessity, the oneness of a cosmic patriarchal spirit comes forward as the focus and center of Nuer religiosity. Consequently, the side of Dinka religion that was related to tension in the son-father relationship is more prominent among the Nuer, while the side of Dinka religion that was related to the spiritual and material powers of fathers is less prominent. The principal ethnographic sources for chapters 5 and 6 are Evans-Pritchard's studies of Nuer politics, ecology, and religion.

The remaining chapters test the conclusions reached in the initial chapters by applying them to examples of East African and Old World stock keepers.

In chapter 6, examples of Bantu-speaking, cattle-herding peoples are reviewed in order to determine why neither the problematical relationship of self and other nor the oneness of a cosmic patriarchal spirit are prominent among such peoples. This review demonstrates that the two effects of a stock-keeping ecology, the enhancement of authority and the enhancement of individualism, are very much at work among Bantu-speaking cattle herders; however, they do not have the same implications as among the Dinka and Nuer. The social systems of the Bantu speakers took shape in a setting of forest dwelling, mixed farming and herding, rather than in a setting of grasslands pastoralism. This different historical background is correlated with more developed institutions of political authority and social rank than were typical of acephalous grasslands pastoralists like the Dinka and Nuer. As a consequence, it is usually the case among

Bantu-speaking cattle herders that strong chiefdoms and kingdoms regulated or restricted contests and conflicts over pastoral resources. There is, then, no compromise of patriarchal authority among these people. Instead, an antagonistic and oppositional individualism is projected from inside to outside society, sometimes in the form of organized military force aimed at expansion and conquest. Chapter 6 is based on a variety of ethnographic sources.

In the two remaining chapters, I hypothesize that the constellation of forces revealed by the controlled comparison of the Dinka and the Nuer were also part of the experience of Old World stock-keeping peoples.

In chapter 7, the pastoral traditions of the northern Somalis are examined. The northern Somalis are an arid-land, camel-herding people in the Horn of Africa who at the turn of the century had been in contact with Old World religious, political, and economic systems for about a millennium. Upon examining the implications of arid-land pastoralism and the use of horses in stock raiding, it appears that the compromise of patriarchal authority is an especially prominent feature of Somali pastoral traditions. So the factor that differentiates the Nuer from the Dinka is characteristic of the Somali, but it is intensified by an arid-land pastoral ecology and by an Old World military instrument. Accordingly, the oneness of a cosmic patriarchal spirit, a segmentary principle of social organization, the problematical relationship of self and other, and the fall in stature of patriarchal spirits and ghosts are prominent features of turn-of-the-century Somali society. The principal ethnographic sources here are I. M. Lewis and Said S. Samatar.

In chapter 8, the question of whether early Indo-European traditions feature the "effect" of a pastoral ecology is raised. Prehistorians have compared Nilotic cattle herders, like the Dinka, Nuer, and Maasai, to early Indo-European cattle herders. In particular, Lincoln has shown that early Indo-Iranian myths and rites feature an opposition between cattle-sacrificing priests and cattle-raiding warriors in the same way as the myths and rites of Nilotic cattle herders. The direct analogy of Nilotic and early Indo-European cattle herders is evaluated in terms of the conclusions of previous chapters. To do so, Georges Dumézil's theory of the *tripartite ideology* of early Indo-European religion is considered. The tripartite ideology features an opposition of authority and individualism in terms consistent with the effect of a pastoral ecology, but the form which this opposition takes is closer to the configuration of tradition and ecology among Bantu-speaking cattle herders than among Nilo-Hamitic-speaking cattle herders.

The design of the study owes something to Weber's comparative analysis of the relationship of religious belief and economic action among early Protestants. In fact, one of my conclusions might be seen as a qualifying footnote to Weber's view of the origins of monotheism. For Weber, monotheism was unique among the theodicies of world religion because it was the result of an attempt to resolve the problem of religious meaning from a standpoint of rigorous logical consistency. In this respect, he saw the doctrine of predestination as the completion of a project which had been initiated by the Hebrew prophets. Weber is perhaps correct in believing that Calvin approached a monotheistic theodicy from the standpoint of rigorous logical consistency, but the origins of such a theodicy lie as much in sentiment and emotion as in logic. This is demonstrated by the place of an opposition of monotheism and individualism in the experiences of certain stock-keeping peoples. There was, then, a profound difference between Calvin and the Hebrew prophets. Unlike the former, the latter were not so much ruthless religious rationalists as eloquent spokesmen of a form of religiosity that figured prominently in the intuitions and experiences of early Middle Eastern peoples.

Acknowledgments

I would like to express my appreciation to faculty, students, and staff at the University of California, San Diego, who have always been a patient and attentive audience in the course of several revisions of my project. In particular I would like to thank F. G. Bailey, Paul Dresch, Melford Spiro, and Marc Swartz, who took the time to read previous drafts of the present book. They provided useful advice and strong criticisms which helped me strengthen my argument. I would like to thank Roy D'Andrade, Robert Levy, and Don Tuzin for listening to me think through my ideas over the years. I am indebted to Kathleen Barlow and David Lipset, who patiently answered my questions about a society unaffected by a pastoral tradition. Thanks are also due to the University of Wisconsin Press readers who helped me to make cuts in a manuscript which had become large and unwieldy. Special thanks are also due to Robert Levy and Marc Swartz, who provided unstinting support and encouragement at those times when the end seemed not to be in sight. I am grateful to the staff of the Department of Anthropology, Kae Knight, J. C. Krause, and David Marlowe for their readiness to be of help. Very special thanks are due to Marian Payne for many services and for seeing this project through while I was out of the country. Finally, I would like to thank my wife and daughters, who have patiently endured my absorption in the problems of this study for several years. When the spell was broken, they were always willing to welcome me back from my intellectual sojourns.

Istanbul
12 January 1988

Note to the Reader

The present tense is often used to refer to social conditions which prevailed at the time of ethnographic observation or just before the imposition of colonial authority. The usage should be clear from the context.

The orthography of non-English words generally follows that of the quoted source.

*The Pastoral Son and
the Spirit of Patriarchy*

1
Youths, Songs, and Personality Oxen

THE RELATIONSHIP OF PERSON TO SOCIETY AMONG THE DINKA

Until recently, the way of life of the Dinka was based on primitive forms of farming, fishing, and herding, each of which made a substantial contribution to the food supply. Lienhardt's (1961:5–10) account of Dinka subsistence activities during the 1950s mentions the following phases of a yearly cycle: When the wet season begins in March and April, most of the Dinka are in their permanent homesteads planting crops of millet. Some weeks later, when the rainy season is at its height, young men take the herds to pasture in savanna forests where they form cattle camps. Eventually, as the rivers and streams rise and much of the land floods, the cattle herders gather into larger camps away from their homesteads. By October, when the rains come to an end, the herders begin to return to their homesteads to help with the harvest and to pasture their animals on the millet leaves and stalks. At this time, beer is brewed and fishing is possible. In January, when the floods have receded and the grass near their homesteads has withered, all the people then move toward the rivers where they establish temporary shelters.

Although Dinka subsistence was based on a combination of farming, fishing, and herding, they considered themselves a herding people, not a farming or fishing people (Kelly 1985:47–49, 94–99). Furthermore, cattle, not millet or fish, figured most prominently in Dinka personal identity, family system, kinship and marriage, political organization, and religion (Lienhardt 1961:10–27). In this respect, cattle had a significance for the Dinka that transcended their relative importance in the food supply. Why was this so? Why should cattle have been such a prominent dimension of social relations when farming, fishing, and herding all made an important contribution to subsistence?

4   Youths, Songs, and Personality Oxen

In the following chapters, I demonstrate how Dinka pastoralism is a subsistence technique that intensifies a question about the relationship of person to society. As an important food resource, cattle require a high degree of cooperation and reciprocity. But as a form of wealth, cattle serve as a vehicle for articulating individual autonomy and independence. The prominence of cattle in Dinka cultural traditions and social institutions follows from these two contradictory features of a pastoral way of life.

It is men, more than women, who find in cattle a symbol of their personal autonomy and independence, and it is the relationships of men with others, more than the relationships of women with others, that are unsettled by this feature of a cattle-herding way of life. This is apparent from the situation of the young man who is coming of age. At this time, a man is granted his first opportunities to see cattle as a vehicle for expressing his personal identity, even as he also becomes subject to the authority of his father and other elders who would place strict limits on the extent to which he might exploit these opportunities.

These matters have been discussed by F. M. Deng, an ethnographer of his own people, in studies of Dinka social organization and oral tradition (see especially Deng 1973; also Deng 1971, 1972). Deng's account of two sides of Dinka experience involves an ethic of sociability and expressions of individuality. While these two sides are a significant aspect of the experience of all the Dinka, young and old, male and female, they are an especially prominent feature of the life situation of the young man who is no longer a child, but not yet an elder.

AN ETHIC OF SOCIABILITY AND EXPRESSIONS OF INDIVIDUALITY

According to Deng, a basic ethical principle of the Dinka, as denoted by the term *cieng*, requires that individual interests should be set aside in favor of sharing, harmony, respect, and loyalty. Translating *cieng* as "good human relations" or "sociability," Deng (1973) observes that it requires

> more than avoidance of conflict and violation of other people's rights; it imposes an obligation to foster a solidarity in which people co-operate in shaping and sharing values. (15)

Deng goes on to illustrate the many ways in which the Dinka individual is subject to social controls and constraints that require him or her to obey elders and to get along with peers. However, at one point he indicates that the Dinka principle of *cieng* is only one of two sides of Dinka experience. This is where he explains the masculine qualities denoted by the term *dheeng*.

Deng first glosses *dheeng* as "gentlemanliness" and illustrates how it is a standard of masculine behavior governed by and consistent with *cieng*. But then he provides a different account of *dheeng*, revealing that it is a complex concept in which qualities of individuality are melded together with qualities of sociability. In some contexts, *dheeng* designates personal manners and expressions and touches upon personal honor, dignity, and pride. As in the case of any good ethnography, Deng's description reveals more than the points it was intended to illustrate:

> Honour, dignity, and inner pride as well as their outward appearance and bearing are part of what the Dinka call *dheeng*, which has many meanings. Singing, as an expression of one's personality, is *dheeng*. Initiation ceremonies, celebration of marriages, the decoration of "personality oxen," dancing, indeed any personal demonstration of an aesthetic or sensuous quality is considered *dheeng*. The way a man walks, runs, talks, eats, or dresses expresses his *dheeng*. As a noun, *dheeng* means such things as dignity, beauty, nobility, handsomeness, elegance, charm, grace, gentleness, richness, hospitality, generosity, and kindness. The adjectival form of the word is *adheng*, which may also be used as a noun, and is often used to mean a "gentleman." (16)

The Dinka notion of "gentlemanliness" (*dheeng*) cannot be altogether collapsed into the notion of "sociability" (*cieng*). The former clearly lends a value to individual character and personality, even though the latter obliges a man to sacrifice personal desires and feelings in the interest of "good human relations."

Of the examples that Deng gives of the individualistic side of "gentlemanliness," those referring specifically to the activities of young men coming of age have a prominent place. Around the age of sixteen or eighteen, a young man endures a painful initiation rite, becomes a member of an age-set, and assumes the status and performs the role of a warrior. At this time, he begins to enjoy a leisure that is not the privilege of boys who are obliged to herd and milk cattle. This leisure includes flirtations and romances with young women, the performance of songs and dances before others, and adventures with members of his age-set who provoke and challenge other groups (42).

Even though the Dinka youth assumes a new identity, acquires a new freedom, displays his talents before others, and engages in exciting projects with his peers, he remains subject to rigid social controls and constraints. Adolescence is then an occasion when personal ambitions and energies are in tension with the ethical principle of "good human relations" (*cieng*). This conflict is in various ways closely associated with the admiration and adoration of cattle, a special characteristic of the life situation of young men.

At the time of his initiation, the father of a youth gives him a special ox of his own, one that has been styled a *personality ox* by ethnographers. The youth takes an ox-color name from this animal as well as other names

6 Youths, Songs, and Personality Oxen

which are metaphors of his ox-color name. He prepares and grooms his ox so that it has a pleasing appearance, training its horns in a distinctive way, sharpening them to a point, and decorating them with tassels. He composes songs in praise of his ox and performs them before others.

It is in his songs that a young man is able to make the most explicit references to his own individuality:

> Dinka songs are remarkable in that they freely reveal things which are not normally spoken of. Such affairs as a man's sexual experience, or his observations of other people's sexual activities, are normally discussed only in the most intimate circles. The language of courtship is indirect, and rich with parables, sayings, and metaphors. Yet in songs one discusses a sexual experience with surprising candour and with no feeling of embarrassment. In everyday life, it is almost unheard of for a man to speak of his riches, praise himself, his father, or his lineage. Yet in songs it is often done and even exaggerated. Equivalent to this is the degree of freedom to complain without inviting conflict. Normally, a son very rarely criticizes his father, but in songs, even when a father has not neglected his paternal duties, a son will criticize him by alleging his father's failure to respond to his demands, and the father, far from being provoked, will attend to the son's request with enthusiasm. (Deng 1973:87)

In songs, which he both composes and performs, the youth portrays personal feelings, glorifies personal attributes, and lodges personal complaints against others. In these respects, his songs take the form of a self-representation.

It is remarkable that an art form of self-representation is to be found among a people who otherwise insist on "attuning of individual interests to the interests of others" (15). Still, because the songs in praise of cattle are one of the few permissible contexts in which vigorous expressions of individuality are acceptable, they also illustrate that self-representation is narrowly restricted among the Dinka. The youth is permitted to make a strong statement of his own personal identity only on the occasion of a stylized performance and only by means of a formalized mode of expression.

Songs in praise of cattle are not the preoccupation of all the Dinka. Apart from a few older specialists, this kind of singing is primarily the activity of adolescent males. This means that songs, as a privileged context for self-representation, must reflect some feature of the life situation of young men. Deng's study of the place of songs in Dinka society provides an analysis of this life situation.

THE RELATIONSHIP OF ADOLESCENCE, SINGING, AND CATTLE

According to Deng (1973), personality oxen and the singing of songs are social devices for sublimating adolescent energies that are in conflict with social controls and constraints:

Since young men are the most aggressive and disposed to violate the norms of society as defined by elders, they particularly use the peaceful outlet for dissatisfaction which I have already discussed as the function of songs. Furthermore, much of their vitality, which is potentially destructive to the system which subordinates them, is sublimated in their preoccupation with cattle, and the creativity centring around them. In particular, much of their potential aggressiveness and violence is satisfied through the bulls with which they identify. Young men sharpen the horns of their bulls and oxen, and while the castrated bulls, that is, oxen, are pivotal in the aesthetics of cattle and symbolize the opposite qualities of gentleness and submissiveness on the one hand and aggressiveness and physical courage on the other, all of which represent the personality traits of young men, they are praised mainly for their aggressiveness and physical courage even as men superficially criticize them. That oxen, though castrated, occupy such a highly important place among cattle sufficiently symbolizes the position of young men who, though subordinated to their elders, have a very high aesthetic value and gain satisfaction from the recognition of this in songs. (82)

The Dinka male adolescent, perhaps a little like male adolescents everywhere, would rebel against convention and authority but is prevented from doing so. This predicament, according to Deng, is eased by a social device. His father gives the young man an ox in which he is able to discover an image of himself. The ox itself, a beast of enormous strength that has been castrated by its owner, reflects the ambiguous position of the youth who would assert himself but remains inhibited by the authority of elders. The young man admires and adores his ox because he is in fact able to identify himself with the ox.

Deng makes an important point when he notes that a young man's preoccupation with cattle reflects his ambiguous position in society. But one might question whether this preoccupation is properly described as a "sublimation" of adolescent vitality that cannot be directly expressed. Deng demonstrates that the young man's personality ox is a vehicle for representing not only his "gentleness and submissiveness" but also his "aggressiveness and physical courage." In this respect, these representations themselves feature the tension between sociability and individuality that we have seen in the Dinka concepts of *cieng* and *dheeng*. This means that the personality ox is not so much a social device that provides for the sublimation of forbidden energies as a vehicle for self-representation that brings into focus and gives a particular meaning to adolescent vitality. The Dinka youth portrays himself as someone who would be part of society and accept convention and authority, but at the same time he also portrays himself as someone who would assert himself before others, resisting or criticizing the demands they place upon him. Rather than sublimating an adolescent vitality that conflicts with social morality, the youth's preoccupation with cattle expresses this very conflict.

This point would be of little consequence, a quibble with Deng's passing ethnographic observations, were it not that the young man's emotional involvement with his ox is of greater significance than an adolescent episode. As Deng notes, the young man's ox "stands as a symbol for [its] owner and his social status" (97). However, the way in which the personality ox represents a young man's personal identity and social status is but one example of such a relationship between men and cattle among the Dinka. The young man's father, who has presented his son with the ox, is himself a cattle owner, cattle exchanger, and cattle sacrificer, that is, someone for whom cattle "stand as a symbol of their owner and his social status," to paraphrase Deng. In other words, the Dinka adult, like the Dinka youth, represents his person through a relationship with cattle. The difference is that the adult does so through actually controlling and managing cattle while the youth does so merely through adoring and admiring them.

The similarity between father and son, with regard to their relationship with cattle, suggests that the youth is in effect imitating the father, insofar as it is in his power to do so. While waiting to become a cattle owner in his own right, the son is granted a palliative by his father, a personality ox. The young man is by virtue of this gift not a real cattle owner even of this very ox, since his father retains the right to take it back or to give it away. Still, the youth is able to play or act out his aspirations. Given the proper occasion, the young man composes and performs songs in the praise of his ox, making direct and indirect references to his own individuality. The young man imagines — just as his father realizes — personal power and will through cattle.

The young man's devotion to his ox is only superficially a result of a parallel between his life situation and the castrated ox, as Deng and other ethnographers have suggested.[1] More fundamentally, it is a consequence of the important place of cattle in the articulation of Dinka masculine identity. Among the Dinka, adult men gain a sense of their personal autonomy and independence as a consequence of their prerogatives over an object on which the security and welfare of all the Dinka are dependent. The Dinka adolescent does not, in caring for his ox and singing praises of his ox, "identify" with this animal, but rather with his cattle-owning father, whose figure lurks behind the son's representation of himself through praises of an ox.[2]

There is, however, an important difference between the son's and the father's relationship with cattle even though the former is striving to imitate the latter:

Control of wealth and the productive exploitation of resources rest with the elders. Adults share something of the adoration for cattle, but they do not share the *obsessions* [my italics] of youth even though they sanction them. It is through [elders] that cattle and other forms of livestock are acquired. It is they who sacrifice them, slaughter them, sell them, barter with them, pay them in marriage, and give them away in many other ways. (Deng 1972:105)

The relationship of an older man to cattle is one of self-assertion through their control and management, a rational instrumental practice. The relationship of a younger man to cattle is, in contrast, one of self-representation through an "obsessive" adoration and admiration of an object that he might one day, but does not yet, control and manage.

For the youth, whose ownership of cattle is temporarily blocked, but eventually anticipated, a sense of self is expressed through an obsessively figural rather than a rationally instrumental relationship with cattle. Because the adolescent remains dependent on his cattle-owning father, his personal autonomy and independence can be symbolized only by his relationship with his personality ox. His ox is only a figural, rather than a material, resource. That is, the son's songs are representations of a desire that is forbidden as a practice.

Because the young man's songs are a figural rather than a material exploitation of his ox, their value is ambiguous for the Dinka. They are not considered counterfeit and frivolous, but neither are they considered genuine and substantial. This ambiguity is reflected by a somewhat confusing, but nonetheless revealing, distinction that Deng (1973) makes between true "gentlemanliness" (*dheeng*) and false "gentlemanliness" (*alueeth*) as a quality of young men's songs and dances:

A man is referred to as *alueeth* (liar), though in a less derogatory sense than the word normally indicates, if he is not particularly good at singing or dancing, or is not especially handsome or wealthy or objectively distinguished as an *adheng*, but puts on an impressive show of being a good singer or dancer, bears himself as though physically attractive, exaggerates his hospitality as though wealthy, or acts in an excessive manner in any area where *dheeng* is involved. At the same time, a man who is distinguished in singing, dancing, or in any aesthetic field, and acts as though aware and proud of his distinction, is also referred to as *alueeth*. Every young man and woman is considered an *alueeth* by virtue of preoccupation with aesthetic values, and such an evaluation is not really a criticism to the Dinka. (83-84)

There is a difference between the figures of men who are truly "gentlemanly" (*adheng*) and those who are only accomplished "liars" (*alueeth*). And yet, as Deng adds somewhat contradictorily, all young men (and young women as well) are "liars" (*alueeth*) by virtue of their preoccupation with esthetic values, which are, as Deng has already told us, an important dimension of "gentlemanliness" (*dheeng*). This contradiction arises because the self-representations of youths are basically similar to those of cattle-owning fathers, except that their substance, the ownership, exchange, and sacrifice of cattle, is lacking. The songs of youths are then ambiguously very "true" and yet "lies."

FATHERS AND SONS AMONG THE DINKA

If, in fact, the young man's decoration, parading, and praising of his personality ox are inspired by his desire to be like his cattle-owning father, the precise character of this man that the son is seeking to emulate must be determined.

Among a people like the Dinka, for whom food is itself a major form of social wealth, those individuals who own cattle have in their hands an object on which the security and welfare of others is dependent. The "cattle-owning patriarch," as Deng appropriately calls the Dinka father, is therefore an impressive figure of authority who is respected and obeyed by other family members.

But is it correct to say that the father's authority is derived from his "ownership" of cattle wealth as a form of capital or property, as we understand these things in modern society? Given the special features of cattle herding among a people like the Dinka, one might object that it may not be correct to speak of the "ownership" of cattle. Cattle, as a food resource, cannot be monopolized by a few individuals at the expense of the majority of Dinka. Rather, they are more or less at the disposal of all the members of a homestead.[3] Furthermore, cattle are not hoarded by single individuals, but are constantly circulated as part of a social process, one that involves the communication, cooperation, and solidarity of groups (Deng 1971:273-74, 1972:105-6). Since cattle are not monopolized or hoarded but freely used and constantly circulating, they are not really owned in the same way that capital and property are owned. And if cattle are not really owned, they cannot be the basis of direct power over others. They are a social usufruct and a social currency that must be shared and exchanged. The character of Dinka cattle wealth affirms that the Dinka individual is embedded in a web of social responsibilities and obligations. Therefore, it is not possible for the father to assert his authority over others through his rights to cattle.

Deng's ethnography makes it clear, however, that these objections to applying the term "ownership" to rights in cattle among the Dinka are not sustainable. Dinka patriarchs play a large role in determining when cattle circulate and for what purposes they circulate, even if their decisions are subject to many kinds of pressures. Though cattle among the Dinka are not exactly like capital and property in our own society, they are nonetheless controlled and managed by specific individuals who can be said to "own" them as their personal capital or property (Deng 1971:241–65). Deng (1971) writes:

Whereas rights in land are more communal in nature, ownership of cattle is more personal. Such ownership is vested in the head of the family, subject to the use of family members. Cattle are allocated by him according to the seniority of the houses. Within a house, cattle are redivided among the individual wives, but needs of individuals are provided for by whoever can afford to meet them. Any cattle that are not allocated by the head of the household are collective property of the family. The sons of each house inherit from their father the cattle under their control. While the father is alive, neither the wives nor the children can dispose of cattle without his consent. (273)

The patriarch owns the cattle of the family, not by limiting usufructuary access to them, but only by determining their circulation and distribution. Nevertheless, his control over cattle expresses his personal authority over others, even if it is sharply delimited by his social responsibilities and obligations.

Consequently, Dinka cattle-owning patriarchs do have an impressive power over other individuals, even though cattle are constantly circulating, and this power impinges most directly on youths through the institutions of bridewealth and inheritance.

The preeminent occasion of cattle exchanges is the payment of cattle as bridewealth. On the occasion of a marriage, the groom's group is obliged to transfer, on average, twenty-five or thirty head of cattle—and sometimes as many as one hundred or two hundred head—to the bride's group.

While cattle should serve a common interest, their normal control is less widely shared and is vested in a few. The right to such control is determined by one's position in the kinship values. Since adult males are charged with the payment of bridewealth, they are pivotal in the control of cattle. But it is a chicken-and-egg riddle as to which one comes first: responsibility for payment or [adult] male dominance. (Deng 1972:106)

Since marriage requires cattle to be given by the groom's side to the bride's side, a father is likely to be far more reticent to marry a son than to marry a daughter. Accordingly, a young man must often bide his time for some years before his father agrees to assemble the cattle for bridewealth. Furthermore, the willingness or unwillingness of a father to furnish bridewealth affects a young man quite differently than a young woman. The payment of cattle as bridewealth is only one of many institutions by which men control the fate of women, but it is one of the crucial institutions by which older men retard or advance the fortunes of younger men.[4] When a woman marries, she is not free of the problem of masculine dominance. One male is succeeded by another; father is replaced by husband. But for the young man the situation is different. Upon marriage, the young man takes a step toward freeing himself of his own father and becoming himself a father of sons, that is, toward becoming a patriarch like his father. The institution of bridewealth thus places the fate of the young man in the hands of male elders who arrange cattle exchanges.

The transfer of rights to cattle by inheritance also affects young men more directly than young women, since the former, but not the latter, are their father's heirs. For the young man, the possibility of inheriting a father's cattle before or after his death is an avenue of escape from subjection to paternal authority, but here too the young man must typically bide his time for many years. Sometimes a father will provide a son with cattle before his death, but frequently an inheritance is postponed (Deng 1971:35-38, 245, 273-74). When this is the case, the young man will be dependent on his father's brothers to give him his due, and they are likely to be even more reluctant than a father to provide it.

In awaiting his inheritance, whether before or after his father's death, a young man has a profound experience of the difference between his own interests and those of other men with whom he is in direct competition, his brothers and half brothers. Cattle paid as bridewealth for their marriages and cattle set aside for their inheritances are subtracted from the common patriarchal herd. So the young man has not only many years during which he might both admire and envy the power of his cattle-owning father, but also much time to reflect on how his rights to cattle are in conflict with those of other men.

TENSION IN THE SON-FATHER RELATIONSHIP

Among the pastoral Dinka, a ruling father whose personal autonomy and independence are expressed by virtue of his ownership of cattle has as his subject a son whose own personal autonomy and independence are conditional upon his acquisition of cattle. The power and will of an adult are therefore opposed to the ambition and energy of a youth.

Given that a desire for personal autonomy and independence is both fostered and blocked by patriarchal example, one would expect that the son-father relationship would be marked by tension, perhaps even by an undercurrent of the "aggressiveness and violence" that Deng observes in the behavior and attitudes of young men.[5] In fact, the son-father relationship among the Dinka has features that are at least reminiscent of the psychoanalytic concept of Oedipal conflict. Describing the relationship of father and child, Deng (1971) writes:

In father-child relationships, the father wields familial authority by threatening severe deprivations. In the case of younger children, corporal punishment is employed. Where children are older, other punitive measures, divine or secular, are imposed. The Dinka link the father's power with his permanent identity and influence, particularly in his capacity as the procreator. A wronged father or a senior relative will pat his belly with the words "child of my belly" to justify his claim to authority. (35)

The Dinka father, who as cattle owner holds the security and future of the family in his hands, can also be a punitive and depriving disciplinarian, resorting to both physical and spiritual sanctions. Beyond this, the Dinka father claims to be the very origin of the child's person by virtue of his procreative powers. Thus the youth's experience of a father who refuses to advance the son's position in society may well be preceded by the child's experience of the father as stern disciplinarian who asserts his sexual prerogatives.

Despite the impressive power of the cattle-owning father who sometimes punishes, curses, and belittles, the son may well contemplate competing with or even replacing his father, not only as cattle owner, but also as wife possessor and child procreator:

Although he is a protector, the father is also an impediment to the son's value position, which depends largely on the father. On his side, too, the father is threatened by the son, who is his successor. It is the son who will inherit the father's young wives and beget his half-brothers for the lineage. This is often a threat *inter vivos*, for as the father ages, his fear that young wives will be attracted to his sons increases. Adultery by sons, though a serious offense, does occur. (125)

There are, then, at least hints of both sides of the Oedipal relationship among the Dinka: a father jealously safeguarding his monopoly of wives, children, and wealth and a son enviously contemplating their usurpation.[6]

Tension in the Dinka son-father relationship, it can be concluded, is magnified by cattle as a form of social wealth that can be individually managed and controlled. At the same time, another feature of cattle herding, described below, makes tension in the son-father relationship even more crucial as a feature of Dinka traditions and institutions.

So far, the Dinka father has been considered as a potential key to an understanding of the Dinka son. This approach assumes that the situation of the son is unilaterally determined by the situation of the father, implying, in effect, that the Dinka father figure is primary and original while the Dinka son figure is secondary and derivative. But the father figure is as much determined by the son figure as *vice versa*.

Youths, Songs, and Personality Oxen

THE SPONSORSHIP OF CATTLE-WARRING YOUTHS BY CATTLE-OWNING ELDERS

Cattle herding among a people like the Dinka involves a paradox. On the one hand, it reinforces the authority of cattle-owning patriarchs, making them powerful figures of authority in Dinka society. On the other hand, the vulnerability of stock to confiscation makes cattle-owning patriarchs dependent on the vitality of warrior youths who would protect and defend this important resource.

As a consequence of this, the Dinka elders go to some lengths, not just to allow, but to instill the qualities of the warrior in young men. They do so primarily through initiation rites that constitute a group of young men as an age-set. Taking boys who are dependent on and attached to their families, elders change them into youths who are self-assertively aggressive and courageous. After their initiation, young men are henceforth warriors who on specific occasions take pride in their ability to antagonize and oppose others. With the members of their age-set, they engage in symbolic challenges and fights with young men who were initiated before them, and when away from father and elder in the territory of other Dinka or non-Dinka, they also engage in actual raiding and warfare with other young men.

While Deng provides an account of Dinka initiation rites and age-set formations, he does not analyze how the "militaristic" side of these institutions is connected with Dinka pastoral ecology.[7] This is probably because he felt it unnecessary to insist on such a commonplace ethnographic fact. Sixty years ago, Herskovits (1926) published the first systematic demonstration of the correlation of pastoral ecology with military organization among East African cattle herders.[8] A little later, in his well-known monograph on politics and ecology among the Nuer, Evans-Pritchard (1940) gave a simple explanation for this correlation:

> Cattle are a form of wealth that not only lasts a long time and reproduces itself, but is, also, easily seized and transported. Furthermore, it enables invaders to live on the country without commissariat. Crops and dwellings can be destroyed, but cattle can be confiscated and taken home. This quality, which has given pastoral peoples a bias in favour of the arts of war rather than the arts of peace, has meant that the Nuer are not entirely dependent on their own cattle, but can augment their herds . . . by raiding; a condition that has shaped their character, economy, and political structure. (50)

More recently, Maquet (1972) has reiterated Evans-Pritchard's explanation, generalizing it in such a way that it applies not only to a preeminent cattle-raiding and cattle-warring people like the Nuer but to pastoralists all over East Africa, from the Sudan to the Cape:

This valuable and movable property [cattle] may be easily lost and easily acquired. A pastoral society without means of defense would run a strong risk of being completely dispossessed. Farmers' harvests may also be taken by force and granaries may be robbed, but this booty consisting of consumer goods is less attractive than capital in the form of cattle. Thus it is not surprising that military organizations should be developed in pastoral societies, especially as pastoralists, less compelled to spend their whole time producing the necessities of daily living, have more leisure to train themselves in the profession of war and to practise all the activities associated with it: war dances, making of equipment, memorization and reciting of war poems. (121)

This general feature of cattle herding, the necessity that young men specialize in the arts of war, is another essential dimension of the son-father relationship among the Dinka. Elders are obliged to instill and encourage the aggressive and violent side of young men, preparing them, as Deng (1973) puts it, for the "warring period ahead" (185). Primarily through the institutions of initiation rites and age-set formations, young men's sentiments of antagonism and opposition to others are not only intensified but directly linked with protecting or expropriating pastoral resources: cattle, pasture, and water. The self-assertion of youths is an important side of Dinka pastoral ecology.

The father's impulse to assert himself through the control of cattle is decisively shaped by this dimension of the adolescent life situation in at least two ways. First, the insistence of Dinka fathers on the submission and obedience of sons is intensified by the prominent place of hostile self-assertion in adolescent experience. These activities of youths are closely supervised and narrowly restricted to specific contexts by fathers. Second, the father has himself at one time been a son and as a youth had significant experiences of antagonism and opposition to others. Consequently, he rules his son in terms of an assertion of his own personal power and will, the very qualities that were in question during his own youth.

In effect, then, a son figure determines a father figure just as much as a father figure determines a son figure. Or rather, neither the father nor the son, but the relationship of the two, as it is affected by cattle wealth, is the crucial feature of Dinka pastoral traditions and institutions.

DINKA SONG GENRES

This section reviews the genres of Dinka songs as described by F. M. Deng, considering in some instances excerpts from songs that he has translated. The review confirms the correlation of self-representation with tension in the son-father relationship and illustrates how these matters are linked with initiation rites, age-set formations, and the warrior identity.

16 *Youths, Songs, and Personality Oxen*

In his ethnography of Dinka songs, Deng (1973) describes ten different song genres and provides translations of songs from each genre. The five genres to which Deng devotes most of his study are those sung by young men. These are "ox songs," "cathartic songs," "initiation songs," "age-set insult songs," and "war songs." These can be divided into three groups:

1. Tension in the son-father relationship is a central theme of ox songs and cathartic songs.
2. Generational tension between elders and youths, rather than familial tension between fathers and sons, is the central theme of initiation songs.
3. Verbal challenges and actual hostilities among groups of young men, both inside and outside society, are the central theme of age-set insult songs and war songs.

Taken together, the three sets of young men's songs illustrate how a sense of self apart from and opposed to others is represented in different social contexts, between father and son, between elder and youth, between youth and social other, and between youth and alien other.

A sixth genre, which Deng describes as "women's songs," is sung by young women. Deng does not provide a close analysis of this genre. As a category, it may lump together several types of songs sung by women. Whatever the case, Deng does show that at least some of the songs composed and performed by young women have features in common with those composed and sung by young men. This suggests that young men and young women have similar experiences of individuality. It appears, however, that the antagonistic and oppositional dimensions of these experiences are far more exaggerated in young men than in young women.

The four other song genres described by Deng, children's game songs, school songs, fairy-tale songs, and hymns, are not considered in this chapter. The first three have no close relationship with the issue of how tension in the son-father relationship is affected by the ecology of pastoralism. The fourth, the hymn, is crucial for an understanding of this problem, but is discussed in the next chapter, which deals with Dinka patriarchy and religiosity.

Ox Songs

A young man is given an ox of his own by his father at the time he is initiated, sometime around the age of sixteen or eighteen. The ox song, in which a young man celebrates himself by praising his personality ox, is the song genre most closely associated with this phase of his life. The ox song should be composed and performed by the young "owner" of the animal that it describes. It is a shame and a disgrace for a man to present another man's song as his own. The song is not exclusively concerned with the young man's ox, but refers both explicitly and implicitly to the singer's desires, feelings, and achievements as well as to his relationships with other individuals, especially with his father. Singing without the accompaniment of drums, the youth sits with his hands raised above his head to suggest the horns of the ox and moves his body to imitate the movements of the animal. As he sings, a friend might ring the bell hung about the neck of an ox or make sounds that resemble the bellowing of an ox.

The ox songs that Deng (1973) translates are alternately humorous and touching, oftentimes allusive and beautiful. However, it is not my intention to discuss their esthetic qualities, which can be reliably addressed only by an expert like Deng. Citing two translated excerpts, I show below how ox songs reflect the relationships of adolescence, cattle wealth, and paternal authority.

The first excerpt is from a song which Deng titles "How Grow the Horns." It begins with these lines in which the singer praises his ox:

> How grow the horns spreading!
> How grow the horns sweeping the earth!
> The horns of Mangar [the ox] are straying
> The horns of Mangar are straying like a lost
>   man
> The horns go to greet the things in the sky.
> The rafter-horned Jok, I call him "The
>   Breaker of the Ropes,"
> The breaking ropes of the Flour-White one
>   thunder-clap like shots on the rifle
>   range.
> The trotting Curve-Horned One has a voice
>   like trumpets
> And like the gourd of the wind.
> Why my Mangar roars in the evening
> Why my Mangar roars in the evening when the
>   cattle are tethered
> I do not know whether this will be a
>   permanent way of bellowing
> Or whether it is being gorged which rings the
>   head of my father's Ngar [an ox]
> Like a man drunk with *aregi*.
>   (99)

The singer first expresses astonishment at the horns of the ox spreading and sweeping the earth (lines 1–2). Then there is a hint at alienation and disorientation. The unrestricted movement of the horns in the world at large is compared to the straying of a lost man (lines 3–4). Next the singer evokes another vision of the unrestricted movement of the horns as they rise away from the earth into the sky (line 5). A theme of dissidence or rebellion follows. The rising of the horns is associated with the breaking of tethers, which echoes like a thunderclap or a rifle shot (lines 6–7). The "voice" of the ox is described next—it is powerful and mysterious, like trumpets or like the wind (lines 8–9). It is then obliquely linked with the son-father relationship. The bellow of the ox disturbs the peace of the camp when the cattle are tethered (lines 10–11). The son wonders whether this behavior of his ox is permanent or temporary (line 12). He compares the bellows of his well-grazed ox to a drunk man and refers to its annoyance of his father's ox (lines 13–14).

The young man's images of the aggressive weapons (spreading and rising horns), rebellious energy (breaking of ropes like a thunderclap or rifle shot), and disruptive voice (roaring and bellowing) of his ox are not inspired by the essential qualities of oxen, but by the ambitions and energies of the young man himself. Just as the young man has trained, sharpened, and decorated the horns of the ox to lend them qualities that they do not naturally have, so he has composed and performed praises of his ox which attribute to it a range of qualities that it does not actually exhibit. The subject matter of the ox song is not, therefore, the similarity between a young man and his ox, but rather the subjective experiences of the young man himself, which he expresses obliquely by portrayals of his ox. It is the young man, not the ox, who has the impulse to break away from his father in the homestead, represent himself through the power of his voice, and move abroad in the world as a warrior. It is the young man's own identity which is in question when he compares his ox to a straying man lost in the wilderness or a boisterous and shouting man drunk in the homestead. And it is the young man's own identity which is in question when he wonders whether his ox will remain the same or someday change. The adolescent singer is troubled by his feelings of alienation and rebellion. Might there someday be an end to this? Might he someday become a cattle-owning patriarch like his father, the archrepresentative of Dinka society?

Unable to become a patriarch who controls cattle wealth, the young man is reduced to representing a desire for freedom from paternal authority and social constraints in portrayals of an ox. A self-representation based on the medium of his personal "voice" substitutes for the acting out of a social status and role within the community. The young man turns to features of the animal, its horns, its physical strength, and its bellowing, and portrays them in a way that figures his desire for personal autonomy and independence.

Here is another excerpt from an ox song which Deng titles "Gathering Violence like a Rising Storm":

Youths, Songs, and Personality Oxen 19

My Miyar [the ox] has troubled us.
I say, "Within three years
Even if your heart is as stout as mine
Miyar, you will abandon violence [and submit to me]."
Mangar is gathering violence like a gathering storm.
When I accepted the challenge [to subdue the ox]
I collected fibre [for a rope] in the moonless part of March
And I soaked it into the river like a hyena hiding its prey.
I will not surrender, I will teach the Curve-Horned a lesson
I made the rope so that the skin peeled off my hands
Like the [skin on the] neck of the vulture.
I walked twisting myself like people carrying a tree-trunk for a drum
I accepted the challenge.
He is the ox for whom my father praised me
And said, "It is not good for the ox of a gentleman to be unruly;
Now that he roams the cattle-camp
If he should become wild like a lioness
And like a rabid dog
He will make you hate the camp."
And I said, "Father, he is not unruly,
He is a gentle ox."
My father said: "Well, if you will smile
Call him not unruly, but he will make you hate the camp."
The word of an elder is not futile
The word of my father has come true in one month
He has become exceedingly violent
So that I abandoned the camp as though it were that of strangers
I will not go to the camp.

(102)

The singer describes himself as attempting to subdue his ox, matching his own strong heart against that of the animal. Enduring physical trials in dangerous situations, he carefully and arduously fashions the rope that will harness and tame the animal. But it is finally the ox that overcomes his owner, instilling in him a wild and savage nature. The singer acknowledges the wisdom of his father who warns him that the ox will make him hate the camp. But this realization comes too late. The ox carries him away from the camp.

Here the young man sees himself as lured away from his father by love for his ox. From a psychoanalytic perspective, it is not really the ox that makes the young man rebellious. Instead, the young man has projected his feelings onto the ox, thereby avoiding any recognition of his unconscious wish to break away from the father whom he loves and respects. But in fact the youth has a point. It is indeed the relationship of men and cattle that precipitates the content and form of the Oedipal conflict here and it is the youth's desire to have an ox for himself that fosters rebellion against patriarchal constraints and alienation from the society of the camp. So the youth is right when he attributes his behavior to his devotion to his ox. The Dinka youth not only understands his plight but articulates it with delicacy and insight in his ox songs.

Cathartic Songs

In the ox songs translated by Deng (1973), the youth is hesitant about breaking away from his father and is not at ease with his feelings of social alienation and rebellion. In the cathartic songs, another side of masculine adolescent identity becomes apparent. Although the youth still hesitates to assert himself, he is nonetheless very much aware of the constraints which his father and other elders place upon him, and he is keenly frustrated by them. Cathartic songs are complaints and appeals addressed to a father or elder. These songs, which the Dinka call "cleansing" (*waak*) songs, are composed during a period known as "lying in" (*toc*), when youths "isolate themselves in far-off camps and gorge themselves with milk supplemented by meat" (159). The youth flees the camp for the bush. He gorges himself on the products of cattle he cannot control, and he composes and recites songs of complaint and injustice.

The most common subject of cathartic songs is the inability of a young man to marry because of the lack of sufficient bridewealth or the opposition of his father or other elders. Most of the examples of cathartic songs that Deng provides take the form of a complaint addressed to the elder who would sponsor a young man's marriage. In the songs, the elder is first praised and then requested to grant the singer's wish.

According to Deng, when the youth reenters the camp, he is fat from the milk and meat that he has consumed, and the object of intense curiosity. Having gained attention, he sings his song appealing for sympathy and understanding. Sometimes his wishes will move the man whom he addresses in his song to grant his wish. The following lines are an excerpt from such a song:

> The name of my father is big
> The name of my father is big in the tribe
> His name always is on people's lips.
> Father, that is right
> Great Chief, that is right.
> Father, you will make me lose the name in
>   Marial [his rural area]
> You will make me lose the name among the
>   tribes
> You will make me not be known by our girls.
> Let me go into the tribe
> To observe the girls of Marial.
> Father that is right,
> Great Chief, that is right.
>
> (166)

After an encomium in which his father is described as one of the foremost chiefs of the Dinka, the young man addresses the patriarch directly, begging him to permit him to marry and uphold the name of his lineage.

This example of a cathartic song illustrates how the young man's ambitions are measured against his perception of the father's power and influence. To have his desires fulfilled, he must appeal to the father, praise him as a mighty chief, and extol his reputation in the tribe. His own subjection then takes the form of anticipation of personal power and influence, a striking model of which is provided by the man to whom he must submit.

Initiation Songs

At the time of his initiation, the young man assumes the status and role of a warrior and joins an age-set constituted by all those youths who were initiated as a group. Since his tie to his family is to some degree replaced by his tie to his age-set, the young man becomes less emotionally dependent on close family relatives, his own mother and father in particular. However, the initiated youth is not, by virtue of this replacement, fully "emancipated," free at last of the checks of his seniors. The initiation period itself is closely supervised by elders, and the relationship of the age-set to its sponsoring elders is an especially important one. Deng (1973) sketches the opening phase of the months-long initiation period as follows:

Initiation among the Ngok begins with the designation of a "father" and a name for the emerging age-set a few years before their initiation. This "father" is usually an elder member of one of the chiefly lineages. The intending initiates then request their father and the chief to permit their initiation. (185)

The real father is to some degree left behind and replaced by an age-set "father." This is but an example of a relative shift of patriarchal responsibility, from father to elders, which takes place at the time of initiation.

As family controls weaken, social controls are strengthened. Accordingly, tension in the son-father relationship now has its counterpart in tension in the youth-elder relationship.

Initiation songs basically describe the introduction of the initiate to the warring period ahead, his elevation to a more respected position in consequence of his courage, and his conflict with the older generations because of this step toward emancipation. (185)

Similarly, just as the relationship of son and father involves a mixture of dissidence and submission, the relationship between youths and elders also has two sides. As Deng points out, the initiation ceremony itself features both conflict and enmity as well as harmony and affection between older and younger generations:

The initiate in turn combines his zest for greater freedom with the gentle submissiveness required of a younger man. This concurrent conflict between, and harmonizing of interests of, different generations are symbolized in initiation and articulated in initiation songs. The initiator, who represents the older generations, is seen with both affection and enmity. He is pictured as one with the upper hand who must be faced with courage. (186)

But there is also a difference between the son-father and the youth-elder relationships. The first is an opposition of a father to a son, who in seeking his independence is imitating a patriarchal example, but the second is an opposition of elders to warriors, who would assert themselves in contests and conflicts. Accordingly, the tension between younger and older generations is more wide-ranging than the tension between son and father. In the ox songs, the rebellion and alienation of an ox are described as obliquely affecting the behavior of a loyal and loving son. In initiation songs and dances, however, a violent energy erupts within the young man, who nonetheless struggles to control it. Deng provides an especially striking illustration of this shift in tone in his description of an initiation dance:

Among the Ngok [Deng's own tribe], the initiation dance in which initiation songs are sung consists of a lifting and dropping of the legs with a jerk of the body to imitate the movement of a horse under tight rein. This is accompanied with exclamations (*mioc*), such as "I blunt the knife." The singer, representing the horse and the rider, makes sounds as though subduing an unruly horse. Sometimes he portrays the whipping of the horse with the reins held tight so that the struggle becomes more marked. These are symbols of their coercive power, their pride in their forthcoming status as powerful warriors, and, it would seem, their desire for emancipation. (186–87)

The youth feels within himself a power which he is obliged to release and to display, but which he must also strive to control.

In age-set insult songs and war songs, these "aggressive and violent" energies of warrior youths are associated with symbolic conflicts inside the circle of society and actual hostilities outside it.

Age-Set Insult Songs

According to Deng (1973), the age-set insult song is "an attempt by the age-set immediately preceding the last initiated age-set to hold back the rise of the younger age-set by defamatory songs" (198). He continues:

When presenting these songs, the older age-set dance the women-dance to represent the younger as womanly. The result is an institutionalized fight (*biok*) between them. Such fights are not only provoked by songs. They are a general manifestation of the conflict between age-sets. In the eyes of the Dinka, they are mock-fights. Only clubs or sticks, not spears, are used, but severe injuries are often inflicted. The effect of the insults is rather to encourage the younger group towards aggression than to deter them from it. (199)

From these comments, it is clear that the age-set formation, which is constituted through the close supervision of elders, is an institution that both expresses and controls antagonism and opposition.

The form in which hostility between age-set formations is acted out is significant. It is the older youths who attempt to hold back the younger youths, conforming to the pattern of tension between senior man and junior man, where the former attempts to block the self-assertions of the latter. Now, however, in this setting, the tension involves an open hostility, which is not just playfully symbolic but tends to lapse into intense seriousness. To prove themselves, the newly initiated youths, fresh from their dependency on mothers and fathers, are obliged to challenge and oppose those who are senior to them. In this way, initiation rites and age-set formations involve a controlled setting for learning to assert oneself before those whom one is accustomed to respect and obey.

War Songs

The war song reveals that self-assertion by young Dinka men, though supervised or restricted by cattle-owning fathers and elders, can be fully expressed outside society, beyond the purview of elder and chief, in a setting of interpersonal aggression and hostility. Deng's (1973) collection of war songs illustrates quite clearly how the adolescent's blocked ambition to gain personal autonomy and independence through cattle wealth finds expression both in fantasy and in acts of murder and theft beyond the domain of society where the authority of elders prevails. Consider, for example, the following war song which Deng titles "The Heart of a Buffalo":

> The Grey One [vulture] flies in the *toc*
>   [grassy plains],
> I killed a man [literally, a small black
>   bird]
> And his mother got into a mourning skirt.
> I gathered my spears.
> And I killed a man.
> There is the Bird!
> The Bird with a heart has killed a brave
>   warrior
> The Bird of Deng, Designer of Black Colour,
> The Bird with a heart has killed a brave
>   warrior.
> I am a bad man
> I fly in the *toc*
> My heart is like that of a buffalo.
> I danced around the herds I captured
> And vultures followed my spears.
> I do not honour the spears of the *Door*
>   [Sudanic peoples].
> We met while Miyom [ox name of chief], the
>   chief, was away
> What is lacking when I have protected the
>   river
> The River of our chiefs?
> Miyom [see above] is away,
> I will not wish he were here;
> The Star Man [praise name of sectional chief]
>   is away,
> I will not wish he were here;
> The Assembly of the chiefs is away,
> I will not wish they were here;
> I am a big bull.
>
>   (207)

In this war song, a young man praises himself for having killed another young man and caused his mother to mourn. He represents himself as a creature of nature (lines 1–11), a bird who flies in the plain and preys without fear upon like beings: other birds, other warriors. He concludes this first image with the lines, "I am a bad man, I fly in the [grassy plains]." Antisocial attributes are linked with free movement in the world beyond the camp. Shifting from the image of wild bird to wild ruminant, the singer claims the courage of a buffalo and celebrates his capture of herds which he slaughters for meat (lines 12-14). Next, he refers to his bravery before hostile warriors in a borderland in the absence of cattle-owning authorities (lines 15-25). The tribal chief, the sectional chief, and the assembly of elders are away, and he does not regret their absence. He claims the honor of protecting the tribal boundary without their help or advice. In the open grassy plains, on the fringes of the tribal domain, he identifies himself with "a big bull," a figure that is elsewhere applied to father, elders, and chiefs.

Where the young man is no longer under the eye of his seniors, he tests his power and will over other men by challenging them in battle and by contesting their ownership of herds. In effect, an antagonistic and oppositional self incompatible with the Dinka concept of "sociability" (*cieng*) is the focus of the young warriors' ideals and values.

The enactment and representation of murder and theft are, however, qualified by a social context. The war songs refer to an "I" as the performer of heroic exploits, but the "I," Deng tells us, refers to an age-set, not an individual. Moreover, when men compare themselves to bulls, buffaloes, vultures, and lions in the war songs, the names of the beasts in question are typically the names of age-sets. For example, in the war song cited above, the "Grey One," a metaphor for the vulture, is an age-set name. Thus the heroic "I" is ambiguously enunciated as an expression of a collectivity rather than an individual. Among the Dinka, the ecology of pastoralism is clearly linked with the emergence of a self apart from and opposed to others, and yet this sense of self is also regulated and channeled by an institutional framework.

Women's Songs

While Dinka pastoral ecology directly affects men, their experience of individuality is part of social relationships in general and is therefore indirectly communicated to women. Women's songs indicate that cattle wealth shapes the relationships of men and women (and no doubt those of mothers and daughters) just as it shapes the relationships of fathers and sons.

Even though young women do not have a personality ox like young men, they have sweethearts and husbands who have such personality oxen. The complex of male adolescence, singing, and cattle among men becomes a complex of female adolescence, singing, and man/cattle among women. As young men represent themselves through praising their oxen, so young women represent themselves through praising their sweethearts, husbands, and their cattle:

> Women's songs . . . are usually a form of ox song centring on the oxen of husbands or dancing-partners. In this respect, the fiction of the unity of the spouses is applied to the extent that the singing woman keeps shifting between referring to her husband as "I" and as "he." Her identity is thus reflected through him. (Deng 1973:218)

Though the woman would appear to identify with the man when she refers to him as "I," her praise of him in song is otherwise best understood as an analogy of the youth's praise of his ox, that is, as a representation of her individuality. The young man essentially identifies, not with his ox, but with the ideal of personal autonomy and identity represented by his cattle-owning father. Similarly, the young woman does not lose herself in her devotion to her husband or sweetheart, but shares his own ideal of personal autonomy and independence. Deng observes that the young woman prides herself on possessing her man in her songs much as the young man expresses pride at possessing an ox:

> The singer often praises her husband and through him herself, with surprising snobbery. The praises are usually exaggerated and the husband overvalued, so much so that this is only possible in songs. (218)

Women are not limited to a vicarious participation in men's experience of individuality as they praise their sweethearts or husbands and their oxen, for women are not by any means wholly dependent on men. They have a power over their sweethearts or husbands, who are dependent on them, if not devoted to them. So women's sense of individuality is not wholly a matter of their identification with men.

In passing so quickly over the question of women's personal identity, I do not mean to imply that it is not highly significant. Indeed, it may be a key to the deeper implications of the Dinka pattern of self-representation through cattle. This issue, however, would require a separate full-length study.

TWO EFFECTS OF A PASTORAL ECOLOGY: AUTHORITY AND INDIVIDUALISM

Among the Dinka, cattle are a vehicle for two different forms of personal identity among fathers/elders and sons/youths. For older men the control and management of cattle are the basis of authority over others. For younger men the admiration and adoration of cattle are the basis of a sense of self apart from and opposed to others. These two different forms of personal identity are not compatible with one another, but they are sustained nonetheless by contradictory sides of the Dinka pastoral way of life. Cattle-owning fathers and elders are key social actors, given the necessity for reciprocity and cooperation among pastoral groups; cattle-contesting sons and youths are key social actors, given the insecurity and vulnerability of pastoral resources. Consequently, the relationships of older men and younger men are characterized by tension between patriarchal authority and adolescent individualism.

While this tension colors Dinka pastoral traditions and institutions in general, it is an especially prominent aspect of the various ways in which a young man represents himself in poetic composition and performance (see fig. 1.1). He hesitantly aspires to personal autonomy and independence by praising his personal ox, but remains keenly aware of his subjection to his father (ox song). He openly expresses his resentment and frustration in the face of patriarchal controls and constraints, but has no alternative other than to beg his father's favor (cathartic song). He experiences a violent and rebellious energy within himself, but only on an occasion when he is under the supervision of elders he respects and loves (initia-

Father, Elder	
patriarch	personal authority expressed through
cattle ownership, exchange, and sacrifice	control & management of cattle

Youth, Warrior	
ox songs	autonomy and independence hesitantly
praise of a personality ox	expressed by adoration of an ox
cathartic songs	resentment & frustration in the face of
complaint and appeal to father, composed out of camp	patriarchal authority
initiation songs	assumption of warrior identity,
themes of violent energies tenuously controlled	both rebellion against and submission to elders
age-set insult songs	symbolic antagonism and opposition
threats and ridicule	inside society in presence of elder and chief
war songs	actual antagonism and opposition outside
self-representation as man slayer and cattle raider	society in absence of elder and chief

Woman	
women's songs	self-identity expressed by identification
various dimensions not examined	with man or by praise of man

Fig. 1.1: The Genres of Dinka Songs as Self-Representations

tion songs and dances). He joins his peers to engage in fights and battles with older youths, but in contexts which are defined by convention (age-set insult song). He participates in acts of expropriation and aggression, but only in a tribal borderland beyond the authority of elder and chief (war song).

2
Elders, Creation Myths, and the Cosmic Patriarchal Spirit

THE TWO SIDES OF DINKA PATRIARCHAL
RELIGIOSITY

Dinka patriarchal religion has two sides,[1] one reflecting the impressive power of the father in society and the other the tension in the son-father relationship. The first has much in common with the religious beliefs and practices of cattle-herding people all over East Africa from the Sudan to the Cape. But that side which results from tension in the son-father relationship is more exceptional and less widely distributed. It is found among some of the pastoralists in the Sudan, Ethiopia, and the Horn of Africa, but it is more unusual, and perhaps not found at all, among the Bantu-speaking cattle herders to the south.

As the controllers and managers of cattle wealth, Dinka fathers hold the fortunes of other Dinka in their hands. Accordingly, the father is a central figure of the family, the homestead, the camp, the lineage, the tribe, and so forth. This material power of Dinka fathers is associated with a spiritual power. Virtually every social group is seen as derived from and protected by a father figure, such that Dinka religion features a multiplicity of high and low patriarchal spirits. Sometimes these spirits are represented as patriarchal gods who protect and punish. Sometimes they are represented as actual patriarchal ascendants of families, lineages, and clans. Sometimes they do not have any specific connections with real fathers, living or dead, other than the fact that the Dinka identify them as "spirits of the father."

While the Dinka father monopolizes an important resource, his relationship with his son is a point of weakness. As cattle owners, fathers are dependent on and must encourage the ambition and energies of their sons as warrior youths. In doing this, the wishes of sons to imitate and replace their fathers blossom in the form of an antagonistic and oppositional individuality. Consequently, fathers, having themselves sponsored a man-slaying, cattle-raiding warrior identity, must also strive to limit and restrict the expression of that identity, which constitutes a direct threat to the control and management of cattle. The other side of Dinka patriarchal religion, the concept of the oneness of a cosmic patriarchal spirit, has to be viewed in conjunction with tension between one man who would control and manage cattle and another man who would contest and fight other men.

Drawing on Godfrey Lienhardt's (1961) ethnography, *Divinity and Experience: The Religion of the Dinka*, the two sides of Dinka religion are analytically distinguished and discussed in this and the next chapter. The following section describes that side of Dinka religion which is related to tension in the son-father relationship, the idea of the oneness of a cosmic patriarchal spirit.

THE COSMIC PATRIARCHAL SPIRIT

Among the Dinka, both the father and the son represent their personal identity through a relationship with cattle, but that of the former is instrumental, whereas that of the latter is figural. On closer inspection, this neat opposition proves to be not altogether satisfactory. It implies that the father's control and management of cattle is an unproblematical reality, while the son's adoration of cattle is a problematical ideal. In fact, like the son, the singer of songs, the father is just as deeply implicated in representations, but of a different kind. These representations raise the question of the legitimacy of an antagonistic and oppositional individualism. In this regard, they are a reaction to, and an argument against, the self-representations of the son.

Lienhardt (1961) begins his account of Dinka patriarchal religiosity with a gloss of the term which designates the cosmic patriarchal spirit to which the Dinka recite prayers and offer sacrifices:

> The word which any inquirer into Dinka religion will first and will most frequently hear is *nhialic*. Literally, the word is the locative form of *nhial*, meaning "up" or "above," and *nhialic* is the word used in many contexts in which we should speak of "the sky." Part of the meaning of *nhialic*, then, is conveyed by "sky" and "in the above."
>
> But further, *nhialic* is addressed and referred to as "creator" (*aciek*) and "my father" (*wa*), and prayers and sacrifice are offered to it. It then has a masculine and a personal connotation, and is used in contexts where, for ordinary purposes, it would be suitably translated as "God." (29)

Elders, Creation Myths, and the Cosmic Patriarchal Spirit   31

These few lines mention three important characteristics of *nhialic* as a Dinka concept of the divine. It is situated in the heavens, over and above the affairs of humans in general. It is a "creator" which is conceived as the ultimate origin of human beings. It is addressed as "my father" and hence in some way identified with or compared to real fathers. Noting that the Dinka concept of *nhialic* is similar to the Judaic, Christian, or Islamic concept of God, Lienhardt considers the appropriateness of translating *nhialic* by this very term:

> It would be easy, it is true, to translate *nhialic aciek* and *nhialic wa* as "God the creator" and "God (my) father," for the attributes of *nhialic* and "God" there closely coincide, as do many others — unity (of a kind), power, justice, "highness," for example. When, however, numbers of "spirits" later discussed are all said in Dinka to be *nhialic*, it would not make similar sense in English to say that they were "all God." The word *nhialic* is meaningful in relation to a number of Dinka terms with which our "God" has no such association. *Nhialic* is figured as a Being, a personal Supreme Being even, and sometimes as a *kind* of being and activity which sums up the activities of a multiplicity of beings, while the word "God" has no such extended meaning in our common speech. (29–30)

There is a difference between the Dinka cosmic spirit, *nhialic*, and the Judaic, Christian, or Islamic God. The former is associated with multiple spiritual powers, whereas the latter is a more solitary monotheistic concept.

As described in the next chapter, the spiritual powers with which *nhialic* is associated consist for the most part of various patriarchal spirits. They are the other side of the Dinka patriarchal religion that reflects the impressive power of the father in Dinka society. The Dinka cosmic spirit is similar to a monotheistic concept of God, but the prominence of this second side of Dinka patriarchal religion is not a feature of Judaic, Christian, and Islamic monotheism. Lienhardt therefore elects not to translate *nhialic* as "God," deviating from what was almost a standard practice when he wrote. Since the last century, various Western officials, missionaries, and ethnographers have perceived some similarity between the concept of a Supreme Being among certain groups of Nilotic- and Cushitic-speaking peoples in East Africa and the concept of God in Middle Eastern monotheisms.[2] Lienhardt acknowledges that a case can be made for translating *nhialic* as "God." He records that the Dinka themselves follow such a practice, identifying *nhialic* with the God of the Christians and Muslims that they have encountered (56). Still, as an ethnographer of Dinka religion, Lienhardt is obliged to consider differences as carefully as similarities. Faced with the task of providing an accurate description of Dinka religiosity, Lienhardt chooses to translate *nhialic* by the less charged, more neutral English singular "Divinity," written with an uppercase "D." At the same time, he translates the general term *yeeth*, the multiplicity of spirits asso-

32 Elders, Creation Myths, and the Cosmic Patriarchal Spirit

ciated with Divinity, by the English plural "divinities," written with a lowercase "d."

Lienhardt's reticence in translating *nhialic* as "God" is fully justified by his ethnography. And yet, he also clarifies precisely those aspects of Dinka religion that inspired comparisons with the Middle Eastern monotheisms. He illustrates how the Dinka place a remarkable emphasis on the thesis of the oneness of a Divinity as a focus and center of spiritual power: "All Dinka assert that [*nhialic*] is one [*nhialic ee tok*]" (56). At the same time, he also demonstrates that this thesis is not consistent with Dinka religious beliefs and practices in which multiple spirits figure very prominently. Lienhardt does not, then, entirely reject the claims of other observers—including such distinguished ethnographers as the Seligmans, Crazzolara, and Evans-Pritchard—that the Dinka and other Nilotic peoples believe in a Supreme Being that is reminiscent of Middle Eastern monotheisms. Instead, he strives to be more precise about similarities and differences.

Having made the point that *nhialic* is conceived as a oneness, even though associated with numerous spirits, Lienhardt (1961) next proceeds to discuss Divinity (*nhialic*) in its own right, as a religious concept quite apart from the various spirits with which it is associated. He does so by examining those features of Dinka religion specifically related to Divinity: stories of Divinity's creation of man, hymns sung to Divinity, and how Dinka individuals think about and refer to Divinity. In the course of his examination, Lienhardt develops an interpretation of the social function of the Dinka concept of Divinity, arguing that it "reinforces the position and authority of the actual human father" (42).

In what follows, Lienhardt's conclusion is not challenged, but the significance he attaches to it is altered. For Lienhardt, the Dinka concept of Divinity supports one of the most basic norms of Dinka social life: the submission, obedience, and resignation of children before fathers. But these behaviors are only one side of a filial life situation, at least in the case of sons, if not of daughters. The other side is the fascination of young adolescents with expressions of personal autonomy and independence. If the concept of Divinity supports a basic Dinka norm, that norm is placed in question by a dimension of Dinka experience.

Lienhardt's analysis can be revised in recognition of this aspect of Dinka experience. The representation of Divinity on the part of father/elder directly opposes the representation of self on the part of son/youth.[3] This is a slight revision, but it has an important implication. It means that the representation of Divinity by father/elder is a reaction to and an argument against the life situation of son/youth. Consequently, the concept of Divinity is implicated in the tension between controlling and managing cattle as a social resource and killing men and seizing cattle as an expression of personal autonomy and independence.

CREATION MYTHS AS FATHER-STORIES

After introducing the Dinka concept of Divinity, Lienhardt (1961) first discusses a "creation" myth, aiming to demonstrate that the relationship of "Divinity and man" in the myth is analogous to that of fathers and children in experience (implicitly the experience of both male and female).[4]

The creation myth is not always told the same way among different groups of Dinka, but all the versions have a common theme: An original conjunction of Divinity and man is followed by a disjunction. Near to Divinity, man is without need or fear, but lacks freedom and is incomplete in himself. After some offense on the part of man, such as disobedience, quarrelsomeness, or carelessness, Divinity removes himself from man, with the consequence that sky and earth are differentiated and separated from each other. This initiates the beginning of human affairs as the Dinka know them. Man acquires his full powers and gains his freedom, but henceforth he is also subject to suffering and death.

Lienhardt summarizes these features of the myths as follows:

Man is thus represented as having been originally confined and constricted by his closeness to Divinity. He might not eat more than a permitted grain of millet each day, and had to move carefully (this cautious movement is sometimes enacted by the Dinka when telling the story, and resembles in spirit the quiet and modest demeanour they adopt in situations in which they must now customarily show formal respect); or he was enclosed within a fence or wall or pot, from which he eventually came out; or, in the Agar version, he could not "see" properly. There were thus no independently human affairs until Man had "come out," or become separated from Divinity. But freedom then brought with it toil, suffering, and death which he had not previously known. When Man was with Divinity, he wanted freedom. When he became independent, he was still dependent, in that he had to accept suffering and death. (36–37)

Lienhardt next argues that the depiction of the primordial condition of man near Divinity closely resembles the early relationship of son and father. There is, Lienhardt observes, a "parallelism between the separation of Man from Divinity and the separation of men from their fathers when the time comes for them to marry" (36). Near to Divinity, man's access to resources is restricted and his movements are inhibited. Apart from Divinity, man has more freedom, but, separated from the creator's protection and nurturing, must now face the hazards of life on his own. Thus man stands to Divinity in the myth much as son stands to father in experience.

Lienhardt provides solid documentary evidence that the Dinka themselves typically draw the parallel that Divinity is to man as father is to son. At the same time, his explanation of their insistence on this parallel can be questioned. Lienhardt argues that the Dinka mythic portrayal of the Divinity/man relationship is modeled on the father/son relationship

34 Elders, Creation Myths, and the Cosmic Patriarchal Spirit

in Dinka experience. For Lienhardt, Dinka religious concepts and principles both reflect and reinforce an order in Dinka experience, and the order in Dinka experience is derived from the inherent stability and coherence of Dinka communal life.

This interpretation of the Dinka creation myths can be readily undermined. It could be easily argued that the relationship of Divinity and man is a more perfect model of the mother-child relationship than of the father-son relationship. Divinity is the creator (like the mother, not like the father) of man. At first, man is protected and nurtured, but remains in darkness and cannot come out (like the fetus). Later, after separation from Divinity (like birth), man loses this protection and must face first suffering and then death. Lienhardt does not mention this possibility, either here or in various other places where the Dinka account of Divinity and man brings to mind the relationship of mother and child more than the relationship of father and son. He does not do so because it would show how Dinka representations are not reflections of experiential realities, but constructions placed on experience. And once this feature of Dinka religion is recognized, it is apparent that Dinka religious ideals are an argument about, rather than a depiction of, Dinka experience.

What then is the argument of the Dinka story of man and Divinity? The story describes the relationship of man and Divinity as though it were a relationship of child and mother. At the same time, Divinity is identified not as a mother figure, but as a father figure. In other words, the story asserts that a father figure resembles a mother figure. What motivates this assertion?

By describing the relationship of man and Divinity in the guise of child and mother, the story is designed to drive home the point that man has no inherent identity in his own right apart from Divinity. As Lienhardt himself concludes, "there were thus no independently human affairs until Man had 'come out,' or become separated from Divinity" (37). To make this point, the story does not portray the actual experiences of the Dinka, but instead places a construction on Dinka experience. By insisting that man originates close to Divinity, very much as a child is born from a mother, the notion of man having any individuality apart from Divinity is rhetorically diminished. Significantly, however, the denial of man's individuality is associated not with a mother figure but with a father figure. So this is a story that addresses the relationships of sons and fathers but carries a message inconsistent with actual experience. Dinka fathers are not at all like mothers who give birth to children. Dinka sons are not at all lacking in any individuality apart from their connections with their fathers. Through rhetorical strategy and procedure, the creation myths persuade us to see the father-son relationship in one way and from one side.

The creation myths follow their depiction of a transcendent father who resembles a transcendent mother with a moral lesson about the illusion of individuality. Man is impelled by a desire for freedom and so is eventually separated from Divinity. The freedom he gains by this separation proves to be false and illusory. Severed from Divinity, there is only hardship, suffering, and death. Again, however, the story is not a reflection of Dinka experience. Sons do indeed desire freedom from their fathers, from whom they are in the course of their adolescence increasingly separated. But the result is not uniquely "hardship, suffering, and death." They have some bad times but also some good times. There are exciting romances. There are parades of oxen. There are song performances. There are adventures with peers.

The creation stories of Divinity and man are therefore not a depiction of reality but an argument that attempts to reinforce, by means of a construction placed on experience, the position and authority of the father. But more than this, as an argument the creation stories are aimed, not at children in general as Lienhardt sometimes implies, but specifically at the son. They depict a patriarchal "other" that denies the possibility of a filial "self." This means that they are father-stories, in direct opposition to son-songs. The creation myths address, not the general problem of fathers and children, but the specific problem of fathers and sons.

This slight, but fundamental, recasting of Lienhardt's interpretation requires clarifying a point of confusion in Lienhardt's analysis. While the Dinka themselves draw the parallel that Divinity is to man as father is to son, they do so in a way that inverts Lienhardt's interpretation of this parallel. For the Dinka, it is fathers that resemble Divinity, not Divinity that resembles fathers. This Dinka inversion of Lienhardt's interpretation suggests in itself that Dinka religious belief is an argument about, not a portrayal of, experience. This is quite clear from an example which Lienhardt (1961) provides to illustrate how the Dinka draw the analogy that father is to son as Divinity is to man:

Divinity, as father, is needed to look after, or bring up (*muk*), his people, like a human father with his children. The Dinka speak of themselves as being resigned in the same way to the "word" — that is, decision or will — of their fathers, and to the will of Divinity. For example, a father allowed his son, whom I knew, to be imprisoned rather than consent to his marriage with a girl whom he had persistently pursued, and whose father might have accepted a few cattle as an earnest of the youth's serious intentions. In speaking to the son I was rather critical of the father's refusal to help him, which would seemingly have cost him little. The son replied, "Why, is not your father like Divinity? Does he not bring you up and look after you? And if he injures you or helps you, is it not his affair? How should you be angry about it?" (41–42)

Lienhardt begins his anecdote by citing still another way in which the Dinka draw a parallel between Divinity and fathers. Just as the father "brings up" (*muk*) his children, so Divinity "brings up" (*muk*) his people. The Dinka probably put this matter the other way around. Still, the parallel between Divinity "bringing up" his people and fathers "bringing up" their children again suggests that the concept of Divinity, and hence the father who is said to be like Divinity, has the qualities of a real mother even more than the qualities of a real father. The word *muk* is glossed by Lienhardt a few lines later as "caring for, feeding, protecting, and instructing," actions that bring to mind infant and mother as much as, if not more than, son and father (43).[5] Again, the point here is not that Divinity is in fact a mother and not a father, but rather that man has no identity apart from Divinity. By describing Divinity's relationship to man as a relationship of mother to infant, this point is made more persuasively. The concept of Divinity is not a depiction of but an argument about Dinka experience, with a transcendent patriarchal "other" refuting the possibility of "self." As such, it is a father-story in direct opposition to son-song.

These qualifications aside, Lienhardt's ethnographic point must be accepted. The words of a Dinka son plainly confirm that the Dinka draw a parallel between Divinity and fatherhood. Lienhardt next notes that in drawing such a parallel the Dinka justify the absoluteness of patriarchal authority. The son must obey the word and will of the father just as all men, including the foreign ethnographer, are the subjects of Divinity. Lienhardt reaches the conclusion that the Dinka concept of Divinity is motivated by a concern to enhance the stature of the father in Dinka society:

> In the case just described, what the son accepts, in principle at least, is the authority of the Father—of all fathers—an authority associating them with Divinity. The associations of one sort and situation of fatherhood are carried over to the others, and the transcendent fatherhood represented by Divinity *reinforces the position and authority of the actual human father* [my italics]. So Divinity images fatherhood in general, as he images creativity in general. (42)

Lienhardt has not made a good case that the concept of Divinity is modeled on real fatherhood, but he has made an excellent case that it is designed to reinforce patriarchal authority. On the other hand, he has not explained why the Dinka devote so much intellectual energy to this reinforcement, especially given the fact that fathers are unquestionably powerful figures in Dinka society. Eventually, however, he does provide a clue to this problem.

In his account of the creation myths, Lienhardt (1961) sometimes writes that the relationship of man and Divinity is a model of the relationship of child and father. As he develops his case, however, he moves seemingly unconsciously, between references to child and father and references to son and father. Finally, he concludes that the concept

Elders, Creation Myths, and the Cosmic Patriarchal Spirit 37

of Divinity is inspired quite specifically by tension inherent in the son-father relationship:

> The Divinity/man:father/child [sic] analogy of the Dinka may go further than this. The son-father relationship is not simply one of submissiveness, obedience, and resignation on one side, and unquestioned authority on the other, despite the ideal of filial piety which Dinka subscribe to in theory. On the contrary, sons are often in conflict with their fathers, and are not slow in urging their just claims upon them. The *conflict of wills* [my italics] between son and father occurs particularly at the time when the son wishes to marry, and the father refuses his permission, wanting to keep the son long under his own roof and in tutelage. Though the sons of such fathers have ultimately little alternative but resignation or leaving home to find work, they do not pretend to be satisfied with their lot, and a very common theme of ox-songs is oblique criticism of a father or guardian who has thus refused to let his child marry when he wishes and is old enough to do so. (42)

Lienhardt now writes of a difference between the ideal and the reality of the son-father relationship. In theory, there is "submissiveness, obedience, and resignation on one side, and unquestioned authority on the other." In fact, the relationship of son and father involves a "conflict of wills." Lienhardt immediately readjusts his position in the lines that follow. The creation myths depict tension in the relationship of man and Divinity, since it is after all part of the real relationship of son and father. However, in depicting this tension, the creation myths confirm that in experience it is the son who must ultimately submit to the control of the father:

> Here again [in the tension of father and son] the Divinity/man:father/child [sic] analogy is reinforced. Both are relationships with a source of existence and its support; but the support given by the father, or by Divinity, demands also submission, and exacts a control over the dependent son in ways which he may come to find irksome. This situation appears in the stories of Man's initial closeness to Divinity, where he was secure as long as he remained passive, and lost that security by a bid for freedom; it is found in many Dinka families today. Fathers want to have their sons remain dependent on them, while the sons, when of suitable age, are anxious to detach themselves sufficiently from their fathers to set up their own homes and start their own lines of descent. In starting or hoping to start his own lineage, a man is in effect hoping for the day when he himself will be known as "the father of so-and-so," rather than as "the son of so-and-so": he is hoping, that is, for separation, but it is separation which cannot escape conjunction, as in the myth. (42–43)

Without ever explaining why the son-father, as opposed to daughter-father, relationship should figure so prominently in myth, Lienhardt concludes once again that the myth of man and Divinity actually captures the reality of submission, resignation, and obedience of sons before fathers. The separation of son from father cannot escape the conjunction of son and father in Dinka experience, "as in the myth."

Lienhardt has noted that tension exists in the real relationship of son and father and that a parallel to this tension appears in the mythic depiction of the relationship of man and Divinity. These are key points. They suggest that there is a problem specifically in the relationship of son and father, and that this specific problem is addressed in the myth of man and Divinity.

But has Lienhardt otherwise correctly assessed the link between experience and representation? Lienhardt claims that the tension between son and father in experience is imitated or mirrored by the tension between man and Divinity in the creation myths. He asserts that the implication of the myth—man's separation from Divinity cannot escape conjunction with Divinity—reflects the actual reality of the son-father relationship. But is the myth a reflection of the real son-father relationship or a studied construction placed on this relationship? Is the myth mimetic depiction or calculated argument?

In explicating the tension in the son-father relationship, Lienhardt adopts a patriarchal point of view, emphasizing that the son must resolve his differences with his father because his interests are really his father's interests. It is not surprising, then, that Lienhardt's analysis of Dinka experience is affirmed by the relationship of Divinity and man in the creation myths, the latter being themselves Dinka representations of a patriarchal point of view. But neither Lienhardt's perspective nor the creation myths' perspective is the Dinka reality, which has different implications for different social actors. In particular, both overlook the fact that the son assumes, during a well-defined segment of his life cycle, a status and role which question principles with which fathers are identified. The young man, as singer, dancer, raider, and warrior, is a man who, wishing to be like the father but blocked from realizing this ambition, is concerned instead with complaint, criticism, evasion, and defiance, sometimes of his own father, sometimes of fatherhood in general. This means that the portrayal of the man-Divinity relationship in the creation myths, even as it draws on experiential realities of the son-father relationship, is a calculated argument opposing the thinking and experiences of young men. This is why the creation myths are closely associated with tension in the son-father relationship, not in the son-parent, child-father, child-parent, daughter-father, or daughter-parent relationships.

Although Lienhardt does not mention who relates the creation myths, whether it is men or women, whether they are elders or youths, whether they are priests or chiefs, they are clearly father-stories, not son-songs. The myths of Divinity and man are not neutral in their depiction of tension in the son-father relationship and are not disinterested commentaries on the dilemmas of Dinka experience. The cattle-owning, cattle-sacrificing elder, no less than the man-slaying, cattle-seizing youth, is involved in a project of representations.

An anecdote which Lienhardt (1961) cites at this point in his exposition adds further support to this conclusion. In some contexts, says Lienhardt, tension between man and Divinity in the creation myths becomes an outright opposition between man and Divinity. To illustrate the point he refers to a story — and perhaps it is only a story — of youths who set out to contest Divinity. The incident, which was supposed to have occurred in Bahr-el-Ghazal Province, is described in government records:

> The young men of one subtribe, fat with milk and spoiling for a display of their strength, once decided that only Divinity himself was a great enough adversary for them. They therefore attacked (how they did so is not recorded) the rain (*deng*), which is in the report described as the "symbol of God."[6] . . . All were killed except one man, who, it is reported, was left with a hole pierced through his thigh, through which visiting Dinka would pass a stick. (43)

Thus, while the creation myths justify the submission of sons to fathers, other stories of more dubious provenance suggest that sons/youths would openly challenge the very Divinity which requires this obedience. This is further evidence that the concept of Divinity is a thesis of patriarchal authority which is a reaction and response to a counterthesis of filial dissidence. The relationship of son and father is a disturbing one in Dinka experience.

HYMNS AS FATHER-SONGS

In their rhetoric and structure, the creation myths are in direct opposition to songs. They are not the compositions of an author but timeless traditions. They are not dramatically performed by a singer but tales soberly told by a narrator. They do not depict individual experiences but an absolute origin that denies the validity of individual experience. In all these respects, the creation myths are a denial, whereas the songs are an assertion, of self. The creation myths are representations of a transcendent patriarchal "other" which precedes and diminishes an incomplete and evanescent "self." The songs are a representation of a "self" which is differentiated sometimes hesitantly, sometimes antagonistically, and is sometimes murderously triumphant over an "other."

But creation myths are not the only representations of fathers/elders which stand opposed to the representations of sons/youths. Those elders who act as priests are also themselves singers, although of a different sort than sons and youths. On the occasion of collective rites and prayer, they sing songs which take the form of hymns to Divinity. In his introductory remarks to the hymns, Deng (1973) makes the following observations:

> In accordance with Dinka religious expression, in which prayers are not a regular habit but a request for something specific, hymns are sung for the help of [Divinity], lesser spirits, and their ancestors.[7] Thus, except for certain regular occasions of offerings and feasting, they are used as prayers during sickness, war, drought, famine, or any such tragedy, and may be sung by individuals or groups, in public or in private. Divine leaders and other religious functionaries may also sing hymns alone or in company with others as part of their general prayer for the well-being of their people even though there may be no specific threat. Hymns are also sung as part of the inauguration ceremonies for chiefs or as part of the burial rituals of chiefs and certain holy men. (238)

The Dinka sing hymns to Divinity on occasions when they feel helpless, in need of protection and support. They sing both as individuals and in groups, in both public and private. In such circumstances, hymns are not identified with fathers more than sons, or, for that matter, with men more than women. In the absence of dire circumstances, however, religious leaders and functionaries sing hymns, and hymns are sung during occasions involving the succession of authorities, such as inaugural and funeral ceremonies. So even though all the Dinka sing hymns in dire circumstances, they are otherwise particularly associated with positions of authority, that of both priestly and secular elders. They are on the side of the father, not that of the son. They are father-songs opposed to son-songs.

The differences between hymns and songs are revealing precisely because the two are otherwise more similar than myths and songs. Describing the form of the hymn, Deng observes:

> In so far as they reflect situations of public significance, whether involving the public as such or some pivotal individuals or groups, hymns are of historical value. This is especially so because hymns of such public interest tend to be perpetuated even though they may be reinterpreted and distorted to present the viewpoints of interested groups. Even when they are new, hymns tend to build on a legacy and therefore on old hymns. (239)

Unlike the song, a self-representation by its composer and performer, the hymn refers back to events that have been experienced in common. And unlike the song, the hymn preserves and remembers as it incorporates the new, building on a legacy rather than inventing an identity. Hymns are not individual compositions and performances but accumulations of collective tradition.[8]

Moreover, the content of hymns, seemingly similar to that of songs, is on closer inspection quite different. This is a point that Lienhardt (1961) misses, concerned as he is with the parallel of Divinity is to man as father is to son. When citing a hymn, Lienhardt begins by observing:

Elders, Creation Myths, and the Cosmic Patriarchal Spirit 41

It is not, then, merely a European psychological interpretation of the relations of the Dinka with Divinity to compare them in some detail with the relations of Dinka father and son; it appears spontaneously in the context of Dinka religious thought itself. As complaints are obliquely addressed to the human father in songs, and are also often intermingled with pleasing praise (*lec nhom*, literally "to praise the head"), so hymns to Divinity and divinities also include the complaint of an anxious child. The following is part of such a hymn:

> I have been left in misery indeed,
> Divinity, help me!
> Will you refuse [to help] the ants [human
>   beings] in this country?
> When we have the clan-divinity Deng
> Our home is called "Lies and Confusion."
> What is all this for, O Divinity?
> Alas, I am your child.
>
> (44-45)

Just as the son sings the "washing" (cathartic) song, obliquely criticizing but also praising the father, so the supplicant of Divinity sings the hymn which obliquely criticizes but also praises Divinity. At least this is what Lienhardt would have us believe. But the parallel is inexact and therefore misleading.

The supplicant of Divinity does not, unlike the son, speak for his personal desires and ambitions in singing the hymn. Rather, he depicts his situation as one of helpless misery and despair. He does not anticipate attaining social objectives through the aid of Divinity, but distances himself from the "lies and confusion" of human experience. Without advocating his personal autonomy and independence, he speaks of himself as a child of Divinity. And finally, he does not represent his own individual desire and feeling, but identifies his desperate situation with that of all human beings in general. He is but one of the ants.

Deng's (1973) translated excerpts of hymns and songs make this contrast between their content even clearer. In one of these excerpts, for example, Divinity is portrayed as a great cosmic father over all humankind. This vision of a universal human community based on submission, resignation, and obedience is in direct contradiction to the hesitantly dissident, sometimes murderously rebellious, individualism of songs. This particular excerpt, titled "The Lord Thunders," is especially interesting because it seems at first to be so very much like an ox song:

> The Great Lord Madhol [praise name for God]
>   thunders in the byre.
> Thundering in the byre, he is angry with the
>   ants
> He is the Man who brings death.

42   Elders, Creation Myths, and the Cosmic Patriarchal Spirit

> The master whose heart has no grudge
> He attracts all the ants
> People gather on his feet
> And also on his head
> Great Lord of the Gourd
> Put right our land
> The land is shaken
> If the earth is bitterly cold
> If the earth blows with cold wind
> It is the wind of Divinity [the healthy season]
> If a man loves me
> I love him
> And if a man hates me
> I hate him
> But not with all of my heart shall I hate
> For am I not the prosperity of the ants?
> (239)

God is given a praise name by the elder, just as the ox is given a praise name by a youth. God thunders in the byre, just as the ox bellows in the camp. God stands above all the world, just as the horns of the ox spread throughout the land and reach the sky. Here, however, the similarity ends. God presides over the human community which is subject to him, whereas the ox is a vehicle of the individuality of the singer of songs. The human community over which God presides includes both love and hate, and while God loves those who love and hates those who hate, all are his subjects.

The depiction of both divine authority and human community in the hymn is unbounded. Divinity overlooks all men, whether they love or hate one another, whether they be at war or at peace. The hymn's argument directly contradicts the spreading, soaring individualism seen in ox songs and war songs. The hymn asserts the power of Divinity in the world at large, the world beyond homestead and camp where patriarchal authority prevails. This is in direct contrast to the ox song in which the horns of the ox, a symbol of youthful aggression and hostility, are imaged as moving across the earth and rising to the sky, and to the war song in which the predatory bird flies freely in the bush, a symbol of youthful man slaying and cattle seizing. The hymn claims that the space beyond the limits of patriarchal authority in Dinka experience is nonetheless under the dominion of Divinity.

The hymns are centered on Divinity and fixed in their form. They are the property of all the Dinka and are closely identified with the community, unlike the songs, which are individual compositions and performances.[9] The comparison of hymn and song, like the comparison of myth and song, confirms that one side of Dinka patriarchal religion is closely

Elders, Creation Myths, and the Cosmic Patriarchal Spirit 43

linked by way of contrast and opposition to the desire and ambition of sons for personal autonomy and independence.[10] This explains a contradiction in Lienhardt's account of the Dinka concept of Divinity.

THE NONANTHROPOMORPHIC REPRESENTATION OF DIVINITY

Lienhardt is especially attentive to those occasions when the Dinka draw a parallel between Divinity and fatherhood, because they support his thesis that Dinka religion directly reflects Dinka experience, an idea that he illustrates with striking examples. The Dinka do sometimes represent Divinity as a father. In a Dinka hymn excerpt, for example, Divinity is anthropomorphized as a protector and provider, the husband of women and the husband of cows:

> You [Divinity] protect the homestead.
> Shall I not propitiate you with a cow?
> Divinity, father, you protect the home
> Husband of the cows,
> Husband of the women,
> It is you who protect the home.
>
> (44)

The figuring of Divinity as a cattle-owning patriarch is the tendency characterizing the other side of Dinka religiosity that I have not yet examined. It is a result of the impressive power of fathers in Dinka experience, which leads the Dinka to see many spirits, including Divinity, as father figures. But the representation of Divinity as a transcendent fatherhood is only one side of Dinka patriarchal religiosity. From the side arising from tension in the son-father relationship, Divinity is not at all represented in the anthropomorphic form of cattle-owning patriarch.

Toward the end of his analysis of the Dinka concept of Divinity, Lienhardt describes a Dinka representation of Divinity that cannot be squared with his view that Dinka religion reflects Dinka experience. The essence of Divinity, Lienhardt concludes, is nonanthropomorphic:

I must mention here that despite the quasi-human form in which Divinity is sometimes imagined to appear in visions, the figurative references to parts of his "body," and the attribution to him of a kind of universal fatherhood, the Dinka understanding of Divinity is in important respects *the reverse of anthropomorphic* [my italics]. Indeed, it is precisely *as contrasting with men* [my italics] — their judgements, ways, and powers — that *nhialic* is most frequently heard. (53)

How can Lienhardt claim that Divinity is like the father, if Divinity is essentially not like any man at all? This contradiction in Lienhardt's account is the mark of a great ethnographer who does not fail to mention facts inconsistent with his general line of interpretation. Divinity is not like any man at all for the same reason that Divinity is removed from the earth and placed in the heavens where he reigns over the world at large. Divinity is not essentially a likeness of the real father, but a representation of a patriarchal other that opposes the representation of a filial self.

A review of the nonanthropomorphic features of Divinity confirms this. In his account of these features, Lienhardt stresses three principal attributes: creativity, truth, and justice. Each of these attributes is difficult to construe as an essential feature of real fathers, Dinka or non-Dinka, but they are very clearly in opposition to the individuality that appears in the son's self-representations.

Divinity's Creativity

In his discussion of Dinka creation myths, Lienhardt (1961) initially argues that fatherhood and creativity, the two most important attributes of Divinity, are strongly associated. According to his interpretation of Divinity as a transcendent fatherhood, this would suggest that the divine "father" who creates men as his "children" is modeled on the human father who procreates his children. Though such an assumption fits neatly with his argument, Lienhardt later takes some pains to point out that the Dinka very specifically differentiate Divinity's creativity from the father's procreativeness:

> In Dinka there are important interconnexions between notions of creation and of fatherhood, though the verb "to create" is never interchangeable with the verb "to beget." Divinity created (*cak*) men in the beginning, and the men he created begot or bore (*dhieth*) children. Divinity did not "beget" or "bear" men, and it would be a linguistic mistake in Dinka either to use this expression for the creation of men by Divinity, or to say that father and mother "created" their child. Yet the notions are linked. *Dhieth means both "to beget" and "to give birth to," so that verbally the activities of men and women in procreation are not distinguished from each other* [my italics]. When a man was asked to explain what happened in coitus, he described the physical act, and added *"And that is called begetting (dhieth), and Divinity will then slowly create (cak) the child in the woman's belly"* [my italics]. Divinity thus has a creative function in the formation of every human being, and when human beings are barren their barrenness is explained by reference to it; when a woman fails to bear a child despite intercourse with a man known to be able to beget children, it is commonly said that Divinity has "refused" her a child, and at sacrifices masters of the fishing-spear or prophets commonly ask that Divinity may allow women to bear children. (39)

Divinity, as creator (*cak*) of humankind, is associated with, but also differentiated from, the father who begets (*dhieth*) or the mother who bears (*dhieth*). What does this delicate association and disassociation of Divinity's creativity (*cak*) with human procreativeness (*dhieth*) signify?

Elders, Creation Myths, and the Cosmic Patriarchal Spirit 45

Divinity's creativity is, if anything, more directly analogous to the mother's, rather than the father's, procreativeness. The creation of the child by Divinity is said to follow specifically upon the coitus of man and woman. That is, Divinity's creativity is explicitly said to follow the sexual union of the father with the mother. In this respect, the concept of Divinity's creativity certainly recognizes a patriarchal model of human procreation, one that insists on the combination of an unimpressive and inconsiderable — even if necessary — paternal physical function (coitus) together with a far more impressive and considerable maternal physical function (pregnancy). However, the cited Dinka commentary suggests that Divinity's creativity is just as closely associated with pregnancy as with insemination: "And Divinity will then slowly create (*cak*) the child in the woman's belly." Once again Lienhardt overlooks the way in which a patriarchal spirit, represented by fathers, elders, priests, and chiefs, features functions of both fatherhood and motherhood. Not only do the Dinka insist on a difference between Divinity's creativity and paternal procreativeness, but Divinity's creativity cannot be said to be more a metaphor of paternal, rather than maternal, procreativeness. What precisely, then, is Divinity's creativity? What is the significance of the difference between *cak* and *dhieth*?

The explanation is again a fairly simple one, if the opposition between Divinity as father-representation and individuality as son-representation is kept in mind. The concept of Divinity as creator oversees the function of both father and mother in the process of procreation. This representation of Divinity makes the point that the individual has no identity in his or her own right save that given by Divinity. Divinity is — far more perfectly than its representative, the real father — the origin of the person. Consequently, the individual has no individuality apart from his creator. This means that self-representations by sons are false and illusory, while Divinity, whose earthly representative is father, elder, chief, and priest, is essential.

Lienhardt (1961), after concluding from his analysis of *cak* and *dhieth* that the "ideas of 'creator' and 'father' are fused with each other" (39-40), returns to the creation myths for further clues to the nature of Divinity's creativity, but without discovering any answers to this problem. He therefore resorts to the etymological level, addressing the meanings of the very term, *cak*, by which the Dinka refer to Divinity's creativity. Here again, he is unable to reach any definite conclusion, but the issues which arise are especially interesting. The Dinka sometimes speak of Divinity as having made or fashioned human beings "as women fashion pots and children fashion toy oxen of mud" (41), but the word the Dinka use for Divinity's creativity, *cak*, does not have such a meaning. It refers instead to creativity on the level of the verb:

The only circumstances in which it is possible to use the verb to create, *cak*, of a *human* activity are those in which what is created is the product of the imagination or thought, that is in songs, prophecies, and the naming of things and children. Composers and prophets are equally *aciek*, "creators." A man skilled in fashioning material things is not a "creator" but a craftsman (*atet*). As creator, Divinity may also be spoken of as having created human dispositions to lust, malice, and so on. (41)

The creativity of Divinity is not comparable to the activity of a craftsman fashioning physical material, but to the activity of a "verbal craftsman" — a singer, a prophesier, or, more prosaically, a namer. Divinity's power of creativity is somewhat like an author's power of composition. Furthermore, this power of creativity (composition) is seen as the origin of human identity, which is glossed as lustful and malicious. I will attempt to "unpack" these remarks by venturing into territory not fully verifiable from Lienhardt's ethnography.

Lienhardt has exemplified the meaning of the word *cak* by the terms which refer to singing and prophesying. At this point he might have reminded us of an important contrast. The singer of songs is usually a youth with a reputation as a dancer, singer, and warrior. The prophesier who speaks for Divinity is usually an elder with an exceptional religious reputation. That is, the meaning of *cak* is divided between very different forms of verbal craft, one identified with sons and youths who speak for themselves and another with fathers and elders who speak for Divinity. In other words, the opposition of son/youth to father/elder involves an opposition of rhetorical strategies and procedures, apparent in the contrast between son-representations and father-representations.

The Dinka observation that Divinity has created (composed) human lust and malice is itself an example of this rhetoric of the father. It pictures divine creativity as having determined a human identity, and it specifies this human identity as consisting of egotism. Thus, divine creativity is made the absolute origin of man at the same time as man is given attributes which place him in opposition to Divinity.

This conclusion is reinforced by other nonanthropomorphic attributes of Divinity. These attributes link the possibility of equity and harmony among all human beings with a cosmic "other" who stands for a peculiar form of representation that is quite different from and even opposed to self-representations. This peculiar form of representation is the "truth."

Divine Justice and Truth

As Lienhardt (1961) brings his discussion of Divinity to a close, he mentions two other nonanthropomorphic attributes of Divinity, "justice" and "truth." Divinity stands for a form of perfect representation, truth, which is

Elders, Creation Myths, and the Cosmic Patriarchal Spirit 47

opposed to the misrepresentations of human beings, who are sorely troubled by egotism and hostility in their relations with one another:

> If creativity and fatherhood are the attributes of Divinity most commonly referred to, justice (despite the complaints in hymns mentioned earlier) follows them closely. Divinity is held ultimately to reveal truth and falsehood, and in doing so provides a sanction for justice between men. Cruelty, lying, cheating, and all other forms of injustice are hated by Divinity, and the Dinka suppose that, in some way, if concealed by men they will be revealed by him. In the line from a hymn quoted above, "Our home is called 'Lies and Confusion,'" lies (*lueth*), and the misunderstandings, suspicions, hostilities, and malice which accompany them, are mentioned to show that Divinity is specially needed to intervene in human affairs, to put them straight by making the truth appear. *Wet nhialic*, the "word" of Divinity, is the truth, or what really and absolutely *is* so; and the Dinka think that in certain circumstances men may speak this totally objective "word," representing to others the true nature of things, whether of present, past, or future situations. *Cit nhialic*, "like Divinity" or "as Divinity," is one of the common expressions men use to guarantee the truth of what they say, and "Divinity will see" is what any Dinka will say if he suspects another of lying or cheating him and can take no further action of his own in the matter. In some of the invocations reproduced later it will be seen that Divinity is made the final judge of right and wrong, even when men feel sure that they are in the right. Divinity is thus the guardian of truth—and sometimes signifies to men what really *is* the case, behind or beyond their errors and falsehoods. (46–47)

Divinity is itself linked with a form of representation, just as Lienhardt's discussion of Divinity's creativity (*cak*) suggests. This form of representation, the truth, is not a form of self-representation—a composition which reveals individual feelings, attributes, and ambitions—but is totally objective, absolutely free of subjective desire and wish. Furthermore, this total objectivity, which Divinity brings to light, is the foundation for justice in human affairs.

One further comment on the part of Lienhardt provides a valuable insight into the truth of Divinity as total objectivity. Ethnographers are given to pressing their friends and acquaintances to place constructions on their experiences. The most valuable and interesting part of ethnography is, after all, the indigenous point of view, to paraphrase Clifford Geertz. But sometimes this questioning can be not just annoying but morally inappropriate. Such is the case among the Dinka, where a father or elder is prone to be cautious when asked to place a construction on his experience:

> If any question as to why things happen or have happened is pressed home, the Dinka answer will eventually refer them to *nhialic*, a point in explanation beyond which further questioning is meaningless. In the ordinary course of life, however, and not in such an artificial questioning from cause to cause, Divinity is spon-

taneously referred to primarily when men have to adjust themselves to situations in which they involuntarily find themselves, and where clear oppositions and ambiguities of thought and experience occur. (55)

Here, in a moment of frustration, as his informant refuses to respond to his questions, the ethnographer stumbles both literally and figuratively on the "truth." Divinity stands opposed to self-representations. And so to refer to Divinity is also to set aside the possibility of placing constructions on experience. In the same way, the Dinka have an experience of Divinity, the ethnographer explains, when they are caught in circumstances not to their liking but demanding adjustment and adaptation. When they cannot make of something what they would like, that is when they have an intimation of the presence of a patriarchal other.

Analyzing the opposition between the rhetorical strategies and procedures of father and son reveals one side of Dinka religion. This is an opposition between a patriarchal religion reminiscent of monotheism and a secular individualism consisting of experience of the self apart from and opposed to others. To the extent that Dinka patriarchal religiosity is dominated by this opposition, tension in the son-father relationship is a dominant factor in Dinka experience.

Comparing Dinka and Nuer religion and society provides additional support for this interpretation. Chapters 4 and 5 show how this side of Dinka religion, the opposition of monotheistic religion and secular individualism, is a more prominent feature of Nuer religion, while the second side of Dinka religion, respect for a multiplicity of patriarchal spirits, is less prominent. This contrast between Nuer and Dinka religion is directly correlated, moreover, with a greater practico-cultural emphasis on cattle raiding among the Nuer than among the Dinka. In effect, among the Nuer, the control and management of cattle, the basis of patriarchal authority among the Dinka, is weakened as a consequence of access to cattle wealth by stealth and force. Since, however, the control and management of cattle are as important a dimension of Nuer as of Dinka society, the result is that the opposition between father-representations and son-representations moves to the foreground of Nuer religious life.

Before considering the greater prominence of Divinity in Nuer religiosity, however, the extent to which Divinity is not altogether the focus and center of Dinka religiosity must be examined. This is the second side of Dinka patriarchal religion, associated with the impressive power of fathers in Dinka society. The next chapter reviews Dinka patriarchal symbolism and verifies this association.

3
The Multiplicity of Patriarchal Spirits and the Power of Cattle-Owning Fathers

THE LIMITS OF DIVINITY AS FOCUS AND CENTER OF DINKA RELIGION

Lienhardt (1961) begins his analysis of Dinka religion by setting aside the possibility of translating *nhialic* as God, because the Dinka believe in a multiplicity of other nonhuman powers not compatible with a monotheistic principle. The most important of these nonhuman powers (*jok*) are numerous "spirits" or *yeeth* (singular *yath*), which the Dinka explicate as those "powers which are related to people" (30, 31, 104). These "spirits" generally fall into two broad classes which Lienhardt categorizes as *free-divinities* and *clan-divinities*.

But is Lienhardt's case completely acceptable? The concept of God is always more or less associated with popular beliefs in a multiplicity of spirits. In Judaism, Christianity, and Islam, a truly monotheistic concept of God is embraced by only a minority, while the majority is always involved to some degree with numerous spirits in the form of angels, saints, and genies. Perhaps the situation is not very different among the Dinka. The Dinka recognize a variety of *yeeth*, the most important of which are anthropomorphized. And yet Dinka elders also assert the oneness of Divinity and argue that all nonhuman powers are merely different manifestations of Divinity and hence subordinate to it. Perhaps, then, Lienhardt has been too fastidious in refusing to translate *nhialic* as God.

I raise this issue not to revive the interpretation of Nilotic religion as monotheistic, but only to note that the Dinka belief in a multiplicity of spirits is not the only reason, or even the best reason, that Lienhardt cites when he refuses to translate Divinity as God. More important is the specific character of these spirits.

In discussing the Dinka free-divinities and clan-divinities, Lienhardt warns his readers not to look for a unified pantheon or creed in Dinka religiosity (96). In effect, Dinka beliefs and practices regarding nonhuman powers are difficult to outline in a systematic way. Part of the difficulty involves questions of whether the free-divinities and clan-divinities are as compatible with the concept of Divinity as the Dinka claim them to be. It is this relative lack of consistency and organization in Dinka religion that differentiates it from monotheistic religious traditions, not just the Dinka belief in a multiplicity of spirits. The Dinka often argue that Divinity is the focus and center of all spiritual power, but this idea has not touched every facet of their spirituality.

Yet, Lienhardt is not always mindful of his own warning to the reader. Having taken some pains to avoid translating Divinity as God and to insist on the lack of pantheon and creed in Dinka religion, Lienhardt himself tends to fall under the sway of the thesis that Divinity is the center of Dinka spirituality. He overorganizes his account of Dinka religious beliefs and practices, suggesting that incompatible and contradictory features of Dinka religion are systematic and integrated.

This is not a failing that deserves censure, but an inescapable hazard of any ethnographic project. Lienhardt has systematized Dinka religion, even though he understood very well that this was a mistake, for two very good circumstantial reasons. First, as an ethnographer, he is engaged in composing an account of Dinka religious thought and experience. In writing a book on Dinka religion that will be comprehensible to a non-Dinka audience, he is under constant pressure to tie things together and to make connections. Second, his informants, many of whom must have been older men, were probably themselves given to systematizing Dinka religion, for such men have a stake in the thesis that Dinka thought and experience are centered on Divinity (*nhialic*). The concept of Divinity is, after all, that element of Dinka religion that reinforces the position and authority of the Dinka patriarch, and so the father, the elder, the chief, and the priest all have a vested spiritual interest in Divinity.

For both reasons, Lienhardt attributes a total system to Dinka religion, violating his own stricture and describing Dinka spirits as organized under the concept of Divinity. In doing so, he favors one particular Dinka thesis: the oneness of Divinity. Even as he describes that sector of Dinka religiosity which clearly limits such a thesis, the belief in free-divinities and clan-divinities, Lienhardt is preoccupied with how they can be reconciled with the notion of the oneness of Divinity.

Lienhardt's (1961) overorganization of Dinka religious thought and experience begins with the first step he takes in his analysis of the relationship of Divinity (*nhialic*) and spirits (*yeeth*). At the outset, he writes that "*in some senses* [my italics] . . . all existences called *yeeth* may be equated with Divinity" (30). Accepting a claim which some Dinka make on some occasions, he determines to translate the Dinka term *yeeth* by the word "divinities," distinguishing them from *nhialic*, which he has translated as Divinity. Note that such a translation makes a more intimate, semantic connection between *yeeth* (divinities) and *nhialic* (Divinity) than that made by the Dinka themselves. Here, then, the ethnographer has added something to what the Dinka do and say which supports one Dinka point of view, perhaps at the expense of others. References to *nhialic* and *yeeth* are always automatically, but perhaps not properly, hierarchically associated, since they are consistently translated as "Divinity" and "divinities."

Lienhardt is certainly able to demonstrate that his linkage of *nhialic* and *yeeth* is not entirely against the grain of Dinka religiosity. His study clearly illustrates how the Dinka typically regard *yeeth* as subordinate manifestations of *nhialic*. Given the totality of the ethnographic evidence that he presents, this view must be regarded as one Dinka thesis, not wholly unpersuasive, but also not wholly convincing. From this perspective, Lienhardt's observation that all Dinka divinities (*yeeth*) may be equated with Divinity might best be modified to mean that the Dinka typically equate all divinities (*yeeth*) with Divinity, even though they are not always clearly compatible or consistent with Divinity.

The following sections discuss the inconsistencies dividing Divinity from free-divinities and clan-divinities. These can be largely understood in terms of the following distinction: Divinity (*nhialic*) reflects the authority of cattle-owning fathers/elders being brought into question by the individualism of sons/youths. For the most part, the free-divinities and clan-divinities (*yeeth*) reflect the fact that cattle-owning fathers/elders are impressive figures in the Dinka community, figures with both material and spiritual powers. Therefore, the prominence of Divinity (*nhialic*) and the prominence of free-divinities and clan-divinities in Dinka religion arise from two not altogether compatible sides of Dinka experience, even though they are typically fused together in Dinka thinking.

THE FREE-DIVINITIES

Among the western Dinka the most important free-divinities are more or less anthropomorphic spirits known by the proper names Deng, Macardit, Garang, and Abuk. Elsewhere in Dinkaland, these and other free-divinities, such as the female spirits Ayak and Loi, may be active, and in Dinka myths inactive free-divinities proliferate even further (Lienhardt 1961:99–100). Uniting these various spirits as a single class, free-divinities, Lienhardt sees them all as similar phenomena.

Having categorized the spirits Deng, Macardit, Garang, and Abuk as a subclass, Lienhardt goes on to describe them as having similar properties. The free-divinities manifest themselves by "causing illness, by possessing human beings and announcing through their mouths their names and their demands, and sometimes by speaking in dreams" (57). The free-divinities are at the same time associated with a variety of religious specialists of varying repute, such as fetishists, diviners, and prophets (80), who may be called upon by those afflicted by these spirits.

Lienhardt overgeneralizes when he places these four spirits in the same class. All are anthropomorphic representations of nonhuman powers which come into some direct relationship with human beings, but each refers to different kinds of concerns. Abuk, who is linked with the productive activities of women, has no connection with either illness, possession, or religious specialists. Garang causes illness—but he usually affects only men, not women, and is represented by prophets and curers of low repute. Macardit is identified with suffering and misfortune in general—but more often with the afflictions of women than of men—and is not represented by any kind of religious specialist. Deng is unlike all the other free-divinities in that he manifests himself in many ways. Sometimes he is identified as Divinity, but sometimes he is more like a free-divinity, possessing individuals so that they become prophets or curers or striking them down because of some fault or delict. Sometimes, he is not like Divinity or a free-divinity, but instead resembles a clan-divinity. Lienhardt's definition of the category of free-divinities is therefore not completely justified by the evidence presented. Abuk does not fall within the boundaries of the definition of this subclass of *yeeth* at all. Some aspects of Deng do accord with Lienhardt's definition, but others do not. Only Macardit and Garang fit the definition, but the differences between them also indicate that distinct phenomena have been merged together.

Drawing on Lienhardt's ethnography, the differences as well as the similarities among the four principal free-divinities are examined below. Deng illustrates Dinka feelings of attachment to and dependency on patriarchal figures. Garang and Macardit reveal Dinka anxiety about their relationship with patriarchal figures. Abuk, who represents a goddess of women's associations and activities, is much less closely identified with Dinka patriarchal religiosity.

Deng: Divinity in the Modality of a Father Spirit Near at Hand

According to Lienhardt (1961), the Dinka see all the free-divinities as manifestations of Divinity, a concept strongly influenced by the idea of the

The Multiplicity of Patriarchal Spirits and the Power of Fathers 53

unity of Divinity. But of all of the free-divinities, it is only Deng, the most developed and elaborated of the free-divinities, for whom this tendency is characteristic and essential. Associated with rain, thunder, and lightning, Deng is explicitly linked with Divinity "as a whole" (90–91). The Dinka see themselves as the "children of Deng or Dengdit, great Deng" (90), and they "say in general that Dengdit (great Deng) is 'Divinity itself'" (93). Deng is called by many names which add various qualifiers to his name, among them *deng nhialic*, meaning "Deng of the above" or "Deng Divinity" (94). Deng, therefore, is clearly and plainly identified with Divinity by the Dinka themselves. What, then, is the difference between Deng and Divinity?

Lienhardt notes that "unlike other free-divinities, but like Divinity itself[,] . . . Deng does not exist only in a single mode, and the Dinka themselves cannot state clearly the relationship between Deng unqualified and the various figures of Deng, which are represented by qualifying the name of Deng with different suffixes" (93). Indeed, Deng seems to be expressed in even more modes than Divinity itself. He is sometimes very much like Divinity, sometimes like a free-divinity who possesses individuals as his prophets or strikes them down with affliction, and sometimes like a clan-divinity, identified with many specific clans and lineages. His name is also given to children and is one of the more common personal names among the Dinka. "There seems to be no limit to such special figures and refractions of Deng" (95).

Relying on Lienhardt's account, I propose a slight revision of his evaluation of Deng. The crucial aspects of Deng are the two properties which Lienhardt stresses (90–103). First, Deng is most closely identified with the cosmic patriarchal spirit *nhialic*. This confirms that he is himself like Divinity, but a different modality of Divinity. Second, the nature of this different modality is revealed precisely by the many refractions which Deng takes. Unlike Divinity, Deng takes the same form as other more intimate and familiar anthropomorphic spirits (*yeeth*) who are down-to-earth and near at hand, that is, who are specifically linked with particular individuals and collectivities. While Deng is like the transcendent patriarchal spirit *nhialic* on high above all humankind, he is a parochial manifestation of this cosmic parochial patriarchal spirit with a specific relationship to specific persons and groups.

In effect, Deng is a high god in the form of a low god. More precisely, he is the refiguration of one side of Dinka patriarchal religiosity—the nonanthropomorphic creator Divinity which is associated with tension in the son-father relationship—in the modality of the other side of Dinka religiosity: an anthropomorphic father divinity which is associated with the impressive power of the father in Dinka social relations.

The similarity and difference between Divinity and Deng highlight the contrast between the two sides of Dinka patriarchal religiosity.

Divinity is a radicalized version of a patriarchal other which takes shape as a reaction to the problem of the son's self-representation. Separated from earth and situated in the heavens over and above human affairs, this remote spirit stands opposed to individualism. In contrast, Deng is a modality of this remote spirit which takes the form of a real father who is in close touch with his devotees. Thus, Deng is identified with Divinity and yet is sometimes spoken of as "our Deng" in contradistinction to the "Deng" of other Dinka (Lienhardt 1961:94), a point that makes no sense whatsoever in regard to Divinity. Correspondingly, while the tone of the relationship of individual Dinka to Divinity is more abstract and ethical, the relationship of individual Dinka to Deng is one of emotional attachment and dependency. Deng, as a modality of Divinity, is a weakening of the rhetorical strategies and procedures behind the representation of Divinity which respond to tension in the son-father relationship. It is a weakening inspired by the second side of Dinka patriarchal religiosity, that arising from feelings of attachment to and dependency on father figures:

Macardit: The Limits of Patriarchal Protection and Nurturing

The interpretation of the similarity and difference between Divinity and Deng is confirmed by the character of the free-divinity Macardit.

Macardit can be understood as the obverse of Deng. Just as Deng reveals how the Dinka sense of well-being inclines them to symbolize their closeness to a patriarchal spirit, so Macardit reveals that the Dinka tend to associate suffering and misfortune with a spirit who symbolizes the absence of patriarchal protection and nurturing. Macardit is associated with individuals and experiences at the limits of patriarchal support.

For the Dinka, Macardit is the "final explanation of suffering and misfortunes which cannot be traced to other causes more consonant with Dinka notions of Divinity as just" (Lienhardt 1961:81). He is bad: "Macardit kills people." He is cruel: "Macardit does not treat people with respect (kindness)." He is not quite "unified" and "singular" like Divinity but is sometimes addressed "in the plural, as *wek*." Unlike Divinity, who is associated with light and radiance (86–87), Macardit is related to the inauspicious color black. He is the "great black one" and requires a black ox as a sacrifice (82). He is also linked with individuals and experiences furthest from the regard and favors of the patriarch — with the junior wife who symbolizes the end of the procreativeness of the family head and with the middle son who is least fortunate in the inheritance of cattle and is denied the "spiritual strength" attributed to the eldest and youngest (82). He is associated with the bush, not the camp, and sometimes wild animals are sacrificed to him in the forest. Finally, Macardit is associated with women in general, whom he most typically possesses or afflicts (83). Macardit represents, not the confirming antithesis of patriarchal other (like the son), but a sense that patriarchal protection and nurturing are not omnipresent but limited in their scope. All those individuals (women, middle son, last wife) and all those experiences (succession, boundaries, procreation) which raise a question about the patriarchal principle are associated with Macardit.

Garang: Punitive and Beneficent Intercession of a Patriarchal Spirit

The free-divinity Garang raises different problems. Garang has the same name as the first man created by Divinity, and he is sometimes spoken of as the son of Deng or the son of Abuk (Lienhardt 1961:87, 88). In contrast with Macardit, Garang generally affects only men, not women (84). When a man is possessed by Garang he first becomes sick. Then after recovery he announces that he is a "man of Garang," and is consulted as a curer and as a guarantor of oaths (86).

Garang is a more unusual and suspect patriarchal spirit than the widespread and multiplex Deng, who is more closely identified with Divinity and is not so strongly associated with either disease or affliction. Garang tends to affect only certain patrilineal lines: "It tends to be inherited by the sons of those who are possessed or troubled by it, and to become a cult-divinity of particular families" (84). Furthermore, men of Garang are considered a little bizarre: "The Dinka do not take all or most men of Garang very seriously, and in their attitude towards them there is often an element of the humouring of eccentrics" (86).

Garang appears to indicate once again Dinka feelings of attachment to and dependency on patriarchal spiritual powers, which they perceive as both punitive and beneficent. They look to men who have been struck down by a sickness as having been visited by a "spirit of the father." They hope through their intercessions to find relief from their afflictions, attributing sickness and health to patriarchal disfavor and favor.

Abuk: An Alternative to Patriarchal Protection and Nurturing

The free-divinity Abuk, who carries the name of the first woman, is "the only known divinity of the Western Dinka who is represented as female, and compared with the others she is of minor importance" (Lienhardt 1961:89). Here, however, one may wonder if Lienhardt is speaking for all of the western Dinka or only for men. Abuk is not associated with men and cattle. She is instead the "patroness of women and of women's produce, the produce of the gardens" (50, 160, 204). In the larger scheme of the Dinka pastoral patriarchy, Abuk is assuredly of minor importance ("I have not found shrines to Abuk, nor cattle dedicated to her" [90]), but she does come forward in certain contexts which have a deep meaning for at least some of the Dinka: "Songs are sung by women to Abuk in connexion with the harvest. She is asked to bring plentiful grain so that the women (who are notoriously fond of beer and in any case are the brewers) shall be made happy with beer, sesame, and other fruits of the earth" (90).

Abuk is poorly described by the categories of Lienhardt's ethnography. "The archetypal woman and mother" (89), she has no clear place at all in his basic definition of the free-divinities, since she does not either "possess people or bring sickness as do the other free-divinities" (90). Furthermore, her uniqueness as a female divinity is questionable, since Lienhardt cites two songs in which there is a reference to her mother, Ayak (87, 183; cf. 87 n. 2). In fact, Abuk is something of a problem for Lienhardt because she is something of a problem for the Dinka. In her is found an alternative center of Dinka religiosity, one that diverges, even if it does not entirely break away from, patriarchal religiosity.

Taken together, the three free-divinities, Deng, Macardit, and Garang, confirm that the Dinka are indeed very much preoccupied with divine images of fatherhood. These three free-divinities also reveal that this side of Dinka religious thought and experience issues from anxieties about their relationship with an idealization of fatherhood which they see as the foundation of both personal and collective well-being.[1] The fourth free-divinity, Abuk, confirms that while fatherhood is a prominent feature of Dinka religious thought and experience, it is not exhaustive. The existence of powerful fathers on both secular and religious levels is not inconsistent with the existence of powerful mothers on those levels.

Finally, the four free-divinities illustrate that the notion of the oneness of the cosmic patriarchal spirit Divinity does not absolutely dominate Dinka society and culture. This finding leads to the following conclusions.

The lack of organization in Dinka religion noted by Lienhardt is not just because it has not been rationalized by scholars and priests. It lacks coherence and organization also because the concept of Divinity, as a focus and center of religious authority, is not absolutely dominant.[2] This is because tension in the son-father relationship is but a side of Dinka social relations rather than a crucial problem which resolutely shapes communal traditions and institutions. Consequently, the Dinka remain mystified by real and actual patriarchs, who, as cattle owners, are figures of considerable power in the Dinka homestead.

If tension in the son-father relationship were a crucial problem — and I will eventually consider other people among whom it is — we might expect one side of Dinka religion to be dominant. That side which responds to tension in the son-father relationship, the cosmic patriarchal spirit, would be magnified. That side which reflects the impressive power of patriarchs,

The Multiplicity of Patriarchal Spirits and the Power of Fathers 57

the multiplicity of spirits, would be diminished. As a consequence, the Dinka would be less mystified by real and actual patriarchs than by the remote, more abstract and ethical representation of a patriarchal other. In effect, Dinka religiosity would more closely resemble Middle Eastern monotheisms.

Anticipating the confirmation of such a process among the Nuer, neighbors of the Dinka, the example of the multiplicity of spirits in Dinka religiosity leads to a somewhat surprising conclusion. The Dinka are preoccupied with their relationship to patriarchal spirits, but this preoccupation is not an exclusive one. The considerable importance of the cattle-owning father in Dinka experience is not inconsistent with the importance of still other dimensions of Dinka experience. Hence the presence of Abuk, the maternal free-divinity associated with the productive activities of women. Somewhat paradoxically, the prominence of this alternative to the patriarchal principle is possible precisely because the power of the Dinka father is relatively unquestioned. But were his power more resolutely opposed by the individualism of sons, this issue would dominate Dinka religiosity to the exclusion of any women's goddess like Abuk.

The impressive power of Dinka fathers is therefore correlated with an elaborate patriarchal symbolism, but not with the absence of any alternatives to it. It is the weakening of patriarchal authority in a setting in which such authority is still perceived as the foundation for communal prosperity and security that results in a religion of a cosmic patriarchal spirit to which there are no legitimate alternatives, patriarchal, matriarchal, or otherwise. A crisis of patriarchal authority, not the impressive power of fathers, leads to the domination of society and culture by the spirit of patriarchy. Society and culture are thoroughly patriarchalized when the father is a crucial, but questionable, foundation of communal traditions and institutions.

THE CLAN-DIVINITIES

The clan-divinities throw light on the issues of tension in the son-father relationship and the representation of communal groups among the Dinka. The clan-divinities are symbols of the experience of community, of the caring and nurturing qualities of an intimate and familiar human environment. This experience of community is persistently associated by the Dinka with both paternal ancestors and agnatic relationships, or what anthropologists call "patrilineal descent groups." In effect, when the Dinka associate a representation of community, the clan-divinity, with a patrilineal descent group, they are suggesting that community is linked with common patrilineal descent.

This linkage is, however, problematical. Tension in the son-father relationship, which takes the form of a sense of self apart from and opposed to others, raises the problem of father opposed to son, brother opposed to brother, and agnatic cousin opposed to agnatic cousin. As a result, clan-divinities as representations of the experience of community are not precisely coordinate with agnation (common descent through a male line), even though the Dinka are not inclined to recognize this fact, insisting instead that clan-divinities are "of the father." Moreover, even though the Dinka claim that the agnatic relationships of patrilineal groups are the essence of an experience of community, these relationships can be seen to be tinged by sentiments of competition, if not antagonism and opposition.

According to Lienhardt (1961), clan-divinities are an intimate part of the patriarchal principle of Dinka social organization. The clan-divinities are identified with the experience of the protection and support of agnatic relations:

What the Dinka say about clan-divinities connects the notion of those divinities very closely with their lived experience of the relations between agnatic kin, and of the values of agnatic kinship. (135)

Accordingly, the clan-divinities are appropriately linked with father, father's father, and father's father's father:

They [clan-divinities] are what the Dinka call "divinities of the father" (*yeeth wun*), usually addressed in the singular as *yaan wa*, "divinity of my father," and it is by this, their direct and original association through the father with all the paternal ancestors, that the Dinka distinguish what we have called clan-divinities from free-divinities. (106)

When the clan-divinities are closely examined, however, they are not altogether compatible with agnatic groups or paternal ancestors.

Lienhardt notes that the clan-divinities "resemble the 'totems' of anthropological literature" and "are represented in material forms — in animal and other species" (30). Among the Dinka "priestly" clans, Lienhardt lists the following clan-divinities: Flesh, Hedgehog, *Awar* grass, a certain river spirit (*Malek*), Fresh-water Oyster, Thigh-bone, Sausage-tree, Winnowing-tray (of women), a red cobra, *Wec*-grass, brooms (of this grass), head-rings (of this grass) and the act of Sweeping, Sycamore-tree, Cattle-tick, Catfish, Elephant, Crocodile, and Fire (108–9). Among the Dinka "warrior" clans are the following: Heglig-tree, Giraffe, Black Cobra, Gourd, Lion, Ant-hill, Cattle-egret, Hippopotamus, Fire and Water, Patuic (a species of moth), Mudfish, Paluac (a type of grain), Pestle, Deleib Palm (from which mortars for grinding are made), Pelican and Viper, Deleib Palm and Viper, Monitor Lizard, Tamarind Tree, *Apac* grass, Vulture, Head (of animals), Heart (of beasts), a species of grain-eating bird,

The Multiplicity of Patriarchal Spirits and the Power of Fathers 59

Termite, Jackal, Stone, a species of lizard, Needle, Saddle-billed Stork, Crested Crane, Slow-worm, the river Nile, the Forest, the planet Venus, and Comets (109-10).

These plants, animals, or items, which are styled "divinities of the father" by the Dinka, are not related in a direct way with the symbolism of fatherhood. Indeed, there are probably more of them explicitly related to women than to men. So it is not their inherent symbolism which links them with paternal ancestors and agnatic groups, but rather, as Lienhardt points out, a Dinka commentary on clan-divinities. Lienhardt gives a further example of this commentary in the following passage:

If a Dinka is asked what his divinity is, he may, if he has been personally affected by one of the free-divinities, mention its name; but if he is asked what the divinity of his clan is, or the divinity of his father, or of his ancestors, he will give the name of his clan-divinity, that which he inherited from his paternal ancestors and which he thinks of as linking him with all of them. The clan-divinity, "that of the father," follows (*bwoth cok*) those who have inherited it, supporting and protecting them. They rely upon it to help them when they are travelling and lonely. They may call upon it for help in misfortune or danger, and if they neglect sacrifices to it, they expect it to bring sickness. (106)

Lienhardt concludes that clan-divinities, which are addressed as "you of my father," "you of my ancestor," or *wadit* ("my 'great' father"), are "the very type of agnatic ancestor" and represent "the ideal and permanent values of agnation for the Dinka" (135).

Given the close association of clan-divinities with the father, and through him with paternal ancestors and agnatic groups, Lienhardt (1961) is able to argue that they can be thought of as spirits which mediate between Divinity (*nhialic*) as a form of transcendent fatherhood and more familiar and immediate notions of fatherhood. For example, he advances this point of view when describing the young man who was jailed because his father refused to consent to his marriage. Equating the will of his father with that of Divinity, the young man asks, "Why is not your father like Divinity?"

The Dinka form of the argument by analogy here is consistent with the fact that the ancestors and the clan-divinities, which stand in the relationship of "the fathers" to their descendants and descent-groups, are more closely assimilated in thought to Divinity than is the living human father, and the authority of the living father is for the Dinka connected with their transcendent fatherhood. (42)

For Lienhardt, ancestors and clan-divinities are mediators between Divinity (who represents a form of transcendent fatherhood) and actual fathers (who are the figures of authority in the family and in the homestead). In Lienhardt's view, clan-divinities are part of the machinery of the transcendentalization of fatherhood as represented by the concept of Divinity.

Divinity represents the principle of divine fatherhood for all Dinka, while the clan-divinity represents this principle with respect to a specific patrilineal grouping, which is either broadly or narrowly defined. This view, it should be noted, suggests that Dinka religion is a systematic patriarchal creed with a systematic patriarchal pantheon. That is, Lienhardt surrenders to the impulse to describe Dinka religion as a coherent and integrated set of representations. If the details of his ethnography of clan-divinities are examined, however, little or no evidence is presented which justifies this interpretation. Lienhardt's interpretation of the clan-divinities as mediators between Divinity and fathers appears almost fifty pages away from his detailed account of the clan-divinities. In the ethnography itself, he does not repeat or even refer to this claim, and his ethnography in no way suggests that clan-divinities can be so construed. In his detailed account, Lienhardt notes that clan-divinities are said to have been given to a clan by Divinity (116) and that both Divinity and clan-divinities are simultaneously addressed in rituals and sacrifices (106). But these two observations are as close as he comes to demonstrating or even claiming that clan-divinities are mediators between Divinity and the father.[3]

It is questionable, then, whether the clan-divinities are properly conceived as mediators between a fatherhood on high and a fatherhood down below. It is also questionable whether clan-divinities are as strictly linked with agnation as Lienhardt would have us believe. The Dinka, Lienhardt states, are inclined to respect not just their own clan-divinity but the clan-divinity of their mothers, their maternal kin (110), their husbands (121), their wives (130), and even their neighbors. This indicates that people who are close to one another, whether they be agnatically related or not, symbolize their experience of community through respect for a common clan-divinity. If so, the clan-divinity is only incidentally, rather than essentially, related to agnation.

In raising this question of whether agnation and clan-divinity are altogether compatible, I do not mean to quibble unnecessarily with the ethnographer of the Dinka. A basic feature of Dinka agnation cannot be understood without raising this issue. In fact, Lienhardt himself eventually contradicts his repeated assertions that clan-divinities are "the very type of agnatic ancestor" and represent "the ideal and permanent values of agnation for the Dinka." He makes it clear that agnatic relationships feature problems inconsistent with the kinds of communal sentiments that are represented by clan-divinities.

THE CLAN-DIVINITIES AND AGNATION

The clan-divinities symbolize an experience of community. This is why individuals tend to respect the clan-divinities of all those with whom they are closely associated, their mothers, their maternal kin, their husbands, their wives, and their neighbors. But communal sentiments among the Dinka are themselves strongly influenced by patriarchal ideals and values, as is demonstrated by the important role of patriarchy in defining various communal groups, such as the family, the homestead, the lineage, and the clan. It is therefore not surprising that the clan-divinity, as a symbol of an experience of community, is strongly correlated with agnatic groups, but this does not necessarily mean that it is "the very type of agnatic ancestor" and represents "the ideal and permanent values of agnation for the Dinka."

According to Lienhardt (1961) himself, there are clear differences between agnatic symbolism and clan-divinity symbolism. For example, while agnatic symbolism is public, clan-divinity symbolism is more private:

I have never heard Dinka inquire spontaneously into the divinities of strangers, though they inquire into their clan-affiliations and their homelands.
A clan-divinity thus does not face outwards to other clans, so to speak, appearing as a label or sign by which outsiders may know with whom they have to deal, but relates inwards to the clansmen. By knowing from genealogical evidence that they are agnatically related, they know also that they are united in relation to a common divinity, which for them symbolizes their relationship. (113)

The clan-divinity is more private than clanship, agnation, or homeland, but it is not private to the extent of being a personal or familial symbol. It is, on the contrary, as Lienhardt argues, directly correlated with agnatically defined communal relationships, such as lineages and clans, even if it is somehow different from agnation. The key to this problem lies in the link between the clan-divinity and agnation as alternative representations of an experience of community.

Lienhardt, as ethnographer rather than interpreter of the clan-divinity, observes that "other expressions for the relationship of clansmen with their clan-divinities are that they 'meet' or 'are together' in them."[4] In other words, the clan-divinities express relationships of intimacy and familiarity, like most agnatic relationships. Descent from a paternal ancestor is the definition of some of the most basic social groupings among the patriarchal Dinka, including homestead, lineage, clan, and tribe. But agnatic relationships are not in themselves relationships of intimacy and familiarity, as is evident from the difference between the strictly private knowledge of clan-divinities and the public knowledge of agnatic relationships.

This distinction reveals why the correlation of clan-divinities and agnation is not the same for close as opposed to distant agnatic relationships. There is a tendency for clan-divinities to shift and change so that they always refer to an existing intimate and familiar collectivity, whereas agnatic relationships preserve the historical record of descent more rigidly:

62 The Multiplicity of Patriarchal Spirits and the Power of Fathers

Clans usually have more than one divinity, though one or two in each clan are of primary importance. Different subclans of the same clan often have different secondary divinities, though they have the same clan-name and the same original founding ancestor. The Dinka do not expect all subclans of a clan, which may now be widely separated, to have exactly the same range of divinities; for the divinity is "that of the father," and when ancestors more recent than the founding ancestor of a whole clan have been for a long time separated in different parts of the country, their descendants, as groups, are differentiated in a way which is reflected in their different range of divinities. The divinities of members of a clan thus may differ as the range of those who are recognized as particular agnatic ancestors differ, while they are the same in so far as the same founding ancestor is recognized for any clan throughout Western Dinkaland. Here we see that primary clan-divinities have a close connexion with the Dinkas' experience of the widest groups they recognize, in any area, as having the same agnatic descent. (119-20)

In this passage, Lienhardt insists that clan-divinities and paternal ancestors are closely coordinated. A new clan-divinity appears in conjunction with a new patriarchal ancestor, thereby confirming the Dinka thesis that the clan-divinity is "that of the father." But the evidence could be read somewhat differently. The Dinka symbolize the intimacy and familiarity of the most immediate groupings in their experience by a clan-divinity. At the same time, the Dinka also tend to organize themselves as agnatic groups which are represented by patrilineal ancestors. But these two tendencies must be distinguished, even though there is a strong correlation between clan-divinity and agnatic groups. Three different phenomena reveal this distinction: (1) respect for a clan-divinity is not restricted to the "divinity of the father" but spills over into all intimate and familiar relationships; (2) groups that are distantly related agnates are expected to have a paternal ancestor in common, but are not expected to recognize the same set of clan-divinities; and (3) groups that are closely related agnates are expected to have a paternal ancestor in common and to recognize the same set of clan-divinities. Clan-divinities and patriarchal ancestors are thus strongly correlated only where agnation in common also means intimacy and familiarity in common. This means that representations of groups by clan-divinities and by paternal ancestors are differently motivated. The first attempts to symbolize community as an intimate and familiar experience, whereas the second attempts to organize community under the principle of patrilineal descent.

In fact, clan-divinities might be more experientially "of the mother" than "of the father," for the mother is the inside figure and, as such, a focus and center of the intimate and familiar. But the Dinka do not choose to recognize this, swept away as they are by the father figure as a principle for defining and organizing family, clan, and tribe. Thus, the com-

The Multiplicity of Patriarchal Spirits and the Power of Fathers 63

munity as "mother" is under the constant pressure of being represented as a community of the "father."

If the clan-divinity and agnation cannot be collapsed together, there must be some important difference between agnation as a way of organizing the community and the experience of an intimate and familiar community. Lienhardt (1961) points out this difference in remarks which contradict his own assessment of the clan-divinity and agnation.

Lienhardt's views on the clan-divinities' connection with agnation were quoted earlier: the clan-divinities are directly linked with the Dinka's "lived experience of their relations between agnatic kin, and of the values of agnatic kinship"; they are "the very type of agnatic ancestor," representing "the ideal and permanent values of agnation for the Dinka" (135). But on the same page on which he makes these forceful remarks, Lienhardt contradicts himself by insisting that the essence of the clan-divinity, its symbolism of agnatic relationships as an undifferentiated community, is inconsistent with the experience of agnatic relationships:

The emblems of the clan-divinities, perhaps by virtue of their being non-human, can be thought to form a single undifferentiated group. Each giraffe, for example, is seen by human beings as equivalent to every other giraffe, in space or in time, and is to be treated in the same way by all members of a clan respecting Giraffe. In purely human social relationships this ideal of the equivalence of human clansmen is not fully realized, for they are individuals, and members of families and lineages, and are conspicuously differentiated from each other in these ways. The clan (like the total Dinka world discussed in an earlier chapter) is a divided unity; but in relation to the clan-divinity and its emblem the Dinka transcend the divisions and oppositions between clansmen. As clansmen, not simply as men, they are undifferentiated classificatory half-brothers of an animal or species standing in the same relationship to all, and children of a common ancestor. Hence all the clan "ancestors" become one ancestor in the clan-divinity and all the clansmen become equally "half-brothers," socially equivalent to each other, in relation to the emblems of the divinity. Actual agnatic ancestors give place to each other, changing and dividing the structure of the clan; actual clansmen must be more or less distant from each other, in genealogical space and time. But the clan-divinity and its emblems for the Dinka transcend that space and time, and the differentiations of human clansmen which it produces. (135)

Giraffes are all the same, but men who are agnatically related have different identities. The clan-divinity is not simply an alternative mode of representing agnatic groups but a mode of representing such groups which evades the implications of agnatic representations: son is divided from father, and sons are divided from one another. Thus Lienhardt completely contradicts his own statement that the clan-divinity is the "very type of agnatic ancestor." As shown by Lienhardt's later comments, the value of the clan-divinity as symbol lies in its aspect as a thing of nature, not of man. For as a species, the clan-divinity persuasively represents, as a community, a collectivity within which details of human relationships and identities — as signified by agnation — contradict the experience of community.

Clan-divinities, it can be more confidently concluded, symbolize an intimate and familiar experience of community that is not entirely consistent with agnation. This is why clan-divinities tend to be associated with relatively small agnatic groups, such as the subclan, a collectivity whose members know one another by name and face. Beyond this relatively narrow domain, the experience of community is degraded by mutual competition and suspicion. Accordingly, the clan-divinity signifies, not the way in which the clansmen announce themselves to others, but something shared by the collectivity that is not necessarily meaningful to outsiders. The symbolism of the clan-divinity is therefore parochial and idiomatic, even bizarre and eccentric in its "totemic" form. The clan-divinity makes itself known by distinctive marks on newborn children; it can also be a physical presence close to home, appearing in the homestead or its immediate neighborhood:

Emblems of a clan-divinity are thought to show special preference for the homesteads of their human clansmen, and in some cases are thought to manifest themselves in the clansmen themselves. So it is said that members of a clan with the divinity Cattle-tick are sometimes born with tick-like lumps on their heads, as was their founding ancestor; those clans which have *Rual*, Sausage tree, as their divinity may have children born to them with fleshy lumps resembling the fruits of that tree growing on their fingers. These signs give pleasure to the parents of such children, for, as a Dinka said, it is "as though their divinity has shown itself." Also the emblems of tree, plant, and grass divinities are thought to spring up of their own accord in the homesteads of their clansmen. In fact, one often finds a homestead of Payi with a giant ficus, a homestead of Parum or Padior with a sausage-tree, a homestead of Padiangbar with a heglig, or a homestead of Pajiek in which a tuft of the *wec* grass is growing. . . . The Dinka deny that they themselves have anything to do with planting these emblems; indeed, they think it significant that they should have come *of themselves* to be near their human clansmen, whose faith in their divinities they certainly strengthen by doing so. . . . Again, there often seems to be a certain basis for this belief, in that in places where snakes are particularly numerous, there are sometimes concentrations of members of clans with Snake divinities, and where crocodiles are numerous, there are members of the clan with Crocodile as divinity. (121)

The plants and animals that become clan-divinities are intended to represent what a particular group has in common, not what separates a particular group from other groups. This use of the clan-divinities is clearly reflected by Dinka attitudes toward them. Clan-divinities symbolize feelings of being "at home among friends," and this is more or less the way the Dinka think of them, as representatives of homeliness and friendliness.[5]

The Multiplicity of Patriarchal Spirits and the Power of Fathers 65

The difference between clan-divinities and agnation as two ways of representing social groupings is highly significant and of utmost importance for this study. Clan-divinities, symbols of intimate and familiar relationships, are closely associated with agnatic relationships among the Dinka. But Dinka agnatic relationships feature problems that are inconsistent with the experience of an intimate and familiar community, as Lienhardt (1961) suggests on the same crucial page: "Real human clansmen are in fact differentiated from each other by generation, or by personality, or by family and lineages" (135). Indeed, the symbolism of agnation is double-valued. In one sense, the sense that has most impressed social anthropologists, it defines the boundaries of a human collectivity and the place of the individual within that collectivity. But in another sense, the symbolism of agnation also specifies divisions and oppositions. While the father unites his sons as brothers, his sons also separate from the father to become competing family heads. This is what Lienhardt has in mind in the above statement, which might be rewritten as follows: "Real human clansmen are in fact differentiated from each other by generation [son is opposed to father], or by personality [the individual is opposed to the community], or by family and lineages [brother is opposed to brother]." These oppositions are aspects of any community, of course, but the important point is that symbolism of agnation, that is, the patrilineal genealogy, actually represents them by insisting on degrees of descent. Agnation is not simply one mode of representing patriarchal authority among the Dinka. It potentially reveals that something is wrong with patriarchal authority as a basis of community. What is wrong with it, moreover, is directly related to cattle, since agnation among the Dinka, as among most other animal-herding people, is linked with such matters as herd ownership and inheritance, pasture and water rights, and in general with the defense of cattle, pasture, and water against usurpation or expropriation by others. Among stock keepers like the Dinka, the patriarchal principle is implicated in a concept of personal/collective autonomy and independence, reflected in the problematical dimensions of agnatic relationships, which symbolize both solidarity and opposition. Every agnatic group is both unified and divided, just as the son responds to his father's authority with both submission and rebellion, both assent and dissent.

This feature of Dinka agnation results not from the considerable power of fathers among the Dinka but from tension in the son-father relationship as it is affected by Dinka pastoral ecology. In other words, the "monotheistic" tendency of Dinka religion has as its counterpart the "segmentary" tendency of Dinka social organization. The concept of a divinity over and above the earth which presides over human affairs is a response to the problem of division and opposition within the Dinka community.

This correlation appears in the strong contrast between Divinity and clan-divinity as two incompatible and contradictory ways of representing community. Divinity is not peculiar to the father, the homestead, the lineage, the clan, or the homeland. Divinity is "in the sky" or "on high," not, like so many clan-divinities, on the ground somewhere nearby. The clan-divinities, which represent a patrilineal grouping as a familiar and intimate community, do not refer to concepts of religious authority that govern all men, but rather to sentiments of dependency on and attachment to a face-to-face community.

THE DINKA VIEW OF THE TOTALITY OF DINKA RELIGION

The free-divinities and clan-divinities are for the most part strongly linked with Dinka patriarchal ideals and values. However, unlike Divinity, they reflect not the tension in the son-father relationship but (with the exception of Abuk) the importance of patriarchal authority in defining and organizing social relations. The Dinka themselves do not make such a distinction. They see the matter somewhat differently: "It is asserted by many Dinka that long ago (*watheer*) they knew only Divinity, and Deng who was 'Divinity itself' and the clan-divinities" (Lienhardt 1961:104). When they consider the origin of their religiosity, they see it as comprising Divinity, Deng, and their totems. This excludes the free-divinities with proper names such as Garang, Abuk, and others who, some of the Dinka say, are recent introductions which came to them from other peoples (104).[6]

The Dinka identify their religion with three distinctive kinds of patriarchal spirits: (1) the oneness of a cosmic patriarchal spirit (Divinity), (2) a guardian spirit of a patriarchally defined collectivity (Deng), and (3) totems which represent patriarchally defined collectivities as a protective and supportive community (clan-divinities). Numbers 1 and 3 more or less reflect the two different sides of Dinka patriarchal religiosity: Divinity as cosmic patriarchal other is opposed to clan-divinity as protective and nurturing patriarchal collectivity. The first is up above all human beings. The second is down below, near at hand, belonging to "us" but not to "them." Accordingly, number 2 (Deng) is a spirit which actually fuses the two different sides of Dinka patriarchal religion together. He is "Divinity itself" and therefore the creator of all human beings, but he is also "our" Deng and therefore a parochial, patriarchal protector and nurturer.

The next chapter examines the ethnography of the Nuer, a people who are neighbors of the Dinka and have very similar traditions and institutions. The Nuer's greater emphasis on cattle raiding means that antagonism and opposition to others figure more prominently in Nuer than in

The Multiplicity of Patriarchal Spirits and the Power of Fathers 67

Dinka experience. The life situation of Dinka sons/youths, as opposed to that of Dinka fathers/elders, is more prominent among the Nuer. Consequently, a comparison of the Nuer and Dinka makes it possible to test and extend the conclusions following from an analysis of the relationship of Dinka traditions and institutions to Dinka pastoral ecology.

4

The Nuer Warrior Identity and the Segmentary Principle

THE RELATIVE EMPHASIS ON CATTLE RAIDING
AMONG NUER AND DINKA

Since the nineteenth century, the Nuer have been situated amid the Dinka, dividing the latter into western and eastern groupings (see map 4.1). Although greatly outnumbered by the Dinka,[1] the Nuer had the reputation, among their neighbors and among themselves, of being a warlike people who forayed at will for herds and captives. While various features of Nuer society and history have been matters of debate among anthropologists, this reputation has not been questioned. Before a Pax Britannica was imposed earlier in this century, the Nuer routinely engaged in short- and long-term cattle-raiding expeditions among other neighboring peoples. Moreover, the Nuer contrasted themselves with their neighbors in terms of their greater willingness to engage in fighting and their greater success in seizing cattle by stealth and force. Evans-Pritchard (1940), who worked among the Nuer in the late 1930s, describes the situation in the following terms:

Fighting, like cattle husbandry, is one of the chief activities and dominant interests of all Nuer men, and raiding Dinka for cattle is one of their principal pastimes. Indeed *jaang*, Dinka, is sometimes used to refer to any tribe whom the Nuer habitually raid and from whom they take captives. Boys look forward to the day when they will be able to accompany their elders on these raids against the Dinka, and as soon as youths have been initiated into manhood they begin to plan an attack to enrich themselves and to establish their reputation as warriors. Every Nuer tribe raided Dinka at least every two or three years, and some part of Dinkaland must have been raided annually. Nuer have a proper contempt for Dinka and are derisive of their fighting qualities, saying that they show as little skill as

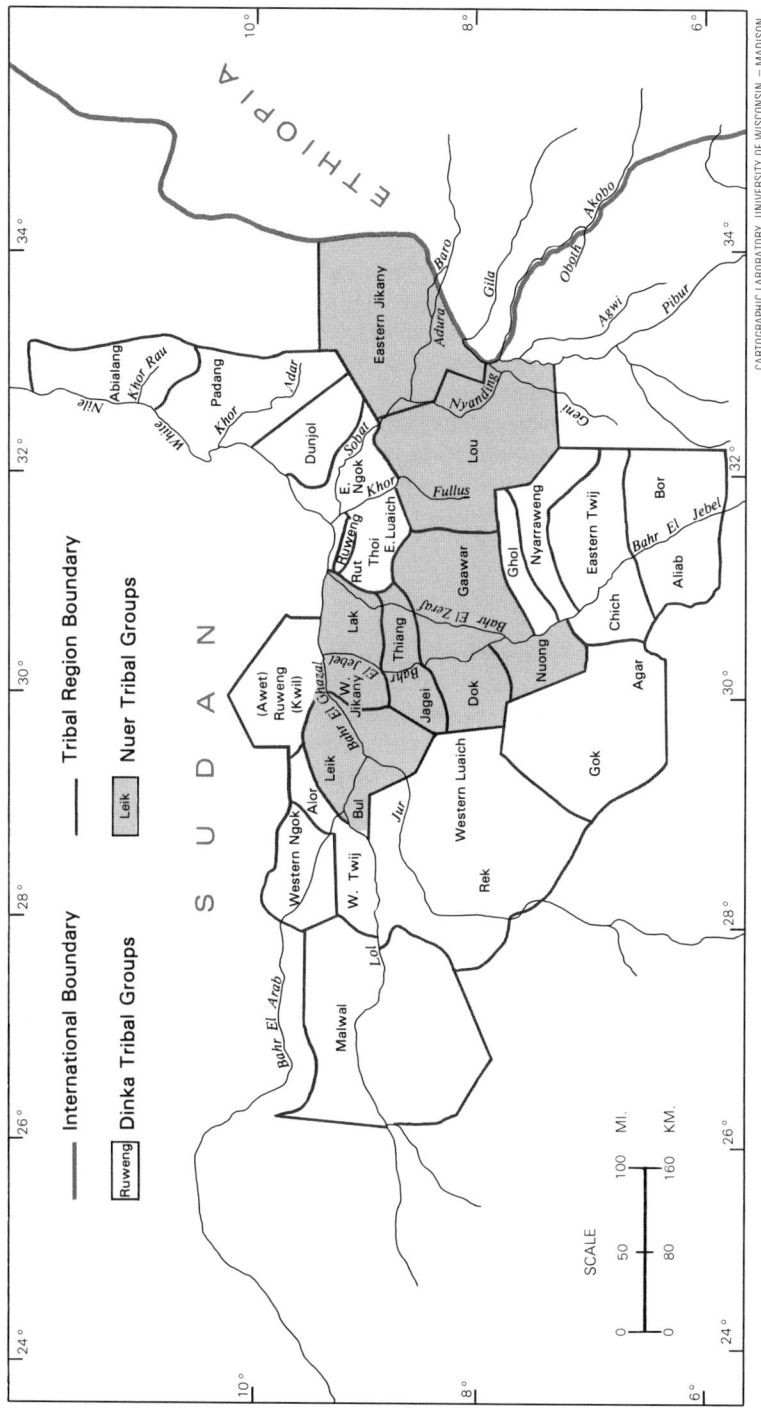

Map 4.1. The Spatial Relationships of Nuer and Dinka (after Kelly 1985)

courage. *Kur jaang*, fighting with Dinka, is considered so trifling a test of valour that it is not thought necessary to bear shields on a raid or to pay any regard to adverse odds, and is contrasted with the dangers of *kur Nath*, fighting between Nuer themselves. (126)

Other earlier and later observers of the Nuer repeatedly make the same points.[2] In comparison with neighboring peoples such as the Dinka, the Nuer saw themselves as a cattle-raiding people and regularly engaged in cattle raids among their neighbors.[3]

The contrasting emphasis on cattle raiding among the Nuer and Dinka is especially interesting because these two peoples speak closely related languages, rely on similar subsistence techniques, and have similar systems of social organization. They even share a myth of their common origins.[4] Indeed, several interpreters of Nilotic ethnography have recently proposed that the Nuer are not distinct from the Dinka at all, but a segment of the Dinka which began to specialize more intensely in military activities.[5] This, however, may be going too far. Linguistic evidence suggests that the separation of the Nuer and Dinka may have taken place no less than two millennia ago, a considerable period of time.[6] Still, the very fact that it has been possible to argue that the Nuer and Dinka are the same people does indicate just how much they have in common.[7]

Southall (1976) and Kelly (1985) have developed the boldest analyses of the common origins of the Nuer and Dinka. Here I summarize Southall's argument because he focuses on the contrasting emphasis on a cattle-raiding, warrior identity among the two peoples.[8] Rejecting the terms "Nuer" and "Dinka" altogether as colonial neologisms, Southall argues that the Nuer do not differ from the Dinka much more than the Dinka differ among themselves.[9] The thesis that the Nuer are not Dinka is based on certain social and cultural contrasts which are apparent only where Dinka and Nuer meet. But where they meet, peculiar politico-economic factors cause these differences. For example, the traditions and institutions of the eastern Nuer are clearly different from those of the Dinka on their borders, but it was here that the Nuer were most active as cattle raiders against their Dinka neighbors. Consequently, Southall concludes, the differences between "Nuer" and "Dinka" are not ethnic in origin, but derive instead from the status of the former as "raider" and the latter as "raided."

As evidence of this point of view, Southall cites Evans-Pritchard's (1940) account of Nuer and Dinka terms of self-reference. The Nuer called themselves "Naath," while the Dinka called themselves "Jieng." At the same time, among the Nuer, the cognate of the Dinka term of self-reference, *jaang*, designated, not just the Dinka, but any people raided by the Nuer. Southall (1976) therefore infers that Nuer and Dinka terms of self-reference should be glossed, respectively, as "those who raid" and "those who are

The Nuer Warrior Identity and the Segmentary Principle 71

raided." For Southall, Naath and Jieng are politico-economic, not ethnic, terms. Here Southall comes very close to an important point, but in my opinion slightly misses the mark. His argument rests on the perspective of the Nuer, who are both picturing and organizing themselves in a certain way. There is no reason to doubt Evans-Pritchard's report that the Nuer prided themselves on being — among other things — "those who raid." But so far as I can determine, there is no recorded evidence that the Dinka saw themselves as the Nuer saw them, as "those who are raided." Furthermore, it seems highly unlikely that they would have taken this view of themselves, being for the most part independent peoples rather than the political subjects of the Nuer.

Despite this qualification, Southall's account of Nuer and Dinka identity brings to our attention an important feature of how the Nuer conceived their own social and cultural identity in contrast with that of their neighbors. He points out that among the Nuer primordial origins and relations — family, lineage, tribe, language, homeland — were often less important than a cultural identity (cattle raider) based on an actual practice (cattle raiding). The Nuer were inclined to believe that the important difference between themselves and other peoples was based on their keen interest in and successful practice of cattle raiding, an activity which the surrounding peoples — most of whom were Dinka — did not favor to the same degree.

Southall's interpretation fits neatly with the readiness of the Nuer to accept Dinka among them. According to Evans-Pritchard (1940), the Nuer were ready and willing to let any *jaang* — "those who are raided" — become *naath* like themselves, "those who raid." As a result of a variety of circumstances, including both Nuer eastward intrusions and Dinka westward migrations, large numbers of Dinka were accepted among the Nuer and assimilated into their social system. Evans-Pritchard estimated that as many as half of the Nuer were Dinka in origin (211). It was not unusual for these Dinka to achieve positions of influence among the Nuer or even to "out-Nuer" the Nuer as cattle raiders. Some of the best known and most influential of Nuer leaders, and some of the most expansive and militant of the Nuer clans, were Dinka in their origins.

Thus, among the Nuer, the terms *naath* and *jaang* are linked with an emphasis on a cultural identity associated with a specific practice. Such a "pastoral warrior identity" is more or less present among all Nilotic cattle-herding peoples, but emphasized among some far more than others. Southall (1976) documents the Nuer's greater emphasis on a pastoral warrior identity as follows:

Commentators on both Jieng [Dinka] and Naath [Nuer] and even on their neighbours, are remarkably unanimous on the nature and importance of Naath raids upon the Jieng. Fighting was one of the chief activities and dominant interests of the Naath (Evans-Pritchard 1940:126) and a method of repairing stock losses (1940:93). Naath youths plan raids to get cattle for themselves as soon as they are initiated, and "every Nuer tribe raided Dinka at least every two or three years and some part of Dinkaland must have been raided annually" (1940:126). Fighting Jieng was a "trifling test" for Naath compared with fighting one another (1940:126). Naath raids were nearly always successful (Howell 1947:133) and Jieng seldom resisted but rather loosed their cattle and tried to drive them away (Evans-Pritchard 1940:127). It is a striking demonstration of the different organisation and orientation of the Jieng that it is "by no means expected that all Dinka within call will rush to the assistance of their fellows against members of a different people" (Lienhardt 1958:129). Lewis confirms a similar reaction of Jieng to attack by the Beir: "If one village is attacked the whole idea of the others is to keep clear" (1972:7). Raiding led to migration and permanent settlement through "the raiders settling permanently in Dinka country and by systematical raiding compelling the inhabitants to withdraw farther and farther from the points of occupation. In the following season a new series of raids was initiated and the process was repeated till the Dinka were compelled to seek refuge with their kinsfolk of another tribe and leave their country to its invaders" (Evans-Pritchard 1940:128). The unconquered Jieng continued to expand, as they moved toward the periphery, and they remained the majority population. They seem to have been more seriously devoted to their agriculture (Stubbs & Morison 1938:252), in addition to their loving care of cattle, whereas Naath agriculture, though resourceful in its way, was more limited [personal communication to Southall from Lienhardt and Howell] and perhaps inhibited by the adverse conditions of the nuclear Naath terrain by which it was originally shaped (Evans-Pritchard 1940:76-7; Howell 1947:131). (Southall 1976: 485)

From the point of view of both images and claims as well as of actual facts and events, the pastoral warrior identity was a more important feature of Nuer than of Dinka culture and practice.[10]

CONTROLLED COMPARISON OF THE NUER AND DINKA

The Nuer emphasis on a pastoral warrior identity means that adolescent experience is strongly associated with contests and conflicts. As a consequence of this, one might expect tension in son-father and youth-elder relationships to be more severe among the Nuer than among the Dinka. But Nuer cattle raiding is correlated, not with such a slight shift, but with a more global reorientation of Nuer traditions and institutions. The Dinka cattle-owning patriarch monopolizes access to cattle through the institutions of bridewealth and inheritance, thereby holding the fate of young men and women in his hands. The situation is somewhat different among the Nuer. Because young men have access to cattle wealth through raiding and warfare, the Nuer cattle-owning patriarch cannot monopolize access

The Nuer Warrior Identity and the Segmentary Principle 73

to it. The authority of fathers and elders over sons and youths is therefore compromised.

The weaker authority of the cattle-owning patriarch among the Nuer is correlated with a weakening of the opposition between cattle-owning fathers and cattle-raiding sons. Among the Nuer, raiding and warfare were not the exclusive interest and practice of newly initiated adolescents, but instead of both younger and older men:

> Boys do not take part in warfare because they would certainly be killed if they did and the same applies to old men. Nevertheless a good number of the older men who are more active than fellow-members of their age-set will accompany expeditions. (Evans-Pritchard 1936:252–53)

In effect, both younger and older men supplemented their cattle herding with cattle raiding so that access to cattle wealth was less monopolized among the Nuer than among the Dinka. The difference between the distribution of cattle among these two peoples is a direct illustration of this. While Dinka cattle ownership was very uneven, some men owning hundreds, other men owning none, Nuer cattle ownership was far more even, there being fewer examples of men who were either very rich or very poor (Kelly 1985:139). And since as cattle raider and cattle herder each individual Nuer was more nearly the master of his fate, Nuer character was somewhat different from Dinka character. Evans-Pritchard (1936) observes:

> Every initiated Nuer is his own lord, paying respect to age and the obligations of kinship, but free and independent, owning no man service. A newly initiated boy may now order his juniors about, see that they do their work thoroughly, and admonish and beat them if they are remiss in any task. Even though he is quite small, and perhaps no older than many who are uninitiated, he is a *wut*, a man, while they are *dholi*, boys. (254)

The relationship of ruling father and subject son has been overshadowed by the figure of an autonomous and independent individual.[11]

The weaker authority of father and elder among the Nuer does not mean that the legitimacy of cattle owning and cattle exchanging were of any less concern to the Nuer than to the Dinka. Cattle raiding was not routinely permitted in the family, lineage, clan, or tribe, but was normally acceptable only among other Nuer or non-Nuer tribes. Closer to home, there was still a high respect and deep concern for the legitimate control and management of cattle, even though disputes and quarrels over this matter were common. Since many Nuer men were both cattle owners and cattle raiders, there was tension, not so much between younger and older generations, but rather between two sides of Nuer behavior and outlook. One side stressed the control and management of cattle and was associated with norms of patriarchal authority, while the other side stressed contests and conflicts over cattle and was associated with an antagonistic and oppositional individualism.

ANTAGONISTIC AND OPPOSITIONAL INDIVIDUALISM AMONG THE NUER

A comparison of Dinka and Nuer songs would no doubt be one of the best places to begin in a study of the implications of a lesser or greater emphasis on cattle raiding. As self-representations, which address personal desires, feelings, frustrations, and ambitions, these songs should be sensitive indicators of any contrast in the experiences of Dinka and Nuer youths. Unfortunately, such a comparison is not yet possible because of the poor documentation of Nuer songs.

Evans-Pritchard (1940) remarks that songs are clearly just as important, if not even more important, for the Nuer as for the Dinka:

Names of cattle, especially oxen, and ox-names of men are used profusely in songs. The Nuer, like most pastoral peoples, are poetic and most men and women compose songs which are sung at dances and concerts or are composed for the creator's own pleasure and chanted by him in lonely pastures and amid the cattle in camp kraals. Youths break into song, praising their kinsmen, sweethearts, and cattle, when they feel happy, wherever they may be. (46)

This passage hints that self-representation is less confined to an appropriate social context and to adolescent males, indicating thereby that Nuer "individualism" is less restricted and limited than that of the Dinka. Beyond such brief remarks, however, very little has been published about Nuer song genres and song texts.[12] Therefore, more indirect evidence, such as Evans-Pritchard's accounts of Nuer character and institutions, has to be relied on, though it has the disadvantage of being a secondhand rather than a firsthand document. Still, the ethnographic portraits that Evans-Pritchard gives us, while lacking the precision and freshness of Nuer self-representations, leave little doubt about the greater importance of an antagonistic and oppositional individualism among both younger and older Nuer men.

Consider, for example, his account of the place of the war spear in the initiation of a young man. Among both the Dinka and Nuer, the father presents his son with both a war spear and a personality ox on the occasion of the young man's initiation.[13] But while Dinka ethnographers have not felt it necessary to stress the meaning of the war spear, Evans-Pritchard (1956) explains that it is a key symbol of Nuer personal and collective identity. In the following passage, he emphasizes the aggressive side of the young man's new status as a warrior:

The Nuer Warrior Identity and the Segmentary Principle 75

When a boy is initiated into manhood and takes on the full responsibilities of that status he is presented by his father with a *mut*, a metal fighting spear, and an ox. . . . It is not just a spear, but a new status that is being given. The boy is now a boy no longer but man and warrior and soon to be husband and father. He takes part in feuds and wars and raids. He also for the first time engages in dances and displays with oxen, both of which among the Nuer are martial exercises as well as play intimately associated with courtship; and also in the pursuits of herding and hunting. (238-39)

Like his ox, the spear is a symbol of the young man's very person:

[The metal war spear is] an extension and external symbol of the right hand, which stands for the strength, vitality, and virtue of the person. It is a projection of the self, so when a man hurls his spear he cries out either "my right hand" or the name of the ox with which he is identified. (233)

In the case of the Nuer youth, the war spear is very possibly an even more essential mark of his attainment of manhood than the personality ox:

A man's fighting spear (*mut*) is constantly in his hand, forming almost a part of him—when he is fighting, hunting, travelling, herding, dancing, displaying himself with his oxen, playing with his comrades, and so on—and when he lays it down it is within his reach; and he is never tired of sharpening and polishing it, for a Nuer is very proud of his spear. (233)

A Nuer youth parades, decorates, and praises his ox only occasionally, but he always has his spear at his side.

While the war spear is an important symbol for the newly initiated adolescent, it is also associated with manhood in general and directly linked with collective life:

Spears, both fighting- and fishing-spears, were something more, and fighting-spears something much more, than weapons of war or of the chase. They were almost parts of the person. I have seen Nuer enraged when neighbours have borrowed their spears without permission, especially if they have lost them, their anger being out of all proportion to the offence if we think of the matter solely in terms of economic value, for the economic value of spears is quite negligible at the present day. It is the audacity and the insult which outrage the owner, as though someone had taken, and perhaps lost, part of his person; and all the more so in the case of the fighting-spear, with which are bound up his manhood and his participation in his lineage. (238)

As a symbol of the person and collectivity, moreover, the war spear emphasizes the antagonistic and oppositional side of both personal and collective identity:

The word *mut*, besides meaning a fighting-spear, has a general sense of taking part in war and raiding: "*ce Nath wa mut*," "the Nuer went raiding"; "*ca mut nang Jaang*," "war was made (by the Nuer) to the Dinka." The idea expressed by the word *mut* in these examples *is not so much the general idea of war and raiding as the idea of a collectivity, the clan or lineage in its political or tribal embodiment, going to war or going on a raid* [my italics]. Hence Father Kiggen [1948:206] correctly translates "*te ke mud mediid*" (his spelling) as "they have a big army." By synecdoche "spear" stands for "battle-host." (245)

Both the Nuer individual and the collectivity are conceived as engaged in contests and conflicts. Evans-Pritchard's analysis of Nuer spear symbolism strongly suggests that this aspect of individual and group identity is more salient among the Nuer than among the Dinka. While this contrast is correlated with a greater and lesser emphasis on cattle raiding, the antagonistic and oppositional side of the Nuer is not wholly restricted to the context of cattle raiding between Nuer and non-Nuer. In fact, in a series of ethnographic sketches, Evans-Pritchard reports that conflicts, disputes, and quarrels, especially with regard to cattle, but spilling over into other matters, are common at various levels of Nuer social relations.

In the following passage, for example, Evans-Pritchard (1940) observes that conflicts over cattle were not at all limited to organized cattle-raiding expeditions among neighboring peoples, but were a more pervasive feature of social relations:

Cattle have also been the chief occasion of strife among Nuer themselves. Indeed, after a successful raid on Dinka stock there is often further fighting over the booty. Thus the Leek raid the Jikany, Rengyan, and other western [Nuer] tribes, and cattle raids are of common occurrence along [Nuer] tribal boundaries elsewhere, for to "steal" (*kwal*) cattle from another tribe is regarded as laudable. Within a tribe, also, fighting frequently results from disputes about cattle between its sections and between individuals of the same section, even of the same village or homestead. Nuer fight on slight provocation and most willingly and frequently when a cow is at stake. On such an issue close kinsmen fight and homes are broken up. When ownership of cattle is in dispute Nuer throw over caution and propriety, showing themselves careless of odds, contemptuous of danger, and full of guile. As my Nuer servant once said to me: "You can trust a Nuer with any amount of money, pounds and pounds and pounds, and go away for years and return and he will not have stolen it; but a single cow—that is a different matter." (49)

This assessment is in sharp contrast with Deng's (1973) account of the preeminent morality of "sociability" (*cieng*) and the subtle individuality of "gentlemanliness" (*dheeng*) among the Dinka. While the ethnographers of the Dinka were impressed with norms of personal submission and cooperation, Evans-Pritchard emphasizes the querulous and combative dimensions of Nuer relationships.

In his most strongly worded passage, Evans-Pritchard (1940) describes the Nuer as having a sense of personal honor and dignity so keen that they are ever prone to resort to violence in defense of it:

The Nuer Warrior Identity and the Segmentary Principle 77

As Nuer are very prone to fighting, people are frequently killed. Indeed it is rare that one sees a senior man who does not show marks of club or spear. . . . A Nuer will at once fight if he considers that he has been insulted, and they are very sensitive and easily take offence. When a man feels that he has suffered an injury there is no authority to whom he can make a complaint and from whom he can obtain redress, so he at once challenges the man who has wronged him to a duel and the challenge must be accepted. There is no other way of settling a dispute and a man's courage is his only immediate protection against aggression. Only when kinship or age-set status inhibits an appeal to arms does a Nuer hesitate to utter a challenge, for it does not occur to him to ask advice first, and no one would listen to unsolicited advice. From their earliest years children are encouraged by their elders to settle all disputes by fighting, and they grow up to regard skill in fighting the most necessary accomplishment and courage the highest virtue. (151)

This account is unacceptable as literal fact. Evans-Pritchard observes that "people are frequently killed" among the Nuer. Does this mean that people are killed hourly or daily? No doubt, Evans-Pritchard only means that each month, or perhaps each year, some homicides occur. But in this respect, the Nuer are not very different from most other peoples, including the Dinka. Evans-Pritchard continues in the same vein of hyperbole. A Nuer will resort to duel at once if he considers that he has been insulted. There is no other way of settling a dispute other than violence. It does not occur to the Nuer individual to ask advice. The child is encouraged to settle all disputes by fighting. Fighting and courage are the highest virtue. All these statements are contradicted by other observations that appear in the very book from which this quotation is taken. Evans-Pritchard is clearly describing only one side of the Nuer, "the fighting Nuer" (Johnson 1981). As a literal account, the preceding sketch of Nuer contentiousness is certainly misleading, if not palpably false. Nonetheless, as comparative ethnographic portraiture, it makes a valid point confirmed by other observers. While the Nuer are in many ways very similar to the Dinka, an antagonistic and oppositional side of Nuer personal identity, directly linked with a practico-cultural emphasis on cattle raiding, left a vivid mark on the quality of Nuer social relations in general. The Nuer could be one of the more, if not the most, contentious Nilotic people of the southern Sudan, but they did not by any means have a monomaniacal focus on fighting. Taken as a whole, Evans-Pritchard's various descriptions of the Nuer demonstrate that they appreciated the virtues of sociability, reflection, humor, friendship, and cooperation, despite the less-than-favorable conditions in which he had encountered them.[14] Indeed, the distinctive feature of Nuer social relations is not simply an emphasis on aggression at the expense of sociability, but rather the precise relationship between the two. Nuer social relations, unlike those of the Dinka, are problematical. At every level—family, lineage, clan, and tribe—norms of cooperation and solidarity are set against contradictory norms of antagonism and opposition. This is indirectly apparent from Evans-Pritchard's account of what he called the segmentary principle of Nuer political institutions.

EVANS-PRITCHARD'S ACCOUNT OF THE NUER SEGMENTARY PRINCIPLE

In his classic study of Nuer politics and ecology, Evans-Pritchard (1940) was exploring the question of how a cattle-herding people without a centralized regime — an "acephalous" people, as anthropologists came to style them — might achieve a measure of political stability. In particular, he was concerned with how serious conflicts which threatened to disrupt their means of livelihood might be controlled and resolved. To deal with this problem, he examined the way in which the Nuer represented the relationships of territorial groups, agnatic lineages, and age-sets, and he developed a theory of how these representations instituted checks and balances which forced opposing parties into settlements with one another. His argument is summarized below.

Among the Nuer there is a strong tendency for collectivities to divide into two or more opposed collectivities on the occasion of some dispute. These collectivities are represented as fighting groups constituted for the purpose of a resort to armed force. Faced with a standoff between two comparable groups, both parties are usually persuaded by a neutral third party to settle their differences and reach some compromise. In this way, a stable political system results, despite the absence of a regime. Since every Nuer collectivity is divided into opposed groups — from the level of tribe down to the level of family — Evans-Pritchard described the Nuer political system as featuring a segmentary principle. And because the segmentary principle led to political stability through a process of confrontation and hostility, Evans-Pritchard called the Nuer political system an "ordered anarchy."

Evans-Pritchard's (1940) study, *The Nuer: A Description of the Modes of Livelihood and Political Institutions of a Nilotic People,* can no longer be accepted at face value. Over the years some telling criticisms have been made of his claim that the segmentary principle was the institutional foundation for political order among the Nuer. At the same time, anthropologists agree that his study does draw attention to a fundamental feature of Nuer society. The segmentary principle says very little about the specific pattern of political processes among the Nuer, but it does reveal an important aspect of Nuer thinking and experience. This consensus is based on the conclusions of various studies over the past twenty years or so.

The Nuer, more than the Dinka, have collective representations which feature a segmentary principle (Gough 1971; Kelly 1985:157–88). These collective representations cannot be presumed to define the actual groups which emerge in the course of Nuer political processes, nor can Nuer political processes be presumed to involve the systematic combining and dividing of any groups whatsoever (Holy 1979a, 1979b). Nuer collective representations are idealizations not necessarily in accord with political realities, and other Nuer political concepts and procedures correspond more closely to actual practice (Holy 1979a, 1979b). Nevertheless, the Nuer groupings which feature a segmentary principle should not be dismissed because they are more "symbolic" than "practical" in their significance. They reveal something about the character of Nuer thinking and experience (Karp and Maynard 1983), especially about their involvement in cattle raiding and cattle warfare (Gough 1971:90; Southall 1976:472–73; Bonte 1979).[15]

This consensus is a broad one which has been emerging since Gough's 1971 article, but it is not unanimous. Harking back to a point of view (Lienhardt 1958; Sahlins 1961; Newcomer 1972) that predates the above criticism, Kelly (1985) has recently addressed the specific issue of the Nuer's success in their raids and wars against the Dinka.[16] Kelly takes the position that the segmentary principle described by Evans-Pritchard was an institutional mechanism for achieving political cooperation and solidarity. Since such a segmentary principle did not exist among the Dinka, he concludes that it was a crucial means for the Nuer's triumph over the Dinka in seizing both cattle and pasture. Thus, Kelly believes not only that the segmentary collectivities of the Nuer do indeed reflect actual political groupings which emerge in the course of Nuer political processes, but also that the thrust of these collectivities was toward the unification of political groups. Because the Nuer had invented an institution that the Dinka had not, he argues, the Nuer were better organized, higher on a scale of social evolution than the Dinka, and destined in time to replace and absorb the Dinka had it not been for the arrival of the British in the Sudan.

Though Kelly's study has many virtues, it is difficult to accept this particular argument, since it rests on a superficial reading of one aspect of Nuer ethnography. In fact, Kelly has not given much consideration to just what Evans-Pritchard meant by a segmentary principle. It is true that Nuer collective representations imply that small groups combine into larger and larger groups. It is also true that Dinka collective representations do not feature this same property on the same scale or to the same degree as those of the Nuer. Kelly (1985:157–88) has admirably demonstrated these points. But the coalescence of small groups into larger and larger groups is only one side of the Nuer segmentary principle as described by Evans-Pritchard, the other side being the disintegration of large groups into smaller and smaller groups which are opposed as fighting groups.

If the Nuer are able to compose larger groups than the Dinka, it might also be argued that all Nuer groups are more fractious and unstable than Dinka groups.

Furthermore, while Lienhardt (1958), Sahlins (1961), and Newcomer (1972) advanced their arguments before criticism of *The Nuer* had fully matured, Kelly (1985) has not adequately addressed this criticism. He has asserted, rather than demonstrated, that Nuer collective representations were the institutional means by which the Nuer were able to assemble larger military groups than the Dinka, enabling the former to overcome the latter in any battle. But no one, including Evans-Pritchard himself, has provided a detailed account of the place of Nuer collective representations in the context of Nuer-Nuer or Nuer-Dinka confrontations. On the contrary, the descriptions of Nuer raids against Dinka that are available make a much simpler point. The Nuer were more determined fighters who looked upon the prospect of a cattle raid in Dinkaland as a trifling affair. The Dinka, upon sighting groups of Nuer intent on seizing cattle, tended to abandon the field to them whether the Nuer were present in either large or small numbers.[17] With regard to their success in raids and wars, the crucial feature of Nuer society is more simply the practico-cultural emphasis on the warrior identity, not collective representations which feature a segmentary principle. Indeed, such representations are more likely caused by, rather than the cause of, the Nuer emphasis on the warrior identity, a point made some time ago by Gough (1971:88, 90).[18]

THE SEGMENTARY PRINCIPLE IN NUER THINKING AND EXPERIENCE

The specific issue which criticism of *The Nuer* has so far failed to resolve is how and why the segmentary principle is linked with Nuer engagement in pastoral raiding and warfare.[19] This problem can be worked out by considering those collective representations which feature a segmentary principle as ideological constructions which are strongly influenced by one specific side of thinking and experience, the pastoral warrior identity.

Among the western Nuer studied by Evans-Pritchard (1940), a tribe consists of numerous separate local groups, each of which is closely associated with a lineage segment of a dominant clan. The members of this dominant clan represent a minority in the local group. Considered to be the original occupiers of the land, they are "aristocrats" (*dil*) with a slightly superior social position in what is otherwise a relatively egalitarian society. The majority in each local group belong to other "stranger" (*rul*) clans whose members are in many cases of Dinka origin. According to Evans-Pritchard, the political relationships of all the local groups of a tribe are

The Nuer Warrior Identity and the Segmentary Principle 81

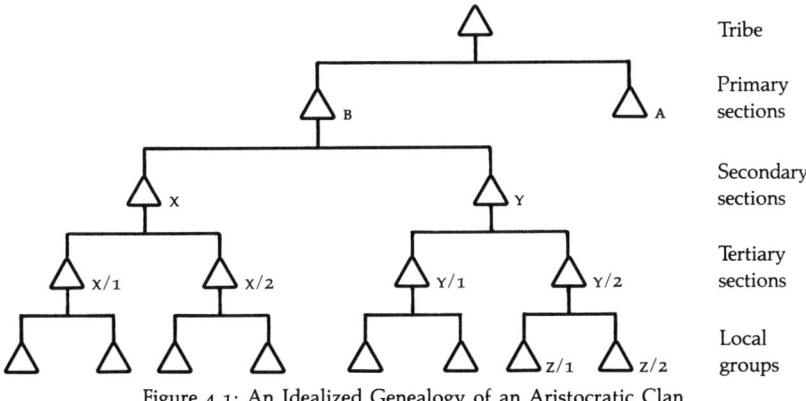

Figure 4.1: An Idealized Genealogy of an Aristocratic Clan

structured according to the genealogical relationships of the lineages of the dominant (*dil*) clan. Thus, the genealogy of the dominant clan serves as a kind of paradigm for the political organization of the tribe, whereby each local group is progressively incorporated into a framework of ever larger political groupings by a patrilineal genealogy (240–41). Figure 4.1 illustrates an idealized version of the genealogy of such a dominant clan. All males represented in the genealogy are the patrilineal ancestors of the members of the dominant clan. Those at the bottom (z/1, z/2) represent the apical ancestors of each local lineage associated with a local group. These local lineages combine into minor lineages at a higher level of the genealogy (x/1, x/2, y/1, y/2). These combine into still larger major lineages at a still higher level (x, y), which combine into even larger maximal lineages (A, B). As a result of this system of genealogical representations, the tribe has a structure which consists (starting now from the top and moving down) of primary sections, secondary sections, and tertiary sections, where each of these divisions is coordinated with the division of the dominant clan into lineages.

According to Evans-Pritchard's interpretation of this genealogical representation of tribal political structure, any dispute among the members of two local groups activates political alliances and oppositions as determined by the closeness or distance of agnatic relationships. Any local group would thus receive the support of all other closely related local groups in its disputes with more distantly related local groups. In principle, this leads to a process of collective fusion and fission. Territorial groups and clan lineages coalesce and dissolve with reference to different political disputes. Presenting the diagram in figure 4.2, Evans-Pritchard cites a Nuer informant's comment on Nuer political procedure and then uses the comment to explicate what he calls the segmentary principle of Nuer politics:

Thus a man of the Fadang section of the Bor tribe exemplified it when he told me, "We fight against the Rengyan, but when either of us is fighting a third party we combine with them." It can be stated in hypothetical terms by the Nuer themselves and can best be represented in this way. . . . When z/1 fights z/2 no other section is involved. When z/1 fights y/1, z/1 and z/2 unite as y/2. When y/1 fights x/1, y/1 and y/2 unite, and so do x/1 and x/2. When x/1 fights A, x/1, x/2, y/1, and y/2 all unite as B. When A raids the Dinka A and B may unite. (143–44)

Note that the Nuer informant speaks in an idiom of conflict and violence among fighting groups instead of the common interests of a section in herds, pasture, and water. This does not necessarily mean that the tribal sections have an existence only insofar as there is raiding and warfare; however, it does suggest that such collectivities, to the extent that they are construed in terms of the segmentary principle, are represented as though they were fighting groups. When the Nuer are talking about their political organization in segmentary terms, the warrior identity is in the background of their thinking.

Such an interpretation insists on giving priority to how the Nuer construct their experience. What is at issue is not the place of their collective representations on the occasion of some particular dispute or conflict, but rather the ideological stance that they assume as they reflect upon their political experiences. A hundred secondhand accounts of Nuer political processes will not resolve this issue unless Nuer reactions in word and deed are also recorded. Unfortunately, Evans-Pritchard's ethnography is somewhat lacking in this kind of material, in contrast with the work of his student Lienhardt, and especially with the work of the student of his student, Deng.[20]

However, the significance which the Nuer attached to segmentary collective representations can be uncovered in an indirect way. Revealing inconsistencies in Evans-Pritchard's account suggest that the Nuer saw a meaning in their collective representations that the ethnographer missed. One such inconsistency involves his observation that the age-sets of the

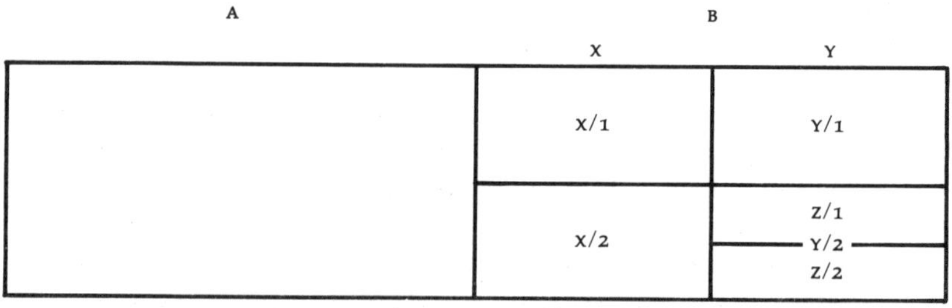

A	B	
	X	Y
	x/1	y/1
	x/2	z/1 y/2 z/2

Fig. 4.2: Evans-Pritchard's Diagram of the Segmentary Principle

The Nuer Warrior Identity and the Segmentary Principle 83

Nuer also feature a segmentary principle, an idea whose import can be understood only with reference to the place of *The Nuer* in anthropology.

THE SEGMENTARY PRINCIPLE OF NUER AGE-SETS

Evans-Pritchard's study of Nuer politics and ecology has had an enduring place in anthropology because it addresses the problem of the relationship of ideological constructions to political processes. However, after its initial appearance, *The Nuer* most intensely interested anthropologists concerned with an excessively narrow approach to this issue. This approach, which can be styled "segmentary lineage theory," involved the study of lineage representations of various tribal peoples from a comparative sociological perspective. Its proponents assumed that the lineage representations of different peoples were a unitary phenomenon of social organization, and, accordingly, they attempted to arrive at generalizations about how the segmenting form of a lineage was the key to understanding political behavior and processes. Thus the lineages of peoples who had different historical backgrounds and who followed different ways of life were nonetheless assessed as reflecting similar principles of social organization.[21] For example, the lineage systems of the Nilotic-speaking Nuer, who are pastoralists, have frequently been closely compared with those of the Bantu-speaking Tiv, who are agriculturalists, without any discussion of the many differences between these two peoples' representation of lineages or understanding of their significance.

In the years following the publication of *The Nuer*, it was more or less forgotten by anthropologists, including perhaps Evans-Pritchard himself, that the segmentary principle was not a feature only of Nuer lineages. In their enthusiasm for applying Evans-Pritchard's analysis to the lineage systems of nonmodern peoples all over the world, the notion of a segmentary principle was torn from its place in an ethnography of the Nuer way of life. A review of this ethnography, however, clearly shows that the segmentary principle was a *culture-specific* phenomenon.[22]

According to Evans-Pritchard (1940), the segmentary principle was a prominent feature of Nuer collective life. It was evident in the composition of territorial groups, where smaller groups combined into larger groups and larger groups divided into smaller groups. It was evident in the composition of clans, where smaller lineages combined into larger lineages and larger lineages divided into smaller lineages. And it was also evident in the composition of age-sets. But age-sets, by Evans-Pritchard's own admission, have nothing to do with the Nuer political system and therefore nothing to do with the resolution of dispute and conflict by the balanced opposition of fighting groups. Why, then, do age-sets feature the form when they do not serve the function? In the final pages of *The Nuer*, where this problem is discussed, Evans-Pritchard concludes that the segmentary principle is more nearly a way of thinking about identity and relationships, not an institutional mechanism of political stability.

In the main part of his study, Evans-Pritchard argues that Nuer territorial groups and clan lineages lead to a "complementary opposition" of fighting groups and therefore play an important role in maintaining order among the Nuer pastoralists. When he turns to the age-set, however, he specifically denies that these groups have any relationship to such a politico-economic function: "The age-set system of a tribe is in no way its military organization. Men fight by villages and by tribal sections and not by sets" (254). He suggests instead that the significance of age-sets is only social and domestic: "It is in more general social relations, chiefly of a domestic and kinship order, and not in political relations that behaviour is specifically determined by the positions of persons in age-set structure" (254). But if the age-set is not part of the political system, why is it included in a study of Nuer politics and ecology? If it is nearer to the issues of the "domestic and kinship order," why did Evans-Pritchard not relegate his account of age-sets to his study of Nuer kinship and marriage (Evans-Pritchard 1951a)? A close look at Evans-Pritchard's (1940) analysis provides answers to these questions. He describes age-sets as yet another illustration of the segmentary principle:

> The age-set system is a further exemplification of the segmentary principle which we have seen to be so evident a quality of social structure. Tribes segment into sections and their sections further segment, so that any local group is a balanced relation between opposed segments. Clans segment into lineages and their lineages further segment, so that any lineage group is a balanced relation between opposed segments. Likewise the institution based on age is highly segmentary, being stratified into sets which are opposed groups, and these sets are further stratified into successive sections. (255)

In this passage the segmentary principle of age-sets is explicitly likened to that of territorial groups and clan lineages. It is a means of balancing opposed groups. But in the context of the age-set system, this balancing of opposed groups serves no clear-cut politico-economic function. The whole point of the balancing of opposed groupings, according to Evans-Pritchard's account of tribal sections and clan lineages, is to provide a measure of political stability and order so that the pastoral way of life can be successfully pursued. But the age-set is a relatively gratuitous expression of the segmentary principle, since it plays no direct and intimate role in the political relationships of local communities.

This assessment of Evans-Pritchard's argument may be confirmed by turning to a passage where he seems to notice that he has been caught

The Nuer Warrior Identity and the Segmentary Principle 85

in a contradiction. Having said that the age-set system is to be associated with the domestic and social order, not the political order (254), he then feels obliged to explain how age-sets do have a function in the political order. He begins by noting that age-sets, while lacking "leadership and administrative and judicial functions," do establish ties across local communities. This means that they do, after all, impinge on the political context. But having said this, he hesitates and contradicts himself once again:

> The age-set system has been briefly treated because of this action [cross-communal ties] and also because, in the larger tribes at any rate, it is a tribal institution. It segments the male population of a tribe into stratified groups which stand in a definite relationship to one another and it cuts across territorial divisions, giving identity of status where there is political disparity and differentiating status where there is political identity. *However, the political system and the age-set system do not seem to be interdependent* [my italics]. (260)

The age-sets do have some political implications, but their implications, the establishment of cross-communal ties, are not particularly impressive nor in any way unique. The Nuer establish cross-communal ties in many ways, so the age-set system cannot be explained by its unique fulfillment of such a function. Indeed, if the general matter of cross-communal ties is to be considered as part of the Nuer political system, Evans-Pritchard should have discussed Nuer kinship and marriage, Nuer religion, and all manner of other subjects that he chose not to examine in *The Nuer* but to describe in other books and articles. His explicit justification for ending his book on Nuer politics and ecology with a discussion of age-sets is therefore an exceedingly weak one. Furthermore, Evans-Pritchard seems to want to recognize the insufficiency of his argument, for he concludes the passage in which he justifies his description of age-sets by insisting that the political and age-set systems do not appear to be interdependent. If the age-set is not, unlike the section or the lineage, a politico-economic grouping, what kind of grouping is it?

Even though the age-set is not the basis of Nuer military organization, it is indisputably connected with the Nuer warrior identity. This is plainly apparent from the interlinkage of adolescent assumption of warrior identity, initiation rites, age-set formations, and ritualized confrontations of opposed age-sets. If, as I am arguing, the pastoral warrior identity is behind the segmentary principle, it is entirely appropriate for Evans-Pritchard to insist that the age-set formations exemplify the segmentary principle. But when Evans-Pritchard observes that the segmentary principle is expressed by age-set formations as well as by territorial groupings and clan lineages, he is implying that a form of personal identity, the pastoral warrior identity, lies not only behind age-sets but also behind these other collective representations. If so, both age-sets and the territorial groupings and clan lineages conceived by the Nuer as fighting groups are more or less orderly expressions of antagonism and opposition within society itself. This means that Nuer collective representations have an ambiguous role in achieving political stability and order among these acephalous peoples. In fact, these collectivities are less an institutional mechanism for stability and order than evidence that antagonism and opposition have broken the boundaries of their ritual containment by age-set formations and become part and parcel of society itself. In effect, cattle raiding has given the Nuer a keener sense of the self apart from and opposed to others and this sense is blatantly featured in their representation of the composition of territorial groupings and clan lineages. Among the Nuer, some men come together in defense of interests challenged and opposed by other men, and this comes about at every level of society, from family to clan and from tribe to *naath* versus *jaang*.

Why did Evans-Pritchard not see this, especially when he realized that the age-set featured the form, even though it did not serve the function, of his "segmentary principle"? He could not accept the implications of the parallel: warrior identity is to territorial group and clan lineage just as warrior identity is to age-set. He could not, precisely because of his unusual perspicacity as an ethnographer; for the parallel undermines the very thesis of his study of Nuer politics and ecology. If Evans-Pritchard were to realize that the pastoral warrior identity of Nuer age-set formations is also behind Nuer collective representations, he would also realize that tribe, section, clan, and lineage played an ambiguous role in maintaining order and stability. In fact, tribe, section, clan, and lineage are as much vehicles of conflict and disorder as stability and order, because they are touched by the pastoral warrior identity. Evans-Pritchard's summation of Nuer politics as an ordered anarchy must therefore be reread to lend it a meaning that its author did not explicitly state but may have implicitly perceived.

It is the opposition of Nuer age-sets according to the segmentary principle that allows a relatively contained and controlled intratribal expression of men's claims to honor and dignity through combat. But the Dinka also have age-sets which obey the segmentary principle, even though they do not have the segmenting lineages, clans, and sections of the Nuer. Thus, the segmentary principle holds true in both societies where the pastoral warrior identity — an identity which depends on self-assertion, antagonism, and combativeness — is influential. Among the Dinka, the segmentary principle is relatively contained and controlled within the domain of age-sets, whereas among the Nuer it has touched and shaped the representation of all collectivities, where it plays a fundamental role in (but does not necessarily determine mechanically) political events and process. The segmentary principle which Evans-Pritchard describes as pervading Nuer society on the level of sections, clans, lineages, and age-sets is in fact the reflection of the greater prominence of the pastoral warrior identity among these cattle-raiding, cattle-warring peoples.

The segmentary principle has to be understood, then, not precisely as the framework of Nuer political organization, but as a mode of Nuer political thinking and experience that was deeply influenced by the pastoral warrior identity. It is a principle which reflects a problematical relationship of person and society. The Nuer are preoccupied with peace and security just as much as, if not even more than, the Dinka. What is different is that solidarity and cooperation among the Nuer are closely associated with division and opposition. The Nuer have a more secularized and politicized concept of social life, in which assertion of the relative autonomy and independence of the individual and collectivity are constantly in play.

The differing character of Nuer and Dinka political organization reflects this contrast. The Nuer had larger tribes and were more cognizant of the world beyond the immediate local group in which individuals lived; Dinka tribes were smaller and more parochially concerned with their own little communities.[23] Antagonism and opposition as dimensions of personal and collective identity are correlated with a greater awareness and concern about human affairs beyond the local group. There is a sense of both safety and danger in the presence of others that refocuses the Nuer imagination on the extracommunal world of politics. Consequently, even though the Nuer may have been capable of organizing larger military expeditions than the Dinka, their segmentary collective representations were not derived for this special purpose. Their collective representations which simultaneously feature solidarity and opposition are more ambiguous results of their involvement in cattle raiding. They show that the Nuer had a sense of themselves apart from and opposed to others, but also a sense of their individual fates and fortunes as linked with others, not only their family and friends, not only their more distant relatives, but even unseen and unknown people.

Sahlins (1961), Newcomer (1972), and Kelly (1985) are not wrong, then, in seeing some connection between the segmentary principle and Nuer pastoral raiding and warfare with the Dinka, but the segmentary principle does not have the utilitarian function they attributed to it. Rather, as an aspect of Nuer social representations, it reflects a moral perception that has a problematical relationship to experience.[24]

THE SECULARIZATION AND POLITICIZATION OF NUER SOCIETY

The greater emphasis on the pastoral warrior identity among the Nuer than among the Dinka is also correlated with a contrast in social relations. Nuer society is not so much composed of local groups, homesteads, and families headed by cattle-owning patriarchs in the manner of the Dinka. More prominent in Nuer society is a political process of combination and division as cattle-owning cattle raiders assert and defend their rights before one another. The religious mode of the Dinka, who revere the impressive power of the cattle-owning father, contrasts with the secular mode of the Nuer, who admire the cattle-raiding son who asserts himself through antagonism and opposition to others.

This contrast between Dinka religiosity and Nuer secularism goes back to the relative power of the cattle-owning patriarch in each society. Among the Dinka, the cattle-owning patriarch holds the security and welfare of his charges in his hands; hence, the collective life of the Dinka is infused with symbols of father figures which represent relationships of attachment and dependency. But among the Nuer the authority of the cattle-owning patriarch has been dealt a blow by an emphasis on cattle raiding. The cattle-owning patriarch no longer holds a monopoly over cattle wealth, individuals have a greater sense of their personal autonomy and independence, and the character of Nuer social relations is altered. The spiritual power of the father figure, which serves to define and organize communal life among the Dinka, is displaced among the Nuer by a secular, political process of alliance and confrontation. Accordingly, the role of religion, which is bound up with patriarchal authority among Nilotic cattle herders, is a less important dimension of Nuer than of Dinka social relations.[25] This can be illustrated by the relative development of a priesthood of elders among the Nuer and the Dinka.

In recent discussions of the Nuer and Dinka, anthropologists have noted that the Nuer "leopard-skin chief" and the Dinka "master of the fishing spear" are similar priestly figures who function as peace makers in their respective societies. However, the former is only a marginal figure among the Nuer, whereas for the Dinka the latter is a central figure.

Lienhardt (1961) was obliged to devote a major portion of his book to the myths, rites, and social functions of the Dinka master of the fishing spear. Like the leopard-skin chief, the master of the fishing spear is a peace maker, but unlike him, his various other offices and duties make him one of the most prestigious figures of Dinka society. He is a priestly elder who is able to bring the Dinka together when they are faced with dire circumstances, including the necessity of uniting for warfare:

The functions of masters of the fishing-spear mentioned by all Dinka are their prayer, invocations, and sacrifice for the cure of the sick and the vitality and prosperity of their people, their driving away of lions and other dangers of the forest and of the river, their mediation between enemies and settlement of feuds, and finally and most important, in the past at least, their invocations for victory in war and raiding. (211)

The Nuer Warrior Identity and the Segmentary Principle 89

The spiritual authority of this priestly elder in the matter of raiding and warfare is consistent with another function of the master of the fishing spear, the opening and closing of age-sets:

> One of the functions of masters of the fishing-spear was to open and close age-sets; and though the age-sets seem never to have had in themselves specific regimental functions, their pride and reputation were and are still connected with their military prowess. Consequently, a renowned master of the fishing-spear was himself at the centre of the military organization of his people, and the inspiration of the most active fighting men. So, though every public sacrifice involves warlike display, at the burying of a master of the fishing-spear the fighting power of his people is particularly emphasized. Members of groups other than those rallied by the ceremony are in danger if they approach it; the young men are fully armed for war; and the cattle are tethered during the day, not taken out in their separate herding groups which are weak in the face of attack. (318)

Among the Dinka, a priestly elder is closely correlated with military victory, military organization, and military identity, even though all these matters are the special sphere of warrior youths. This is consistent with the fact that initiation rites and age-set formations, while being occasions where youths express the warrior identity, are also instruments of patriarchal authority which contain that identity within the framework of social traditions and institutions (see chap. 1).

Significantly, the Nuer have no priestly elder who can compare with the Dinka master of the fishing spear.[26] Instead, the secular and political dimensions of Nuer society are more developed (as indicated by the prominence of the segmentary principle) while its ceremonial and religious dimensions are diminished and marginalized. This is seen in contrasts between the Dinka master of the fishing spear and the Nuer leopard-skin chief. The former is a commanding figure in society who settles differences, achieves unity, organizes military activities, and opens and closes age-sets, but the latter is an outsider, often of Dinka rather than Nuer origin, who is no more than a neutral mediator in the quarrels and feuds among lineages.

Among the Nuer, the leopard-skin chief's activities are strictly limited to settling lineage feuds. In the few pages that he devotes to these marginal figures, Evans-Pritchard (1956) observes that their duties are "tiresome and ill-rewarded, but somebody has to perform them" (293). In the eyes of the Nuer, the leopard-skin chief is not a priestly elder who has an impressive moral authority but more nearly a useful "instrument" of warrior sections and lineages who are obliged to turn to an outsider as a mediator.[27] The Nuer leopard-skin chief does not perform the full range of religious and organizational functions of the Dinka master of the fishing spear.

The characteristics of the Nuer elder who does open and close age-sets, the "man of the cattle," are also revealing. He is a secular rather than a priestly figure. Evans-Pritchard notes that the man of the cattle is "not by virtue of his office a person of social importance" (301) and is an even less impressive figure than the leopard-skin chief (cf. Beidelman 1971):

> It is remarkable that, considering what cattle mean to the Nuer, the man of the cattle is not socially or ritually so important a figure as the priest of the earth [leopard-skin chief]. Doubtless this is because his functions in the organization of the age-sets are not so often brought into play, nor so striking and important, spiritually and socially, as the priest's function in homicides and the feuds that arise from them. (Evans-Pritchard 1956:302)

The important priestly function — such as it is — among the Nuer is associated with hostilities between opposed sections and lineages, not with the opening and closing of age-sets. The latter, however, are major functions of the Dinka master of the fishing spear, for initiation rites and age-set formations are the crucial means by which Dinka fathers and elders supervise the coming of age of young adolescents who are assuming a warrior identity. Therefore, the fact that the Nuer man of the cattle who opens and closes age-sets is not an impressive priestly figure with supernatural powers reveals that the patriarchal supervision of the warrior identity is diminished.

THE PROBLEMATICAL RELATIONSHIP OF SELF AND OTHER

The Nuer representation of tribes, sections, clans, and lineages does not necessarily indicate actual political alliances and oppositions. In fact, by the standard of more recent ethnographies, Evans-Pritchard's 1940 study really tells us very little about Nuer political processes. Furthermore, the segmentary principle exhibited by the Nuer representation of territorial groups, agnatic lineages, and age-sets does not exhaust Nuer political thinking and experience. Among the Nuer, certain individuals do act as "elders," "chiefs," "priests," and "prophets," even if such offices are not so developed as among the Dinka. And, like all Nilotic peoples, the Nuer also have legal customs and legal procedures (Deng 1973:71–73; Howell 1954). Nuer society is therefore inaccurately stereotyped as either acephalous or anarchic. Nevertheless, Evans-Pritchard, in portraying a segmentary principle, does bring into focus one particular mode of political thinking and experience among the Nuer.[28] He clearly demonstrates that features of Nuer territorial communities, agnatic groups, and age-sets reveal a conception of human relationships in which conflict and opposition are just as prominent as cooperation and solidarity.

The Nuer Warrior Identity and the Segmentary Principle 91

Since the Nuer emphasize the pastoral warrior identity more than the Dinka, it might be expected that the resort to force, the specialty of the warrior, might figure more prominently as a dimension of Nuer, rather than Dinka, political groupings. This is the basic principle of the so-called system of segmenting groups. The ethnographer of the Nuer insists that political collectivities are inseparable from conflict and violence in the thinking and experience of the Nuer. In effect, a political group is signified only in terms of potential combat with some other political group. The political system described by Evans-Pritchard is the organizational ideology of the warrior identity. It links the constitution of a political grouping with a resort to armed force. In such an ideology it is the capacity of the warrior that defines the social group, rather than the common interests of breeders and herders of cattle.

But this is not all. The various Nuer political groupings, while constituted as fighting groups, are all at the same time deconstituted by lower-level fighting groups which oppose one another by a resort to force. Where the pastoral warrior identity is the principal form of masculine identity, every level of political grouping, from tribes down to individuals, is associated with expressing autonomy and independence by resorting to force. The result is a secularized and politicized mode of representing collectivities which reflects a problematical relationship of self and social other.

Among the Nuer, then, a practico-cultural emphasis on cattle raiding correlates with a form of social relations in which the authority of fathers is qualified by assertions of autonomy and independence. There is still a concept of patriarchal authority among the Nuer, and Nuer collectivities are defined by patriarchal ascendants more or less in the same manner as Dinka collectivities. But Nuer patriarchal ascendants no longer represent communal groups toward which individuals feel sentimental attachment and dependency in the manner of Dinka patriarchal groups where patriarchal ascendants and clan-divinities are closely associated. Instead, from the point of view of the segmentary principle, Nuer collectivities are associated with acts of antagonism and opposition which qualify collective obligation and membership. Thus, no level of patriarchal authority is stable with respect to the assertion of autonomy and independence, and no sense of dependence on and attachment to community is unqualified.

Comparison of Nuer religion with Dinka religion reveals that the compromise of patriarchal authority and the enhancement of confrontation and hostility in social relations favor one facet of patriarchal religion at the expense of the other. Among the Nuer, the counterpart of Divinity is more prominent than the counterparts of free-divinities and clan-divinities.

5
The Compromise of Patriarchal Authority and Nuer "Monotheism"

THE COMPARISON OF DINKA AND NUER RELIGIOSITY

Fortunately, two fine ethnographies of Nuer and Dinka religion were written in circumstances that required their respective authors to address, implicitly if not explicitly, the other author's work. Evans-Pritchard and Lienhardt wrote with an awareness of each other's views and findings. Consequently each ethnographer was able to direct his attention to the peculiarities of the particular religion he had studied,[1] an important distinction since many aspects of Dinka and Nuer religiosity are broadly similar to one another. All the Dinka spirits, Divinity, free-divinities, and clan-divinities, have their Nuer counterparts; however, the Nuer have a different attitude to each class of spirits and a different conception of their relationship to one another.

Writing some years before Lienhardt, Evans-Pritchard faced the same problem of translating the Nuer term for a cosmic patriarchal spirit, which, like the Dinka Divinity, is similar to the concept of God in Middle Eastern monotheisms. The Nuer refer to their cosmic patriarchal spirit as *kwoth nhial* or as *kwoth a nhial*, which literally mean "spirit of the sky" or "spirit who is in the sky" (Evans-Pritchard 1956:1). This spirit is associated with what is above or on high (1-3). Set apart from man (4, 10), it is attributed unity (48-49) and omnipresence (4). *Kwoth nhial* is also a creator (4-7) associated with justice and peace (22). Its acts of creation are sometimes described by the Nuer word *thath*, which implies a fashioning of something from preexisting physical material, but are more often described by the word *cak*, which means "creation *ex nihilo* and in thought and imagi-

The Compromise of Patriarchal Authority and Nuer "Monotheism" 93

nation" (5-6). *Kwoth nhial* is the "founder and guardian of morality" (16) in whose presence "every statement . . . must be true" (211). Its will and word (5-6, 22) are right in the sense of being moral (16). It is the final Nuer explanation of everything. And its "anthropomorphic features . . . are very weak" so that the Nuer "do not act towards . . . [it] as though . . . [it] were a man" (7).[2]

Evans-Pritchard's stance is in direct contrast with that which his student was to take at a later date. He elects to translate the Nuer concept of *kwoth nhial* as "God," and he insists on the "markedly monotheistic tendency of Nuer religious thought" (49). In taking this step, he points out that Nuer religion, while closely resembling Dinka religion, was otherwise untypical of the religions of Black Africa and exceptional even as a Nilotic religion.[3] Furthermore, he claims that the Nuer *kwoth nhial* is broadly similar to God in the Old Testament, citing chapter and verse as he does so.

Later critics have sometimes dismissed these views, attributing them to the misplaced zeal of a convert. A careful reading of the ethnographic evidence, however, reveals that Evans-Pritchard has more of a sociological case than he has been allowed. Evans-Pritchard was not eccentric in his view that Nuer and Dinka religion were different from other religions in Black Africa but bore some close resemblance to Middle Eastern monotheisms. Similar opinions about the religions of certain Nilotic- and Cushitic-speaking peoples have been repeatedly expressed by numerous observers both before and after him.[4] In fact, the only good case against Evans-Pritchard's view of a resemblance between the Nuer *kwoth nhial* and the Middle Eastern God is the case made by his student Lienhardt in his study of Dinka religion.

As seen from Lienhardt's account, there are two sides of Dinka religion. One side does feature a cosmic patriarchal spirit which resembles the concept of God, but the other side is not consistent with this religious perception. From this second side, the Dinka cosmic patriarchal spirit appears anthropomorphically as a transcendent father figure, protector of the homestead, husband of the wives, and husband of the cows. And again from this second side, the Dinka cosmic patriarchal spirit is linked and even merged with a multiplicity of patriarchal and nonpatriarchal spirits.

Precisely the same assessment could be made of Nuer religion. The Nuer often advance a thesis of the "oneness" of *kwoth nhial*, a nonanthropomorphic cosmic creator who stands for justice and truth, but this is contradicted by other religious beliefs and practices. The Nuer also figure *kwoth nhial* anthropomorphically as a transcendent father who more or less resembles a real and actual father. It is "father, protector, and provider, but not begetter" (Evans-Pritchard 1956:7-9, 22), and it is the "owner of cattle and children" (14). And the Nuer also believe in a multiplicity of spirits, "spirits of the air" or *kuth dwanga* (free-divinities) and "spirits of the earth" or *kuth piny* (clan-divinities), many of which have some association with father figures. In fact, Evans-Pritchard takes some pains at the end of his study to insist on the very dimensions of Nuer religion which contradict the Nuer concept of the oneness of a cosmic patriarchal spirit.[5]

But despite the broad resemblances between Nuer and Dinka religion, Evans-Pritchard's stance toward the Nuer cosmic patriarchal spirit is not unjustified. There are good reasons for believing that Lienhardt's judgments about the Dinka *nhialic* apply less forcefully to the Nuer *kwoth nhial*. From the point of view of comparative ethnography, it is fully appropriate that Evans-Pritchard and Lienhardt differ on the degree to which a cosmic patriarchal spirit should be identified with or distinguished from the God of the Middle Eastern monotheisms.

CONTRASTS BETWEEN NUER AND DINKA RELIGION

The Nuer emphasis on the pastoral warrior identity is correlated with the compromise of patriarchal authority and the politicization and secularization of Nuer social organization. This effect of the pastoral warrior identity can be seen in a broad contrast between Dinka and Nuer religion. Both Evans-Pritchard and Lienhardt agree on the greater importance among the Dinka of priestly elders and collective ceremonies and the greater significance among the Nuer of individual prayer.[6] Citing the opinions of the Dinka themselves, Lienhardt (1961) puts it this way:

> It is rare to see a Dinka pray individually. On occasions of difficulty or danger he may address a short petition for help to Divinity or divinities, but much the greater and most important part of religious practice is collective and formal. I have heard Dinka remark upon their difference, in this respect, from the neighbouring Nuer, whose frequent individual prayer seems to be consistent with their less developed priesthood. (219)

The lesser importance of priest and ceremony among the Nuer illustrates the compromise of patriarchal authority. Relative to Dinka religiosity, Nuer religiosity has retreated to the domain of individual, rather than collective, experience. In a brief footnote, Evans-Pritchard (1956) provides a clue that the politicization and secularization of Nuer social organization are responsible for priesthood and ceremony being less prominent among the Nuer. Speculating on the contrast between the importance of fishing-spear symbolism among the Dinka and the importance of fighting-spear symbolism among the Nuer, he writes:

> One may ask, in the light of this discussion about the *mut* [fighting-spear], why it is that the title of spiritual leaders in Dinkaland is taken from the fishing-spear

The Compromise of Patriarchal Authority and Nuer "Monotheism" 95

(*bith*) instead of from the fighting-spear. An explanation might be put forward in terms of the analysis I have presented. Whereas among the Nuer the fighting-spear is the symbol of the clan because what is being symbolized is exclusiveness and opposition, among the Dinka the fishing-spear is the symbol of spiritual leadership because what is being symbolized is inclusiveness and unity. (245 n. 2)

In effect, Dinka collectivities are more closely linked with the position and authority of fathers, elders, and priests, whereas Nuer collectivities are more closely linked with assertions of autonomy and independence. But while Nuer society is relatively more politicized and secularized than Dinka society, the Nuer are still a religious people, in certain respects even more religious than the Dinka.

A review of the Nuer counterparts of Divinity, free-divinities, and clan-divinities illustrates how the side of patriarchal religion associated with a cosmic patriarchal spirit overshadows that associated with patriarchal symbolism.

THE NUER "DIVINITY": SPIRIT OF THE SKY

While the Dinka *nhialic* and the Nuer *kwoth nhial* are in many ways very similar, Evans-Pritchard's account of the latter is qualitatively different from Lienhardt's account of the former. The Nuer, a people who assert their autonomy and independence before others, approach God with a sense of their own inconsequence and ignorance:

It is in the light of their feeling that man is dependent on God and helpless without his aid and that God, though a friend and present, is yet also remote that we are to interpret a word Nuer frequently use about themselves when speaking to or about God: *doar*. The meanings of this word given in Nuer-English dictionaries, "idiot," "stupid," "fool," and "weak-minded," do not adequately convey the sense of the word, especially when it is used to refer to man's relationship to God. Then it means rather "simple" or "foolish" or "ignorant" — "idiot" in the sense the word used to have in the English language and which the word from which it is derived had in Greek. Nuer say that they are just ignorant people who do not understand the mysteries of life and death, and of God and the spirits, and why things happen as they do. (Evans-Pritchard 1956:11)

God, as patriarchal other opposed to individual self, knows everything, while the person knows nothing.[7] At the same time, the Nuer — who are not hesitant to take Dinka cattle, women, and children by stealth and force — feel that all they possess belongs to God:

When a child dies women lament, but only for a little while, and men are silent. They say that God has taken his own and that they must not complain; perhaps he will give them another child. This is a common refrain with Nuer, especially in their invocations at mortuary ceremonies. They say of the dead man that God has taken him and that he was in the right in the matter, for it was his man; he has taken only what was his own. Also, when a byre is destroyed by lightning Nuer tell him that they do not complain. The grass of the thatch is his, and he has a right to take what belongs to him. Likewise if a cow or an ox of your herd dies Nuer say that you must not complain if God takes his own beast. The cattle of your herd are his and not yours. If you grieve overmuch God will be angry that you resent his taking what is his. Better be content, therefore, that God should do what he wishes, seeing not that he has taken one of your cows but that he has spared the others. If you forget the cow God will see that you are poor and will spare you and your children and your other beasts. (12–13)

Similarly, the Nuer, who are famous in ethnographic literature as a proud, if not overbearing, people, approach God with humility:

In speaking about themselves as being like ants and as being simple Nuer show a humbleness in respect to God which contrasts with their proud, almost provocative, and towards strangers even insulting, bearing to men; and indeed humbleness, a consciousness of creatureliness, is a further element of meaning in the word *doar*, as is also humility, not contending against God but suffering without complaint. Humbleness and humility are very evident on occasions of religious expression among the Nuer—in the manner and content of prayer, in the purpose and meaning of sacrifices, and, perhaps most evidently, in their sufferings. Nuer accept misfortunes with resignation. Whatever the occasion of death and other misfortunes may be, whether they be what Nuer call *dung chak*, the lot of created things, or whether they be the result of what they call *dueri*, faults, they come to one and all alike, and Nuer say that they must be accepted as the will of God. (12)

Evans-Pritchard's ethnographic sketches of the Nuer concept of God are at first surprising because they seem to contradict everything that he has written about the "arrogant" and "combative" Nuer in his study of Nuer politics and ecology. Having insisted on the readiness of the Nuer from childhood to adulthood to defend their honor and dignity at the slightest hint of an insult, he now presents a completely different side of Nuer character and experience. The "fighting" Nuer feel resigned, submissive, and obedient to God, precisely the way that Dinka sons feel before their fathers.

The comparison with the Dinka son-father relationship is in fact the key to the matter. The compromise of patriarchal authority by an emphasis on cattle raiding among the Nuer is not accompanied by any decrease whatsoever in the importance of cooperation and reciprocity in Nuer social relations. Nuer pastoral ecology, no less than Dinka pastoral ecology, requires agreements and understandings among individuals and groups. In effect, then, the Nuer concept of God represents another side of Nuer character and experience which contradicts, but is nonetheless the complement of, an antagonistic and oppositional individuality. This contradic-

The Compromise of Patriarchal Authority and Nuer "Monotheism" 97

tion does not, however, center on a tension in the relationship of sons/ youths with fathers/elders. It is a contradiction in the character and experience of each individual. The Nuer are at one and the same time religious and yet secular. The higher level of contests and conflicts in their way of life has centered their attention more resolutely on a universal right and morality. In their experience, they know that it is not just the norms of a little group that matter, not peace and harmony just among a few families living in intimacy and familiarity, but also among human beings in general. They realize this somewhat more keenly than the Dinka because they live in a society in which aggression and hostility extend from those nearby to unknown and unseen people. And similarly, where this feature impinges on the Dinka, at the borders of Dinkaland and Nuerland, there is a strong tendency for Dinka to become Nuer, to lose faith in the parochial religious tradition of priesthood and ceremony and to embrace a universal religious tradition of an omnipresent and omniscient God.

The relative difference in Dinka and Nuer religion eventually leads Evans-Pritchard (1940) to insist, not on the concept of *cieng*, but on the concept of *cuong*. The concept of *cieng* ("home," "homestead," "hamlet," "village" [136]) is also an important one among the Nuer, but carries a somewhat different meaning from its Dinka counterpart. In terms of their religious conceptions, however, it is *cuong* which is more crucial. The latter emphasizes, not "sociability" and "good human relations," but rather being morally "right" or "correct." It touches on a Nuer taste for litigiousness and is directly linked with redress for offenses against personal honor and dignity:[8]

This brings me to an extremely important Nuer concept, an understanding of which is very necessary to a correct appreciation of their religious thought and practice. This is the concept of *cuong*. This word can mean "upright" in the sense of standing, as, for example, in reference to the supports of byres. It is also used figuratively for "firmly established," as in the phrase *"be gole cuong,"* "may his hearth stand," which has the sense of *stet fortuna domus*. It is most commonly employed, however, with the meaning of "in the right" in both a forensic and a moral sense. The discussion in what we would call legal cases is for the purpose of determining who has the *cuong*, the right, in the case, or who has the most right; and in any argument about conduct the issue is always whether a person has conformed to the accepted norms of social life, for, if he has, then he has *cuong*, he has right on his side. We are concerned with the concept here both because it relates directly to man's behaviour towards God and other spiritual beings and the ghosts and because it relates to God in a more indirect way, in that he is regarded as the founder and guardian of morality. (Evans-Pritchard 1956:16)

Unlike *cieng*, which refers to the parochial norms of an immediately experienced community ("sociability"), *cuong* is a more universal notion of a moral law ("right") of God. This moral law of God, not an experience of community, is for the Nuer the foundation of equity and peace in human affairs:

> What then, Nuer ideas on the matter amount to is, in our way of putting it, that if a man wishes to be in the right with God he must be in the right with men, that is, he must subordinate his interests as an individual to the moral order of society. A man must honour his father and his father's age-mates, a wife must obey her husband, a man must respect his wife's kin, and so on. If an individual fails to observe the rules he is, Nuer say, *yong*, crazy, because he not only loses the support of kith and kin but also the favour of God, so that retribution in one form or another and sooner or later is bound to follow. Therefore Nuer, who are unruly and quarrelsome people, avoid, in so far as they can restrain themselves, giving gratuitous offence. (18)

Thus Nuer "monotheism" stands opposed to Nuer "individualism." Before an all-powerful, all-knowing, and ever-present patriarchal other, human desire and ambition are insignificant and inconsequential. And yet, Nuer "monotheism" is more part of individual, not collective, religious experience, precisely because it is also the religious complement of an emphasis on personal autonomy and independence:

> [Nuer religion] is a distinctive kind of piety which is dominated by a strong sense of dependence on God and confidence in him rather than in any human powers or endeavours. God is great and man foolish and feeble, a tiny ant. And this sense of dependence is remarkably individualistic. It is an intimate, personal, relationship between man and God. (317)

The secularization and politicization of Nuer society are correlated with a focusing and centering of religious conviction. In this sense, the Nuer can be said to be not less, but more, religious than the Dinka:

> [Dr. Lienhardt] tells me that when he was in western Dinkaland he had in his household a Nuer youth whose habit of praying to God for aid on every occasion of difficulty greatly astonished the Dinka. In prayer and sacrifice alike, in what is said and done, the emphasis is on complete surrender to God's will. Man plays a passive role. He cannot get to God but God can get to him. (317-18)

Evans-Pritchard's qualitative account of the Nuer *kwoth nhial* suggests that the opposition between cosmic patriarchal other and worldly individual self has moved further into the foreground of Nuer religiosity, relative to Dinka religiosity. This qualitative difference is consistent with the greater emphasis on cattle raiding among the Nuer, since an antagonistic and oppositional individualism raises a crucial moral problem for a pastoral people whose security and prosperity require cooperation and solidarity. The Nuer counterparts of the Dinka free-divinities and clan-divinities reveal that the multiplicity of patriarchal spirits has receded more into the background of Nuer religiosity, compared to Dinka religiosity.

THE NUER "FREE-DIVINITIES": SPIRITS OF THE AIR

The Nuer spirits of the air, *kuth dwanga*, are the equivalent of the Dinka free-divinities. While they are a significant feature of religiosity, they are consistently of a lower stature among the Nuer than their counterparts among the Dinka. Evans-Pritchard (1956) mentions at least eight spirits of the air among various groups in Nuerland, including *deng* (compare the Dinka "Deng"), *rang* (compare the Dinka "Garang"), *buk* (compare the Dinka "Abuk"). All of them, he observes, "have only the vaguest personalities and lack distinct individualities defined by clear differentiation of attributes, so that Nuer have nothing very definite to say about them" (32).⁹

None of these spirits of the air have the preeminence of the spirit Deng. Among the Dinka, Deng is assumed to be distinctively Dinka. He is the spirit who figures Divinity in the anthropomorphic form of a free-divinity or clan-divinity. Thus there is no important Nuer spirit of the air which represents the cosmic patriarchal spirit anthropomorphically as clan, lineage, or personal familiar.

At the same time no Nuer spirit of the air has similar properties or receives a similar emphasis as Macardit among the Dinka. The Dinka associate Macardit with darkness rather than light, with the bush rather than the camp, and with persons who are distant from, rather than close to, real and actual fathers. No Nuer spirit of the air is associated with anxiety and concern about the limits of patriarchal protection and nurturing.

The combined absence of the counterparts of Deng and Macardit among the Nuer suggests that the Nuer are not so inclined to see *kwoth nhial* in the form of patriarchal ancestor or ghost, just as they do not see so close a connection between their relationship with real and actual fathers and their relationship with *kwoth nhial*.

In general, the Nuer look on the spirits of the air with some skepticism or suspicion. In this respect, they are not different from the Dinka who also have the same feelings toward all their free-divinities, with the exception of Deng. However, Nuer reservations are more generalized and more convincing. Lienhardt (1961:104) observes, for example, that some Dinka considered that some of their free-divinities had come to them from elsewhere, including other groups of Dinka, but he was not able to find any conclusive proof that these opinions were true. Evans-Pritchard (1956) mentions that all the Nuer considered all the spirits of the air as foreign spirits which had come to them from non-Nuer peoples:

The Compromise of Patriarchal Authority and Nuer "Monotheism"

> All [not some] Nuer with whom I discussed the matter said that . . . the spirits of the air had all [not some] "fallen" into foreign countries [not into other groups of Nuer] and had only recently entered into Nuerland and become known to them. (29)

Evans-Pritchard goes on to cite conclusive evidence that the spirits of the air did indeed come to the Nuer from other peoples, primarily the Dinka, during the latter half of the nineteenth century (34). The spirits of the air were especially prominent among the western Nuer where groups of Dinka were closest to, and even merging with, the Nuer (28). The names of these spirits were generally not Nuer and at least four of them, including *deng* and *buk*, were definitely Dinka in origin (32). Some of the spirits of the air, including *deng*, were especially associated with those Nuer clans known to be of Dinka origin (29). Finally, the names of the spirits of the air, which were sometimes given to children among both the Nuer and Dinka, appeared only in the lower, not the higher, levels of Nuer genealogies, suggesting their recent arrival (34 n. 1).

THE NUER "CLAN-DIVINITIES": SPIRITS OF THE EARTH

The spirits of the earth, *kuth piny*, are the equivalent of the Dinka clan-divinities. They are a significant feature of Nuer religiosity, but of even lower stature and even more suspect than the spirits of the air. In contrast, Dinka clan-divinities are revered highly and considered, along with Deng and Divinity, to be among the Dinka's original religious beliefs and practices.

The Nuer believe that many, if not most, of the spirits of the earth are, like the spirits of the air, not originally Nuer but customs carried to them by peoples of Dinka origin.[10] Referring to the spirits of the earth as "totems" (1949c), Evans-Pritchard (1956) affirms that the Nuer are in many instances correct in their opinion.

> I have had frequent occasion to remark that those [Nuer] who respect a totem are Dinka or of Dinka origin, and our discussion of the whole problem of Nuer totemism is complicated, as was our discussion of the spirits of the air, by the fact that Nuer regard their totems as having for the most part come from the Dinka. (82)

In another passage he notes that, besides the attribution of foreign origins to spirits of the earth, the Nuer sometimes seem almost to despise their totems:

> Somewhat to my surprise, Nuer spoke to me, or to others in my presence, about totemic creatures, even of their own totems, not only without deep feeling or high regard but even disparagingly and as though they were ashamed of them, especially where the totem was known to have a Dinka origin. (78)

And still more emphatically in another passage, he observes:

> That they place the totemic spirits on a lower plane of religious thought . . . is shown by the marked tendency we have noted to look upon, we may even say to look down upon, totemic observances as something Dinka, and in the corresponding condescension, almost contempt, sometimes expressed for totemic creatures. (93)

Evans-Pritchard's assessments of the place of spirits of the earth and air in Nuer religion refer to Nuer attitudes which are not always consistent with the full range of Nuer beliefs and practices. It is not difficult to find other passages in his 1956 work, *Nuer Religion*, where the Nuer are described as piously invoking either of these types of spirits. The Nuer argue the thesis of the oneness of *kwoth nhial* and reject spirits of the air and earth as intrusions of Dinka religiosity. But this Nuer idea, although better argued than its Dinka counterpart, is not entirely convincing and not entirely consistent with the facts.

The contrast between Nuer and Dinka religiosity appears once again in the Nuer and Dinka views of the totality of their respective religions. The Dinka assert that originally their religion consisted only of Divinity, the free-divinity Deng, and the clan-divinities (Lienhardt 1961:104). The Nuer also express the opinion that "long ago" their religion was less contaminated by the intrusions of foreign spirits. Like the Dinka, they identify God (Divinity) with this original religion, but unlike the Dinka, they exclude all spirits of the air (free-divinities) and all spirits of the earth (clan-divinities):

> All Nuer with whom I discussed the matter said that in olden times they had no spirits other than God and the *colwic*, and that the spirits of the air had all "fallen" into foreign countries and had only recently entered into Nuerland and become known to them. (Evans-Pritchard 1956:29)

Only God and the *colwic* are assumed to be purely Nuer. According to Evans-Pritchard (1949b, 1956:60), the *colwic* is indeed, as the Nuer claim, a religious notion wholly peculiar to them and not found among their neighbors. If a kinsman (man, woman, or child) is struck and killed by lightning, he or she is considered to have been "taken by God into the sky."[11] In time, the names of these individuals are eventually forgotten, but in the form of a *colwic* they are remembered and revered as a tutelary spirit of their lineages (Evans-Pritchard 1956:52ff., 59ff.). So the Nuer and Dinka views of their original religiosity are clearly different. The Dinka figure Divinity in the form of Deng, a clan, lineage, or personal familiar. They are not content with a remote, nonanthropomorphic patriarchal spirit (*nhialic*) but prefer instead a near-at-hand anthropomorphic father figure. In contrast, the Nuer are less inclined to figure God in the likeness of a real and actual father, but are fascinated with the notion of a direct relationship between God and the person. It is a figure of this direct relationship, the individual struck down by lightning, that they adopt as a lineage spirit, rather than a recasting of God in the form of a real and actual father. So when the Nuer reflect on what religious beliefs and practices are purely Nuer, their views suggest "monotheism," tinged perhaps with "saint-worship."

THE NUER SPIRITUAL HIERARCHY AND THE PASTORAL WARRIOR

In terms of comparative ethnography, Evans-Pritchard does have a case for translating *kwoth nhial* as God and deemphasizing the Nuer spirits of the air and earth, just as Lienhardt has a case for not translating *nhialic* as God and emphasizing the free-divinities and clan-divinities. Still, Nuer religion is not a monotheism in the same sense as the Middle Eastern monotheisms. The concept of cosmic patriarchal other opposed to worldly individual self is only one side of Nuer, as it is of Dinka, religion.

The second side of Nuer religion, as revealed on those occasions when the Nuer contemplate rather than dismiss it, clarifies to what extent Nuer religiosity is not monotheistic and also indicates that the prominence of a cosmic patriarchal other is directly linked with that of an antagonistic and individualistic self.

As discussed earlier, Lienhardt translates two distinct Dinka terms, *nhialic* and *yeeth*, by two very similar terms, "Divinity" and "divinities," respectively. The English terms imply a meaning that the original Dinka terms lack: Divinity is a "big" God, and divinities are "little" gods. While Lienhardt's convention for translating Dinka religious terminology cannot be said to go against the grain of Dinka religious thought, it does overstate one Dinka perspective over others. Among the Nuer, however, this perspective actually appears in Nuer religious terminology. All nonhuman powers are generally referred to by one word, which Evans-Pritchard glosses as "spirit." However, the unqualified singular of this word is used to refer to the cosmic patriarchal spirit *kwoth*, while the plural or qualified singular is used to refer to either the spirits of the air, *kuth dwanga*, or the spirits of the earth, *kuth piny* (Evans-Pritchard 1956:1, 110, 112). So the semantic connections implied by Lienhardt's translations—Divinity, free-divinities, and clan-divinities—do actually exist in Nuer religious terminology. But this is not all. Nuer religious terminology insists on a spiritual hierarchy ranging from the "high" to the "low" and the "strong" to the "weak."[12]

The first sign of this hierarchy is Nuer fastidiousness about the greatness of *kwoth nhial*, the spirit of the sky, as opposed to other spirits who

The Compromise of Patriarchal Authority and Nuer "Monotheism"

are not high and strong, but low and weak. Among the Dinka the particle *dit*, "great," is often added to the names of free-divinities (e.g., Dengdit, Abukdit, Macardit), but the Nuer explicitly avoid any such terminology:

> Also, the particularizing particle *in* when coupled with the adjective *dit*, great, can only be used when speaking of God and is not used when speaking of even the most powerful of the spirits of the air, for which, however, the indefinite particle *me* may be employed. Thus one may say that a spirit of the air is a *kwoth me dit*, a great spirit, compared, that is, with lesser spirits, but *kwoth in dit*, the great Spirit, can only be used of God. It should be noted further that God is always addressed, in a way familiar to ourselves, in the singular and never in the plural. (Evans-Pritchard 1956:50)

Only God is great, even if there are both greater and lesser spirits of the air.

Beyond this, the Nuer associate the transcendence of the spirit of the sky (*kwoth nhial*) over spirits of the air (*kuth dwanga*) with a difference in actual physical height:

> In imagery taken from the physical universe God is symbolized by the sky and the spirits of the air by the air or breezes which are between heaven and earth, and they are also associated with the clouds which are nearest to the sky. (28)

And in a similar manner, the transcendence of the spirits of the air (*kuth dwanga*) over the spirits of the earth (*kuth piny*) is also associated with the former being physically higher and the latter being physically lower:

> The spirits of the air can be referred to collectively as *kuth nhial*, spirits of the above, in contrast to the *kuth piny*, spirits of the below, but we cannot say of any one of them that it is *kwoth nhial* except in making this contrast and in this sense. Otherwise the phrase can only mean "Spirit of the heavens," that is, God. (50)

Evans-Pritchard adds that the spirits of the air are called the "children of God." In this respect, the Nuer go further than the Dinka who also sometimes speak of a free-divinity as a son or daughter of God. Along with imaging the spirits of the air as children descended from God, the Nuer also think of them as being both nearer to God and more powerful than the spirits of the earth.

The Nuer sense of a spiritual hierarchy also influences their evaluation of various kinds of spirits of the earth. Those which are literally creatures of the air are thought to be genuinely Nuer, while those which are literally creatures of the earth are thought to be non-Nuer in their origins. For example, when an individual respects a "lowly" creature as a lineage totem, this is assumed to be a sure sign of his Dinka origins:

> I have often heard true Nuer say that when you find that a man respects reptiles and such things as parts of animals and diseases you may be sure that he is a Dinka or had a Dinka mother or grandmother; and I have found this to be so. Hence

true Nuer tend to despise many totems, especially reptilian totems, as something Dinka. They say that the *kuth* of Nuer lineages are spirits of the above and not earthly spirits. (Evans-Pritchard 1956:82-83)

The Nuer not only reject "lowly" spirits of the earth, such as reptiles, as Dinka in origin, they claim (perhaps falsely) that the true Nuer lineage totems are not spirits of the earth at all but spirits of the above.[13] And if a Nuer is unfortunate enough to have an earthly creature as his lineage totem, he takes pains to explain how its actual spirit is near to God being really of the above, not of the below like the earthly species itself:

Therefore, though totemic spirits are classed as *kuth piny*, spirits of the below or of the earth, people sometimes went out of their way to explain to me that it is not the species themselves, the material things one can see, that they pray and sacrifice to but the spirits associated with them, and to emphasize further the difference between the species and the spirits they added that while the species are creatures on the earth the spirits are with God in the sky. Thus I was told by a man who respects lions[,] . . . "The lion in its body (as a creature) walks on earth, while its spirit is in the sky," and, by a man who respects pythons[,] . . . "The python just crawls on the earth so, but its spirit . . . is in the sky." (78)

The Nuer and Dinka have, then, very different notions about their totems. Among the Dinka, the clan-divinities are associated with intimate and familiar experiences of a protective and nurturing community, and consequently they select as totems localized, near-at-hand phenomena. The Nuer, however, are somewhat repelled by the narrowness and inwardness of the Dinka perspective. They would prefer their totems to be of the air, where they are more mobile and transcendent. The gist of this preference is revealed by the Nuer claim that the spirits of their earthly totems are of the air and therefore nearer to God. In effect, the Nuer would see their earthly totems, not as near-at-hand symbols of parochial social relations, but as participating in a more universal concept of morality represented by a heavenly spirit.

This contrast in the Nuer and Dinka taste in totemic symbols gives a clue as to why Nuer religion features a spiritual hierarchy while Dinka religion does not. The Nuer spiritual hierarchy is part of the focusing and centering of religiosity on a patriarchal other that has come about with the compromise of patriarchal authority. A greater degree of personal autonomy and independence leads to a fraying of sentiments of attachment to and dependency on a narrow and inward collectivity, and consequently to a drop in the prominence of symbols of protective and nurturing social relations. At the same time, because cooperation and reciprocity are if anything even more essential to the Nuer than to the Dinka, religious and moral concepts break free of their communal bearings and are generalized as concepts of moral right and wrong that transcend the intimate and familiar. In fact, the different ways in which the Nuer and Dinka refer to God/Divinity are also affected by this same contrast in experience. The Nuer refer to God as an actual "being." He is *kwoth nhial*, spirit of the sky. The Dinka refer to Divinity only as a quality. He is *nhialic*, of the sky. For the Nuer, God has come into focus as a divine presence, but for the Dinka, Divinity is but an aspect of their religiosity.

Another aspect of the Nuer spiritual hierarchy provides additional evidence of a link between the prominence of the patriarchal other in Nuer religious experience and an emphasis on the warrior identity in Nuer secular experience. The Nuer associate their spiritual hierarchy with a social hierarchy:

The spirits of the air are *diel*, true or aristocratic spirits, the [spirits of the earth] are *jaang*, Dinka-like spirits, and the fetishes [even more lowly magical powers] are *jur*, despised foreigners. (120)

The spirits of the air, which are higher and therefore closer to God, are said to be *diel*, a quality that differentiates Nuer aristocrats from commoners. This attribution has to be understood in terms of the character of the spirits of the air and the distinction between aristocrat (*dil*) and commoner (*rul*).

The spirits of the air are closely associated with the ideology of the warrior identity. They are regarded "as the medium through which God gives orders to fight and victory" and they are said to "accompany the warriors into battle" (Evans-Pritchard 1956:45). They "delight in blood and battle."[14] Likewise the distinction between aristocrat (*dil*) and commoner (*rul*) is based on a more and less close association with the ideology of the warrior identity, not on social dominance or privilege. The aristocrats (*diel*) are the leaders of their tribes. Their spear names are invoked when the tribe goes to war (Evans-Pritchard 1940:215, 235). Their lineages represent tribal political organization in accordance with the segmentary principle (203-5). Thus, when the Nuer say that the spirits of the air are *diel*, they are associating being closer to God with being closer to the practico-cultural orientation of the warrior identity. When they say that the spirits of the earth are *jaang*, they are associating being further from God with being further from the practico-cultural orientation of the warrior identity.[15] And finally, when they say that fetishes are *jur*, they are associating a magical power that is morally questionable with being neither Nuer nor Dinka in origin.[16] Taken together, Nuer spiritual hierarchy and social hierarchy indicate connections between monotheistic religious convictions, the segmentary principle, and involvement in raiding and warfare.

Despite the social distinctions between aristocrat (*dil*), commoner (*rul*), and assimilated peoples (*jaang*), the concept of Nuer as *naath*, "those who raid," ultimately signifies participation in a way of life rather than family or ethnic origin (cf. Evans-Pritchard 1940:235). This way of life requires adoption of the practico-cultural orientation of the warrior identity, and this adoption brings with it both problematical social relations as well as a transcendent patriarchal other. Given the implications of a pastoral ecology among the Nuer and Dinka, to raid is to experience a relationship of self and other that leads one to contemplate God.

The next chapter examines the pastoral traditions and institutions of Bantu-speaking, cattle-herding peoples farther to the south. Among these peoples, the two effects of a pastoral ecology may again be found: patriarchal authority based on the control and management of cattle as well as filial individualism based on contests and conflicts over pastoral resources. Among these peoples, however, patriarchal authority is not compromised by filial individualism. Instead, strong institutions of authority that do not exist among pastoral peoples like the Nuer and Dinka are the basis for a strict regulation by diverse patriarchal figures of both cattle owning and cattle raiding. Consequently, among Bantu-speaking cattle herders the peculiar features of religion, person, and society found among the Nuer and Dinka do not occur. A cosmic patriarchal other opposed to individualism is not prominent, social organization is not based on a segmentary principle, and the stature of patriarchal ghosts and spirits is high, not low.

6

Authority and Individuality among Bantu-Speaking Cattle Herders

DYNASTIC STATES AND CASTE SYSTEMS
IN NKORE, RWANDA, AND BURUNDI

The precolonial Dinka and Nuer were relatively homogeneous and egalitarian peoples. They lacked kingship or aristocracy, their way of life was more or less uniform, and they were isolated from external contacts. Oliver (1977) contrasts them with other pastoral peoples in East Africa:

The core territory of the Nilotic-speaking people lies . . . in the swampy country of the southern Sudan, where the Nuer and Dinka peoples have from time immemorial practised an economy based on fishing and cattle-herding, building their villages on the natural elevations, and in the dry season pasturing their herds upon the half-inundated plains around. The Nuer and the Dinka have no traditions of ancient migrations or contacts with other peoples. Protected by their native marshes, they have never needed to build states or armies to defend themselves against their neighbours. A shallow genealogical framework extending over about twelve generations has sufficed to explain to their living members the main facts of their collective existence since the day of creation when their first ancestors emerged from the ground, together with the progenitors of their herds. (634–35)

The Nuer and Dinka are very similar peoples, with relatively simple societies and no strong influence from other kinds of peoples living different ways of life. These special features have made it possible to examine how a different emphasis on the pastoral warrior identity is correlated with relative differences in concepts of religion, self, and society.

108 *Authority and Individuality among Bantu-Speaking Cattle Herders*

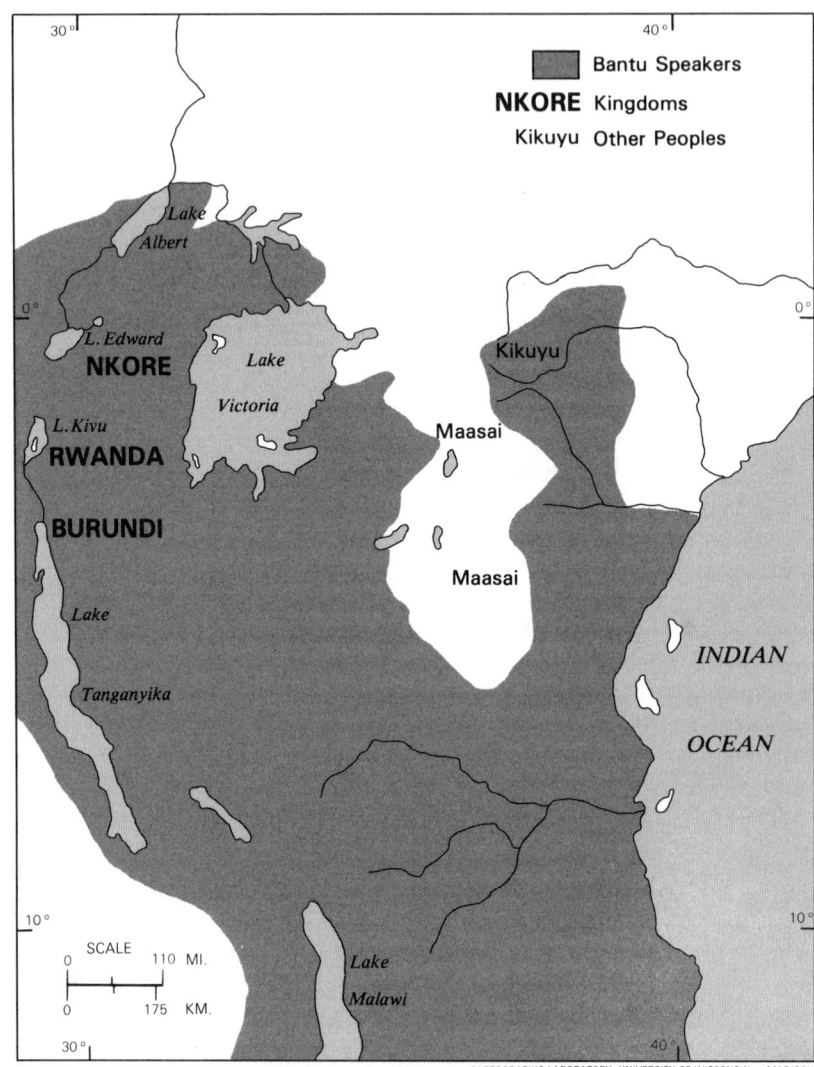

Map 6.1. Kingdoms of the Interlacustrine Region

Farther south, in the area of present-day Kenya, Uganda, Rwanda, Burundi, and Tanzania, this kind of controlled comparison is not feasible. The terrain and climate of the region are more varied. Migrating peoples, some primarily pastoral and some primarily agricultural, repeatedly entered the area and intermingled. In the interlacustrine region, this intermingling led to diversified food-producing economies and to dynastic states and caste systems.

Authority and Individuality among Bantu-Speaking Cattle Herders 109

Not so long ago, these dynastic states and caste systems were thought to have been the result of the conquest of "Bantu" agriculturalists by "Hamitic" pastoralists. According to this conquest theory, the "Hamites" moved south from the Sudan or Ethiopia, reduced the indigenous "Bantus" they encountered to the status of serfs, and set themselves up as feudal overlords. This theory, which was based on evidence of movements of pastoral peoples from north to south, provided an ad hoc explanation of the peculiar systems of social stratification in Nkore, Rwanda, and Burundi (see map 6.1). In these kingdoms, a small "dominant" caste, which was closely identified with pastoral traditions and institutions, lived among the large majority of peoples who were primarily (but not exclusively) engaged in farming or gardening. In Nkore, the pastoral caste, which was known as the Hima, constituted no more than five percent of the population, the remainder being the agricultural Iru peoples. In Rwanda and Burundi similar pastoral castes, which were known as the Tutsi, constituted from ten to fifteen percent of the population, most of the remainder being the agricultural Hutu peoples.

Given the evidence that various northern pastoral peoples had migrated southward into East Africa from an early date, Europeans first concluded that the pastoral ancestors of the Hima and Tutsi had moved into the interlacustrine region and reduced the agricultural ancestors of the Iru and Hutu to tribute-paying serfs. Such a conquest theory was appealing not only as a plausible deduction. Explaining what were apparently racial differences between a "lordly" pastoral caste and a "servile" agricultural caste, it held some appeal for latter-day intruders and would-be overlords. In this way, the conquest theory provided a covert apology both for foreign rule as well as for the racial categories which became part of colonial policy (Oliver 1977:631).

More detailed research has since revealed that the conquest thesis is a gross oversimplification. The interlacustrine region was indeed a setting in which primarily pastoral and primarily agricultural peoples came into contact with one another. However, the meetings of these peoples did not involve conquest and enserfment of the latter by the former. Instead, the precolonial dynastic states and stratified social systems evolved in the course of centuries of social interaction and development (see Oliver 1977; cf. Karugire 1971).

Oliver dates the beginning of this evolution to the first centuries of the second millennium c.e. About this time, Central Sudanic peoples, followed later by Nilotic peoples, began to infiltrate the grasslands of East Africa. While these peoples were primarily pastoralists, they also grew cereals and worked iron. Moving into the grasslands, they displaced in some instances earlier forerunners, Cushitic pastoralists with more primitive, Neolithic subsistence techniques. Upon reaching the interlacustrine region, the Central Sudanic or Nilotic pastoralists came into contact with other Iron Age peoples with different subsistence techniques and different social systems. These were Bantu-speaking peoples who fished, grew fruits and vegetables, and herded small numbers of cattle. They were not grasslands peoples; coming from the west some centuries earlier, they had settled in the forested and well-watered areas of East Africa.

Initially, each of these peoples, one primarily pastoral and the other primarily agricultural, tended to occupy different ecological zones, since the subsistence systems of each were best suited to different environments. But where grasslands and forests bordered one another, a social symbiosis between the two gradually evolved. This symbiosis resulted in a higher level of food production, a rise in population density, and the evolution of regional political organizations. The "pastoralists" of the grasslands were relatively nomadic and acephalous like the Dinka and Nuer, but the "cultivators" of the forests were relatively settled peoples with ceremonial chiefdoms. As the two people intermingled, these chiefdoms served as "brokers" between pastoralists and cultivators, eventually evolving into dynastic states. Oliver (1977) gives the following sketch of this process in Rwanda:

The most fundamental institutions of the Rwanda state—the divine kingship, the sacred fire, the royal drums, the agricultural rituals, the royal burial customs—were taken over from the little kingdoms of Hutu cultivators situated in the districts of Bumbogo and Rukoma at the comparatively late stage when one of several pastoral dynasties ruling in the north-eastern grasslands started to expand into the hilly country of the central watershed, where pastoralism and agriculture had from sheer geographical necessity to be carried on side by side. The great central institution of the *abiru*, the corporation of high ritual officeholders responsible for transmitting the esoteric constitutional and religious traditions of the kingdom, has all the appearance of a classic compromise between invaders and autochthones. The infiltrators, though inferior in numbers, had the military predominance with which to impose their own dynasty, but only at the price of according large constitutional powers to the pre-existing authorities. To judge from their clans and the location of their clan lands, the early *abiru* were mainly Hutu. It was only in the course of their assimilation into a single ruling class that they acquired the status of Tutsi. Likewise, the early settlement pattern was probably based more on economic occupations than on political dominance. The pastoralists settled the hilltops left empty by the cultivators. It was only at a later stage that the cultivators of the lower slopes entered into feudal . . . relationships with the lords of the hilltops, relationships based on the exchange of cattle in usufruct for supplies and services, which left the Tutsi cattle-owners in the position of a leisured ruling class. (643)

The interlacustrine kingdoms, which began to take shape from the fifteenth century onward, were not the result of "Hamitic" conquest and "Bantu" enserfment. Instead, they evolved out of the gradual merging of northern

Authority and Individuality among Bantu-Speaking Cattle Herders 111

grasslands societies and western forest-dwelling societies. While the rulers of the interlacustrine kingdoms had their origins among the dynasties of the Hamitic-speaking pastoralists, state ceremony and tradition were largely drawn from the institutions of Bantu-speaking agriculturalists, among whom state officials and personnel also had their origins.

The contribution of the Bantu-speaking majority could therefore be said to exceed that of the Hamitic-speaking minority. Not only their ruling traditions, but also their cultures and languages, had a more important place in the post-fifteenth-century interlacustrine kingdoms. At the same time, these kingdoms, as state systems, were strongly conditioned by a structural problem inherent in the pastoral ecology of the northern grasslands peoples: the contradiction between authority and individualism.

The ceremonial chiefdoms of the Bantu speakers first evolved among sedentary forest dwellers who practiced mixed farming and herding. This ecological background alone does not explain the existence of strong institutions of chiefly authority among the Bantu speakers, but it is a favorable setting for the consolidation of patriarchal authority among a semi-pastoral people. For just as the mobility of human groups and the open ranging of animals by wandering grasslands pastoralists provide opportunities for evading a stock-owning, stock-exchanging patriarch, so the relative lack of mobility and lack of ranging among sedentary forest dwellers diminish them. In any case, when the "Hamitic" and "Bantu" peoples met in the mixed environment of the interlacustrine region, a forest society with strong chiefly institutions that favored control and management of pastoral resources merged with a grasslands society with strong military institutions that favored raiding and warfare over pastoral resources. The result of this merging was a state system in which a ruling institution suppressed contests and conflicts over stock inside society, while a military institution projected these hostilities outside society.

The following discussion examines the place of cattle herding and cattle raiding in the Kingdom of Nkore. The two effects of a pastoral ecology—authority based on the control and management of cattle wealth, together with an antagonistic and oppositional individualism—were both important features of Nkore society. They appear not on the level of father and son, however, but on the level of king/state and warrior/army.

STATE SUPERVISION OF CATTLE HERDING AND CATTLE RAIDING IN NKORE

The Hima of the Kingdom of Nkore were not, like the Dinka and Nuer, independent cattle-herding peoples. They were a pastoral caste within a state system. Both the ownership and raiding of cattle were strictly regulated by state officials.

In theory, the Mugabe, the head of state in Nkore, was the owner of all the cattle of the kingdom. In practice, the Mugabe, by means of a hierarchy of chiefs and subchiefs, set certain limits on what could and could not be done with cattle:

> A man was considered poor or wealthy according to the number of his cattle, and the places of the chiefs when assembled before the Mugabe were arranged according to the size of their herds. All the cattle were regarded as belonging to the Mugabe, and, though the people to whom he granted them were at liberty to do as they liked with them within the country, they might not sell or give them to any one outside the tribe without special permission of the ruler. Few men would think of killing a cow, so that the only rules necessary were for the protection of bull-calves, which the herdsmen, if they felt a desire for meat, would find some pretext to kill. The chiefs had to keep careful watch lest this liberty should be carried too far, and the Mugabe issued regulations that only a certain number should be killed. (Roscoe 1923:2-3)

The Mugabe has a certain resemblance to the Dinka cattle-owning, cattle-exchanging patriarch in that he controls and manages the disposition of cattle. However, the Mugabe, as the head of a state hierarchy and organization, also has powers that go beyond those of Dinka patriarchs.

Within the scope of his rule, the Mugabe regulated contests and conflicts over pastoral resources. Through state institutions, he provided for the settlement of disputes over cattle and prevented any group from resorting to self-help. He claimed tribute in cattle from conquered peoples, and confiscated the herds of dissident followers. At the same time, he restored the herds of those who lost their cattle by raids or disease. He allowed or disallowed groups to organize cattle-raiding parties, taking a share of all the cattle which these raiding parties acquired. He recruited youths to be trained in his court and to serve in his army. As the leader of his army, he defended his kingdom against the depredations of foreign cattle raiders.[1]

A state apparatus thus favored one effect of pastoral ecology, the exercise of authority by monopolizing cattle wealth, at the expense of the other effect, an antagonistic and oppositional relationship of self and other. Nonetheless, both effects were a feature of pastoralism in Nkore. While the Mugabe "neutralized" contests and conflicts over cattle wealth within his realm, he also displaced them from inside to outside the Kingdom of Nkore. As the sponsor of military expeditions against neighboring peoples, the Mugabe gave rewards for military service. These rewards, which typically consisted of a share in the cattle seized during the expedition, were a principal means for men with few cattle to acquire many:

Authority and Individuality among Bantu-Speaking Cattle Herders 113

[At the return of a military expedition], the leader with the chiefs and his special followers went to the Mugabe to report the doings of the expedition and to divide the spoil. The Mugabe sent his herdsmen to pick out cows for the royal herds, after which the leader might choose what he wanted, and presents were given to any chiefs or men who had specially distinguished themselves. Any which then remained were divided among the other chiefs and the army. The Mugabe might also grant special cattle or even chieftainships to men who had shown great bravery, but any who were accused of cowardice were not punished, though they knew that they might never hope for promotion. (Roscoe 1923:160–61)

For the pastoral Hima, and perhaps for the agricultural Hutu as well, military expeditions outside Nkore made it possible to acquire enough cattle to start a small herd of their own or to pay a brideprice so that they might marry and have a family (see Roscoe 1923, chaps. 7, 11, and 14).

Despite access to cattle through military service, however, the distribution of rights in cattle was very unequal even among the pastoral Hima. The Hima were divided between a very few rich men who owned many cattle and lived a settled life on estates and many other men with far fewer cattle who lived a nomadic life as pastoralists. Not all the nomadic Hima were poor, but substantial numbers of them lacked any cattle of their own, serving as the herders of rich men. As among the Dinka, where the greater power of cattle-owning patriarchs was correlated with an uneven distribution of cattle wealth, so in the Kingdom of Nkore, where the state supervised both cattle owning and cattle raiding, there were some men who were cattle-rich and many more who were cattle-poor.

THE PASTORAL WARRIOR IDENTITY AND HIMA SELF-REPRESENTATIONS

Contests and conflicts over cattle were not entirely suppressed but rather displaced from inside to outside the Kingdom of Nkore. Accordingly, among the pastoral Hima, a poetry of self-representation was well developed and socially important. Morris (1964) has documented and translated what he terms Hima "heroic recitations," which date from the turn of the century, before the independence of the Kingdom of Nkore was seriously compromised.[2] These heroic recitations are a series of metered lines (*enkome*) enunciated according to a strict convention. Holding a spear above his shoulder, jabbing it for emphasis, the performer delivers each line very rapidly with a single breath. The high pitches in the line are much emphasized (the language is tonal), and the reciter's voice tails off at the end of each line. To mark the end of the line, the performer snaps his fingers and his friends add a chorus of "Eeee."

The recitations divide into two different genres distinguished only by their subject matter:[3]

First there is the *ekyevugo*, which is by far the commoner type. Traditionally, this deals with exploits in battle and records not only the composer's heroism but also that of his companions, though these naturally play a subordinate part in the poem. . . . The second type is the *ekirahiro* in praise of a man's cattle. The members of a herd are introduced one by one and their beauty is extolled.[4] (Morris 1964:14)

The two genres reflect the two ways in which the Hima pastoral caste claimed social status: battle exploits and cattle wealth. In the *ekyevugo*, a man represents himself directly in terms of his ability to fight and to oppose other men. In the *ekirahiro*, he represents himself indirectly through praise of his cattle wealth.

Morris describes the value which was placed on this kind of poetry and the social contexts in which it was performed:

In the evening when [the cattle] have been brought back within the kraal, the men relax over their beer and this is when the *omwevugi* (the reciter of the heroic recitations) has his audience. These recitations, or praise poems, are the principal artistic expression of the Bahima, who have otherwise produced so little in the field of art. In the past, every well-brought-up Muhima was expected to be able to compose and recite these poems, for not only was their recitation a pastime for the evening, but there were also certain occasions on which it was necessary for a Muhima to recite a praise poem which he had composed. Among these were such occasions as when a man was given a chieftainship by the Omugabe; when he dedicated himself to the Omugabe for service in battle; and when he visited his future father-in-law the night before his marriage. Furthermore, it was usual for a Muhima in the midst of battle to recite in order to keep up his own and his companions' courage. (12)

Heroic recitations are perhaps the most important art form of the pastoral Hima. They are recited on some occasions by specialists, but are also composed and performed by all the Hima. The singing of heroic recitations which recount battle exploits is closely linked with claims to social status. When a man receives an appointment, undertakes a military office, or prepares for marriage, he is expected to sing a heroic recitation. Moreover, heroic recitations have an explicit connection with fighting and warfare. They are boasts, but they are not entirely empty boasts. They depict acts of bravery that are supposed to have actually taken place, and they are recited in the midst of battle as encouragement.[5]

Ekyevugo can be appropriately described as self-representations. In fact, the very term which designates this genre explicitly describes it as "speaking of oneself."[6] What follows is an excerpt from Morris's transla-

Authority and Individuality among Bantu-Speaking Cattle Herders

tion of eighty lines taken from an early-twentieth-century *ekyevugo* titled *Omusingano* ("The Contest"):

> 66. I Who Am Not Speechless With Fear, with Kaamikyeno, started the fight at Kaamizire;
> 67. I Whom The Foe Does Not Weary, with Kajinja, was encouraged by the cries of the enemy;
> 68. I Who Do Not Desert My Companions, with Kagosi, proclaimed the warriors at Nshagazi;
>
> . . . .
>
> 72. At Kaishebwongyera, I fought hard and they deserted their beasts;
> 73. I Who Waste No Time In The Attack, with The Eager One, recited before the cattle;
> 74. I Who Am Unpredictable, with Rugwengyere, stood fast among the cattle at Ntsiga.
>
> (74)

The reciter describes his actions in battle by identifying himself with different names: "I Who Am Not Speechless With Fear," "I Whom The Foe Does Not Weary," "I Who Do Not Desert My Companions," and so forth. At the same time, there are as many references to positive and negative qualities of speech, the very medium of these self-representations, as to qualities of action: the singer is not speechless from fear (Line 66), the enemy cries out (Line 67), the warriors proclaim (Line 68), and the singer recites (Line 73). Moreover, the names of the singer refer to a specific individual, not to a collectivity as in the Dinka war song considered in chapter 1.

At first reading, Hima poetry seems to feature a far more exaggerated and far less qualified individualism than in Dinka songs. But the above excerpt has some curious features. While the singer is vividly depicted as contesting and opposing others, the enemy is very weakly portrayed. In effect, there is a depiction of an antagonistic self but no depiction of the opposed other. At the same time, while the recitation repeatedly portrays the singer in battle, it also constantly refers to companions who fight alongside him. The praise names of the singer are punctuated by an insistence on companionship: "with Kaamikyeno," "with Kajinja," "with Kagosi."

The figure of the reciter himself as a distinct individual on the field of battle is even more prominent in the following excerpt from a fourteen-line fragment collected by Morris:

1. I Who Am Praised thus held out in battle among foreigners along with The Overthrower;
2. I Who Ravish Spear In Each Hand stood out resplendent in my cotton cloth;
3. I Who Am Quick was drawn from afar by lust for the fight and with me was The Repulser of Warriors;
4. I Who Encircle The Foe, with Bitembe, brought back the beasts from Bihanga;
5. With Bwakwakwa, I fought at Kaanyabareega,
6. Where Bantura started a song that we might overcome them.
. . . .
11. At Nkanga, I seized my spear by its shaft-end;
12. At Kanyegyero, I The Binder Of Enemies took them by surprise;
13. Thereafter was I never excluded from the counsels of princes, nor was Rwangomani;
14. I Who Rescue With The Spear had seized him so that we might fight together.

(42, 44)

Again, the singer stands out on his own in a setting of interpersonal contest and conflict, and again a weak portrayal of the contested enemy contrasts with a strong portrayal of the singer's companions.

The problematical relationship of self and other is largely, if not wholly, absent from the preceding excerpts of Hima poetry and does not appear as a significant factor in the remainder of the recitations documented and translated by Morris. The conclusion of the above fragment provides a clue to the significance of this pattern. The singer there makes a reference to acceptance by authorities (verse 13) and fighting together with others (verse 14). In contrast, all of the Dinka dances, songs, and hymns feature problematical relationships between the individual and authorities over him or enemies opposed to him. In the ox song, the youth loves his ox, but it takes him away from his father and makes him disobedient. In the cathartic song, the youth praises his father as a great chief but also complains that his father is acting improperly, treating him badly, and risking disgrace. In the war song, where collectivity (the age-set) is associated with opposition (the enemy), the youth relishes the absence of chiefs and elders in a border situation, while he takes pleasure in the grief of a woman mourning his victim. In Hima poetry, on the contrary, the portrayal of self opposed to other is correlated with positive, unquestioned

Authority and Individuality among Bantu-Speaking Cattle Herders 117

relationships with others: the accompaniment of peers and acceptance by authorities.

Hima heroic recitations feature a strong image of the individual, one that is directly and indirectly associated with contests and conflicts over cattle wealth. The emphasis on interpersonal antagonism and opposition has no counterpart in the Dinka songs that Deng (1973) has recorded and translated. At the same time, the Hima portrayal of a self opposed to others is not set in the context of a problematical relationship of self and other. When the Hima warrior raids and kills, he thinks of companionship with his peers and acceptance by authorities, rather than of his autonomy and independence from others.[7]

These features of Hima poetry reveal how state hierarchy and organization have altered the relationship of the two effects of a pastoral ecology, authority and individuality. There was, no doubt, tension between Mugabe and chiefs, between chiefs and Hima pastoralists, and between Hima fathers and sons. However, filial individualism, closely supervised by the state and displaced from inside to outside, did not raise a question about patriarchal authority in the Kingdom of Nkore.[8] An extreme individualism was consequently not a threat to authority but instead, narrowly restricted as it was to the context of heroic battle exploits, the basis of acceptance by lord and peer.[9] Thus, in the absence of the compromise of patriarchal authority, religiosity in the Kingdom of Nkore was not focused and centered on a cosmic patriarchal other, and masculine identity was not strongly marked by the problematical relationship of self and other.

While a high god was recognized in the Kingdom of Nkore, a variety of deities, represented by various mediums and curers, received the attentions of both the Hima and Hutu (Roscoe 1923:23–24). Furthermore, the most important side of their religion was their respect and fear of ancestral ghosts:

The really important supernatural beings [besides a variety of deities] were the ghosts. These had their abode in another world which was, however, of little importance, for they spent most of their time hovering around the living, helping them or visiting their displeasure upon them according to the treatment they received from their surviving relatives and friends, and punishing any infringements of law and custom. . . . It was to these ghosts rather than to great gods that the people turned for help and to them they made offerings and prayers. (Roscoe 1923:25)

Religion in Nkore resembles the second side of Dinka religion, the side associated with multiple patriarchal spirits rather than with a single cosmic patriarchal spirit.

Similarly, the relationship of individual to community among the Hima resembles the way in which the Dinka are different from, rather than similar to, the Nuer. The patriarchal clans and lineages of the Hima did not feature a strong segmentary principle, but were linked instead with a system of totemic representations (Morris 1964:8; Roscoe 1923:119).

On the level of both religion and society, Hima sentiments of attachment to and dependency on authority and collectivity are more prominent than expressions of personal autonomy and independence. This contrast between the Nilotic pastoralists and the Nkore pastoralists is especially interesting, since otherwise the Kingdom of Nkore could be considered to be a far more evolved and complex civilization than that of the Dinka and Nuer.

CONTACT WITH THE PASTORAL MAASAI AND THE KIKUYU WARRIOR IDENTITY

The Kingdoms of Nkore, Rwanda, and Burundi illustrate how the pastoral warrior identity of grasslands peoples was incorporated by forest-dwelling, mixed farming and herding peoples with strong chiefdoms.[10] Another kind of setting in which such peoples came into contact with one another was the nineteenth-century interaction of Nilotic-speaking Maasai and Bantu-speaking Kikuyu in southern Kenya.[11] This provides an example of how the pastoral warrior identity among a cattle-herding people could be eagerly assimilated by a mixed farming and herding people with very few cattle.

During the precolonial period, the Kikuyu of southern Kenya lived in fixed village settlements. Kikuyu subsistence techniques were based on both farming and herding, but they are described by their ethnographers as "agriculturalists at heart" although "extremely proud of their cattle, goats, and sheep" (Cavicchi 1977:14). While many Kikuyu families did have large flocks of sheep and goats, most families had no cattle at all.[12] In some respects, Herskovits's (1926) East African "cattle complex" could be said to take the form of a "sheep and goat" complex among the Kikuyu. In the absence of cattle, these smaller animals had a prominent place in sacrifice, in marriage payments, and in restitution for murder, theft, or adultery (Leakey 1977, chap. 7).

Despite the relatively small numbers of cattle among the Kikuyu, the essential elements of the East African cattle complex, patriarchal cattle owner and filial cattle raider, were present because of a border situation. The Kikuyu were neighbors of the Maasai, a Nilotic-speaking people who are similar to the Dinka and Nuer in the Sudan. Unlike the latter, however, the Maasai were a rare instance of an East African people whose subsistence was almost totally based on cattle, the ratio of animals to people among the Maasai being one of the highest anywhere in East Africa.

Even though the Kikuyu did not themselves have large herds, they engaged in cattle raiding among their Maasai neighbors, so that there were

Authority and Individuality among Bantu-Speaking Cattle Herders 119

a number of men of exceptional cattle wealth among the Kikuyu.[13] For example, Kenyatta (1938) writes that cattle were an important basis of a man's prestige and influence in the Kikuyu community (64).[14] In particular, he mentions a form of singing and dancing inspired by cattle wealth:

> Sometimes the owner of cattle hardly had the pleasure of drinking his cows' milk, especially if they were far away from his homestead. In spite of this the owner of a large number of cattle was sentimentally satisfied by praise names conferred upon him by the community in their songs and dances. (65)

These performances are unlike both Dinka songs and Hima heroic recitations. They are songs and dances performed by the community in praise of the cattle wealth of a leading social figure. They are not self-representations performed by the man who desires or seizes cattle but representations of the social rank of a man who is rich in cattle.[15]

Here some caution is necessary. Kikuyu social organization could not be accurately described as centralized and hierarchical. On the contrary, the Kikuyu were a relatively decentralized and egalitarian people (Muriuki 1974:110). Like the Dinka, Nuer, and Maasai (but unlike the Hima in the state of Nkore), they had initiation rites and age-set organizations, signs of a lack of strong and elaborate institutions of chiefly authority. Indeed, they are described by some of their ethnographers as lacking any chiefs whatsoever.[16] Nonetheless, even if they did not have chiefs, which is doubtful, it is clear that they did have a form of "government" based on elders and judges, together with a keen sense of social rank, and that these features were more developed among them than among the Dinka and Nuer. Furthermore, cattle wealth tended to enhance the prestige and influence of those few men who were able to acquire it.

Kenyatta (1938) explains that the cattle-owning rich man had a particularly close relationship with the Kikuyu warrior in that he played the role of their patron and sponsor:

> In former days cattle had very little economic value to the owners, apart from the fact that they were looked upon as dignified and respected rich men. The milk was not sold, but used by the herdsmen and by visitors, especially warriors, who were the protectors of the villages against the Masai or other raiders. The rich men, who naturally had more property to be protected, were responsible for feeding the warriors in the way of milk and providing oxen for meat feasts (*irugo*) to keep the warriors in good healthy condition. (65)

In these lines, Kenyatta describes the warrior as fulfilling a protective and defensive function for the Kikuyu cattle owner; however, elsewhere in his ethnography, where he describes regimental formations, he identifies the warrior with cattle raiding:

> The senior warriors formed front lines (*ngerewani*), while the junior warriors formed the rear-lines (*gitungati*). The council of war went in between the two

forces giving the advice and directions to both sections. The motive of fighting was merely to capture the livestock [cattle] of the enemy and to kill those who offered resistance. In other words, it was a form of stealing by force of arms. (206)

Cavicchi (1977), who questions other observers' conclusions that the Kikuyu had no chiefs at all, throws yet a different light on this matter. In many instances, the rich cattle owner who hosted the young cattle raiders had himself achieved his position by prowess in raiding. Cavicchi translates a text written by a Kikuyu man in 1948:

In the days of the past the men of prowess became-known in the raiding-expeditions with which (one) went to Burugo . . . to rob the Masai of (their) cattle. It was on these (occasions) that there emerged the men-of-prowess and the men-of-wealth, because it was these who brought-home livestock in-great-numbers which they had successfully carried-off themselves through their bravery and courage. There also it was that came-out the leaders of the country (i.e. chiefs), because it was they, the men-of-prowess and the men-of-wealth, who would be able to govern the rest of the population. (94–95)

Another commentary given to Cavicchi by a Kikuyu man in 1946 provides a more exact picture of how the man of prowess attained a position of leadership:

These men (who had been heroes in war, and bought land), once married, would have many young-men (of theirs), because there were who bought [sic] as many as 20 wives and more, . . . and had a greater wealth than the other people. This being so, that is why the leaders of old had quite a name. A man was called a Leader because he had a homestead as big as a town, or had many sons, and decided the law-suits, and at the same time had a wealth of property. (218)

Cavicchi goes on to conclude that an ambitious youth became rich and famous by first demonstrating his prowess in cattle raiding, and then by using the cattle wealth so acquired to buy agricultural land and to pay the brideprices of allies and followers.[17] This picture is ever so slightly reminiscent of the Mugabe in Nkore. Like the Mugabe, only in miniature, the Kikuyu rich man is both the patron of young warriors who raid cattle abroad and a mediator in disputes that arise at home.

The Kikuyu cattle-raiding expeditions reveal the extent of the Kikuyu pastoral warrior identity. What follows is Kenyatta's (1938) account of the aftermath of a Kikuyu military operation:

If the warriors succeeded in a war and captured the enemy's livestock, they returned home as quickly as possible to avoid the recapture of their loot by the enemy. Before reaching home, after the crossing of the enemy's boundary, they halted and counted the cattle they had captured. The council of war then divided the loot among the regiments. In the first place, brave warriors (*njamba*) were rewarded according to the task performed in fighting the enemy. Then a small number of cattle were set aside for the *mothamaki wa borori* (the high councillor or the chief of the country), the medicine man was given his share, and the other members of the council of war. If there were any surplus left, and not enough to go round equally, it was settled by drawing lots. (206–7)

Kenyatta's account of Kikuyu raiding emphasizes its structured character.[18] The expedition is organized in terms of senior and junior warriors and directed by a council of war. The distribution of cattle plunder is supervised by the council authorities and a share of the plunder must be given over to various senior officials. How Kikuyu raiding expeditions compare with those of the Nkore army and the Nilotic Dinka and Nuer is not clear, but the place of the warrior in Kikuyu society is certainly closer to its counterpart in Nkore.[19]

Apart from military service, the warrior corps [among the Kikuyu] formed a reservoir of able-bodied men for performing other public functions. They acted as executive officers to elders, being entrusted with such activities as policing duties in markets and during the festivals, the arrest of habitual criminals and the calling of public gatherings such as *ibata*, during which rules and prohibitions were promulgated and other important pronouncements made. . . . Warriors were also entrusted with the more difficult tasks which were regarded as a man's job. Such duties included the clearing of virgin land and cutting poles for building houses and cattle kraals. They also planted specified crops – such as yams, bananas and sugar cane. Otherwise the warriors were a privileged elite who to a casual observer did nothing else except gorge enormous amounts of food and meat. (Muriuki 1974:120–21)

This picture suggests that warrior youths were more supervised and organized among the Kikuyu than among the Nuer and Dinka. If anything, the relationship of elders to warrior corps is reminiscent of that between the king and army in Nkore. It is not possible to speak of a tension between patriarchal authority and filial individuality as it exists among the Nilotic Dinka and Nuer.

In fact, the Kikuyu are interesting because they present something of a mixed case. They are a Bantu-speaking agricultural people, but because of a border situation they are able to engage in limited cattle raiding and cattle warfare among a grasslands pastoral people. Because of this, their traditions and institutions exemplify how the pastoral warrior identity of grasslands pastoralists is received by peoples whose ecology does not in itself foster it. This indicates that the pastoral warrior identity is a cultural configuration which is fully communicable from one context to another, not a feature of personal identity rooted in a narrowly defined ecological pattern.

Among the Kikuyu, who do not have strong chiefs, the authority of elders over youths is associated with initiation rites and age-set formations. Kenyatta (1938) describes the initiation of a Kikuyu boy as follows:

Before a boy goes through this ceremony he is considered as a mere child, and as such has no responsibility in the tribal organization; his parents are responsible for all his actions. If he commits any crime he cannot be prosecuted personally, it is his parents' duty to answer for him. But this liberty ceases immediately he is circumcised, because he is now "full-grown," and has assumed the title of *mondo-morome* (a he-man), and as such he must share the responsibility with other "he-men" (*arome*). As soon as his circumcision wound heals he joins in the national council of junior warriors, *njama ya anake a mumo*. At this stage his father provides him with necessary weapons, namely, spear, shield, and sword; then a sheep or a male goat is given to the senior warriors of the district, who receive it in the name of the whole national council of senior warriors. The animal is killed for a ceremony of introducing the young warrior in the general activities and the etiquette of the warrior class. (198)

As among the pastoral Dinka and Nuer, the young man's initiation is sponsored by elders and fathers and his coming of age consists of assuming the warrior identity. He is given weapons and becomes a member of a regimental age-group. However, unlike the Nilotic age-sets which are involved in ritualized antagonism and opposition, the emphasis here is on the young man's place in a hierarchy of warrior councils.

Describing the initiation ceremonies themselves, Kenyatta records an oath taken by the young men which reveals a figure of the warrior identity apart from and opposed to both heaven and earth:

The weapons of the young warrior were sprinkled with the blood of the ceremonial animal, then the leading warrior shouted a war-cry (*rohio*), his companions stood up brandishing their spears and lifting their shields upwards; and in a ritual tone they chanted in unison the following warrior's resolution (*mwehetwa wa anake*): "We brandish our spears, which is the symbol of our courageous and fighting spirit, never to retreat or abandon our hope, or run away from our comrades. If ever we shall make a decision, nothing will change us; and even if the heaven should hold over us a threat to fall and crush us, we shall take our spears and prop it. And if there seem to be a unity between the heaven and the earth to destroy us, we shall sink the bottom part of our spear on the earth, preventing them from uniting; thus keeping the two entities, the earth and the sky, though together, apart. Our faith and our decision never changing shall act as balance." (198–99)

Identifying himself with his fighting comrades, asserting his own will as a force in its own right, the Kikuyu warrior would defy both divine and natural powers. With his spear, the symbol of personal prowess, he finds a place for himself in between heaven and earth and therefore on the margins of both. This is a strong statement of the warriors' sense of their autonomy and independence, but Kikuyu self-representations which are associated with the warrior identity do not seem to have much in common with Dinka songs.

After a successful military expedition, some of the warriors were permitted to perform songs which they had composed:[20]

Authority and Individuality among Bantu-Speaking Cattle Herders 123

When this was done the warriors returned to their respective districts singing songs of praise of their own bravery (*koina kaare*). In these every warrior described his action in the war and the number of men he had killed in the battle, and also the position his victims held in their regiments. A warrior who had not killed an enemy could not participate in the singing of *kaare* songs. These brave warriors, as they were called, went round in their districts singing ceremonially the *kaare* songs. They paid visits to their relatives and friends who gave them presents in the form of sheep or goats and ornaments as the recognition of their bravery in the battle. The animals thus given were used for periodical meat feasts (*keruugu*), in which the warriors spent several days eating meat and drinking soup mixed with various herbs and roots which served as a stimulating tonic to keep the warriors in good and healthy condition. (Kenyatta 1938:207)

From this account, which is admittedly sketchy, the Kikuyu *kaare* song seems to be more like the Hima heroic recitation than the Dinka songs. The portrayal of bravery in battle in the *kaare* song emphasizes antagonism and opposition to others, as indicated by the fact that the song can be sung only by those who have been able to kill one of the enemy. Moreover, the battle exploits depicted by the song are the basis of a claim to social status rather than linked with the problematical relationship of self and other in society itself in the manner of the Dinka songs.

The resemblance between Hima heroic recitation and *kaare* song is to be expected for two reasons. First, the configuration of cattle-owning elder and cattle-raiding youth is only a secondary aspect of social organization, since the Kikuyu are essentially an agricultural people. Second, the Kikuyu cattle-owning rich man is largely the sponsor and supervisor of cattle-raiding youths, somewhat like the king in Nkore. On both accounts, access to cattle through military exploits is very restricted among the Kikuyu. Hence, the authority of Kikuyu elders is sometimes enhanced by cattle wealth, but not in the least compromised by cattle raiding. Contact with the cattle-raiding Maasai serves to foster the pastoral warrior identity among the Kikuyu by providing opportunities for cattle-raiding military expeditions, but the pastoral warrior identity, projected from inside to outside society, is not associated with the problematical relationship of self and other.

The Kikuyu warrior identity is basically different from the Dinka or Nuer pastoral warrior identity. Still, the Kikuyu were fascinated by and attracted to the Nilotic form of the pastoral warrior identity which they encountered among the neighboring Maasai. The Maasai probably entered Kenya at some time during the seventeenth century (Oliver 1977:654). Like the Nuer, they were stereotyped during the colonial period as fierce warriors, a reputation that was largely gained by their practice of cattle raiding and cattle warfare, rather than by military conquest and domination (cf. Jacobs 1977). The special attributes of the Maasai, which differentiate them from the Dinka and Nuer, are their more elaborate initiation rites and age-set organizations, but otherwise their religious traditions are similar. Like the Dinka and Nuer, they believe in the unity of a cosmic patriarchal spirit and are less concerned with punitive and beneficent ancestral ghosts than Bantu speakers like the Kikuyu.

Precisely those features of Kikuyu society which were directly and indirectly related to the pastoral warrior identity, such as initiation rites, age-set formations, military tactics, and belief in a unitary high god, were strongly influenced by their Maasai counterparts.

> Linguistically, for example, the Kikuyu language is heavily indebted to Maasai from which it has borrowed nearly all the words relating to cattle, and especially the descriptive ones. Also, certain religious concepts, such as Ngai (God; Maasai, E'Ngai) were borrowed from the Maasai. But the most significant cultural influences were in the fields of initiation and military tactics. (Muriuki 1974:98)

The Kikuyu tended to adopt those Maasai traditions and institutions associated with the pastoral warrior identity.[21] In doing so, they understood and experienced the connections between a distinctive configuration of religiosity, personal identity, and social organization.

But while the Kikuyu flirted with the Maasai configuration of religion, person, and society, it did not become a core feature of their society. They were inclined to subdivide the Maasai cosmic patriarchal spirit into more than one divinity (Routledge and Routledge 1910:225–26). Furthermore, their social organization did not feature the segmentary principle, and their religious beliefs and practices involved beneficent and punitive ancestral ghosts.[22]

The instance of the Kikuyu shows that the two effects of pastoralism, the simultaneous enhancement of authority and individualism, are not necessarily restricted to peoples who are primarily pastoralists, but can spread like a contagion to primarily agricultural peoples. This illustrates the fascination of personal autonomy and independence for peoples living in conditions that otherwise require a high degree of social reciprocity and cooperation. As seen among the Kikuyu, cattle raids and cattle wealth appeal simultaneously to elders who would enhance their prestige and influence in the community and to younger men who would escape the controls and constraints of paternal authority.

CHIEFDOMS AND CATTLE HERDING AMONG SOTHO AND NGUNI PEOPLES

The Bantu-speaking peoples of central East Africa were in close contact with Central Sudanic, Nilotic, and Cushitic peoples who moved southward into the area during the last millenium.[23] But still farther to the south,

Authority and Individuality among Bantu-Speaking Cattle Herders 125

the pastoral traditions and institutions of other Bantu-speaking cattle herders, such as the Sotho and Nguni of southeastern Africa, were less directly influenced by northern grasslands peoples.[24] They can therefore be examined as an example of the effect of cattle herding on peoples who were not in close contact with northern grasslands pastoralists.

The Sotho and Nguni peoples who settled in the grasslands of southeast Africa eventually developed an intensive form of cattle herding, so that by the nineteenth century they were preeminent among those Bantu-speaking peoples whose way of life featured the traits of the East African cattle complex. In comparison with the northern grasslands pastoralists like the Dinka and Nuer, however, the unusual social emphasis on cattle herding among the Sotho and Nguni peoples was a relatively recent development. The Dinka and the Nuer have been pastoralists for millennia, but the spread of intensive cattle herding among the Sotho and Nguni dates from sometime between the tenth and sixteenth centuries C.E. (Birmingham and Marks 1977:606). This late development may explain why the social systems of Sotho and Nguni peoples resemble in many ways those of forest-dwelling Bantu speakers for whom cattle herding is of much less importance. In general, Sotho and Nguni peoples did not practice transhumance or nomadism, but lived in fixed village sites. Agriculture, which was the work of women, was generally of greater importance as a subsistence technique than stock keeping. Men also engaged in hunting, even though stock keeping was their most important occupation. And in contrast with many of the northern grasslands pastoralists, but much like other groups of forest-dwelling Bantu speakers who practiced mixed farming and herding, Sotho and Nguni peoples had strong chiefdoms, some of which evolved into kingships in recent centuries.

There is no systematic ethnography of any Sotho or Nguni people before this century, but the close relationship of chiefly authority and cattle owning is very clear. Among both Sotho and Nguni peoples, chiefs were able to build a following and exert their authority in large part by regulating the usufruct of cattle. Gluckman (1940) describes how this was so among the Nguni peoples who comprised the Zulu nation during the nineteenth century:[25]

I have been told that only important men owned cattle. The rich Zulu loaned out cattle to other people to herd for him; they could use the milk, and also the meat of animals which died, and this contract made them dependent on the cattle-owner because he could inflict great hardship on them by taking away his cattle. [Out of a tribal total of fifty-four thousand head, Gluckman notes, a contemporary chief in Zululand had sixteen thousand cattle loaned out among his people.] When the chief did this, it gave him a hold over his people and prevented them from easily changing their allegiance and going to some other chief. Wealth therefore attracted followers, and as they increased and had children the wealthy man could collect about him a substantial group of dependants which was a political unit. (45)

Schapera (1940) describes a similar situation among the Ngwato tribe, a Tswana-Sotho people, who had a somewhat more elaborate form of government than Nguni peoples:[26]

> In this connexion, the relationship between the chief and his *batlhanka* [headmen] deserves special mention. These men, as we have seen, were placed as common headmen in charge of the chief's cattle-posts. The cattle entrusted to them were the hereditary property of the chieftainship, so that the *batlhanka* were always attached to the ruling chief himself. Each *motlhanka* was required to provide the chief's household with milk and meat from the cattle under his care, and to come with his followers to perform such other work as might be demanded of him. In return, he could use the cattle as he pleased: he kept the rest of their milk, slaughtered a beast whenever he wished, paid *bogadi* (bride-wealth) for his sons out of them, and exchanged them for other commodities, while on his death they passed to his children. He was also given the Sarwa [people of Bushman origin] inhabiting the region where the cattle grazed, and kept most of their hunting tribute for himself. The chief, however, had the ultimate claim not only to these cattle (known as *kgamêlô*, "milk-pail," cattle), but to everything else acquired by the *motlhanka*. The entire property of a *motlhanka* was regarded as *kgamêlô*; and since the chief could withdraw his *kgamêlô* whenever he wished, he could at any time ruin the holder. (77–78)

These features of Nguni and Sotho chiefdoms are thought to have come into existence by the sixteenth century (Birmingham and Marks 1977:615). From the beginning of the nineteenth century, at the latest, systems of states began to emerge as strong chiefs began to discipline and organize their followers.

The first effect of a pastoral ecology, the enhancement of authority, is plainly visible. The second effect, the enhancement of individualism, is suggested by the way in which the praise poetry of Sotho and Nguni peoples differs from that of other Bantu-speaking peoples for whom cattle raiding and cattle warfare were of less consequence.

SOTHO AND NGUNI PRAISE POETRY

The praise poetry of the southern Bantu speakers, "one of the most specialized and complex forms of poetry to be found in Africa" (Finnegan 1970: 121), has been more extensively studied than any other form of sub-Saharan oral tradition. Scholars therefore have a relatively good understanding of its literary and linguistic properties as well as its social significance and functions. However, since Western interest in praise poetry dates from the late nineteenth century, when pastoral raiding and warfare were declining in importance, its links with these activities are less well known.[27] Lestrade (1937), whose work on praise poetry of the southern Bantu

Authority and Individuality among Bantu-Speaking Cattle Herders 127

speakers dates from the first part of this century, describes the genre as follows:

These compositions are regarded by the Bantu themselves as the highest products of their literary art. They are a type of composition intermediate between the pure, mainly narrative, epic, and the pure, mainly apostrophic, ode, being a combination of exclamatory narration and laudatory apostrophizing. In form they consist of a succession of what may be called loose stanzas of an irregular number of lines, each line containing a varying number of words, with, however, a more regular number of strong stresses, the whole being in . . . balanced metrical form. . . . In content they consist of phrases and sentences in praise of some tribe, clan, person, animal, or lifeless object which, as a group or individually, is the subject of the poem. (295)

In surveying the characteristics of praise poetry, Lestrade mentions certain features which are not at all consistent with the attributes associated with songs composed and performed by youths among northern pastoralists, such as the Dinka and Nuer. The praise poems are obviously not self-representations at all.

The difference between the praise poetry of the southern Bantu speakers and the self-representations of Nilotic youths is made even clearer by Schapera's (1965) contemporary description of the genre:

Praise-poems are a form of traditional literature common in all clusters of Southern Bantu (Nguni, Tsonga, Sotho, and Venda). The Tswana term them *mabôkô* (sing. *lebôkô*), a name derived from the verb *-bôka*, "honour by giving titles to a person in poems; sing the praises of." They are composed not only about chiefs, headmen, famous warriors, and other prominent tribesmen, but about ordinary commoners also, including women; there are, in addition, praise-poems of tribes and subdivisions of tribes (such as wards and lineages), of domestic animals (notably cattle), of wild animals (including birds and insects), of trees and crops, of rivers, hills, and other scenic features, and of such inanimate objects as divining-bones. In modern times some have even been composed about schools, railway trains, and bicycles. (1)

The praise poems are composed to honor some person, group, or object that is socially esteemed or respected. Indeed, Schapera's description of the praise poetry of the cattle-herding southern Bantu speakers could also be applied to the praise poetry of other Bantu-speaking peoples for whom stock keeping, not to mention pastoral raiding and warfare, are of little importance.[28] The general pattern of praise poems among southern Bantu-speaking peoples illustrates the importance of social rank among Bantu-speaking peoples in general. The praise poem is a form of honoring individuals, collectivities, and all manner of objects. It is not a figure of the problematical relationship of self and other, but a gift of esteem.

SOTHO AND NGUNI PRAISE POETRY AS SELF-REPRESENTATIONS

Though the praise poem, as genre, is not specifically associated with pastoralism, certain praise poems among the Sotho and Nguni were strongly influenced by these peoples' involvement in pastoral raiding and warfare. Lestrade (1937) describes a particular type of praise poem that brings to mind the heroic recitations of the Hima:

> They narrate, in high-pitched adulatory style, deeds for which the subject has acquired fame, enumerating, in hyperbolic apostrophe, those qualities for which he is renowned; and they include a recital of those laudatory epithets applied to him either as a member of a group or as an individual, and known as his "praise names." . . . Persons of but modest rank in Bantu society usually compose their own praise-poem, and the praise-poems of their cattle, while those of higher status have theirs composed by professional bards, the praise-poets and reciters, the only type of professional literary artist known to tribal Bantu life. (295–96)

In this excerpt, Lestrade describes praise poems in which an individual praises either himself or his herds. Although Lestrade makes no reference to raiding and warfare, this division of genres is reminiscent of the division of Hima genres, the *ekyevugo* and *ekirahiro*, in which a man celebrates his personal prowess and the beauty of cattle.

The comments of other observers also suggest that the praise poetry of the southern Bantu has been in some ways strongly influenced by pastoral ecology. In their book on Sotho praise poems, Damane and Sanders (1974) consider the issue of whether the praise poem took the form of a heroic poem composed by its author instead of the more general form of praise of a chief composed by a subject. They begin by quoting Casalis, a French missionary who arrived in LeSotho in 1833. He describes a "heroic" mode of Sotho poetry that was prominent during the nineteenth century:

> The hero of the piece is almost always the author of it. On his return from war he cleanses himself in the neighbouring river, and then places his lance and his shield in safety in his hut. His friends surround him, and beg him to relate his exploits. He recounts them in a high-flown manner. He is carried away by the ardour of his feelings, and his expressions become poetical. The memory of the young takes hold of the most striking points: they are repeated to the delighted author, who ponders over them, and connects them in his mind during his leisure hours. (Casalis [1861] 1965:328–29, as quoted in Damane and Sanders 1974:18)

This early account suggests that some Sotho praise poems fit the paradigm of self-representation which refers to interpersonal conflicts. However, Damane and Sanders (1974) proceed to qualify the missionary's observations:

> Casalis is correct when he states that in most praise-poems the hero is the author. The exceptions, however, are particularly important, for they are the praises of

Authority and Individuality among Bantu-Speaking Cattle Herders 129

certain chiefs, which were composed for them by their more gifted retainers, who thus became known as their *liroki* (sing. *seroki*) (praise-poets). Some chiefs, it is true, preferred to compose their own, and were highly respected for doing so. "Nowadays the chiefs of the Sotho are praised like cattle," one chief remarked to us, with obvious contempt; "but," he added, with equally obvious approval, "Chief Maama and Chief Lerotholi used to praise themselves." Chiefs who rely on *liroki*, however, sometimes justify this by pointing out that self-praise is no recommendation. In several cases, such as those of Posholi and Lerotholi, praise appears to have been composed both by the chief and by some of his followers, and then to have been jumbled together. (18)

Two kinds of praise poems are of special importance among the cattle-herding southern Bantu speakers, those in which an individual represents his heroic exploits and those in which bards celebrate the qualities of chiefs. The distinctive features of southern Bantu praise poetry are the effects of a pastoral ecology, the enhancement of authority and individuality.[29]

The "heroic" praise poems composed and performed by ordinary individuals during the late nineteenth century or earlier are difficult, if not impossible, to come by. There does not seem to be the equivalent of Morris's (1964) study of Hima heroic recitations. However, praise poems of the heroic exploits of chiefs were recorded and translated. Here is an excerpt of a praise poem of Masopha (Nkau) who is remembered as the most courageous of the many sons of Moshoeshoe, a chief who himself first came to prominence as a cattle raider:

> As the battle caught light and burned,
> And became almost a fiery blaze,
> In went the falcon of my master;
> The dog went in with glaring eyes,
> Baring its teeth in its open mouth;
> As it entered it spoke to the Hawks,
> It spoke to the Plumes of RaTholoana,
> Saying: "Young warriors, stab them with spears,
> Stab them, and divide them among the birds.
> The vultures will rejoice in that land of the Nguni,
> The black vultures that sit in the trees."
> Swarthy avenger, you who are Steadfast,
> brother of Mpinane,
> Fight and avenge the head of your uncle,
> Avenge Makhabane's head.[30]
> So, you have seen, you Koena:
> I've avenged Makhabane's head![31]
> I've killed the chief of the Thembu!
> (Damane and Sanders 1974:134)

The praise poetry of the southern Bantu is a large subject. It would be folly to generalize on the basis of one brief excerpt from one praise poem. What can be said is that the excerpt seems to be far more complex in its structure than the Hima heroic recitation but not in any obvious way reminiscent of Dinka songs. The topic of the excerpt is not the problematical relationship of self and other, but a setting of interpersonal hostility and violence where social honor is at stake. Since further citations would not in my judgment raise any serious problems with these conclusions, but would enter into many difficult and subtle problems of religion, society, and person among the southern Bantu speakers, they need not be considered here.

The pastoral traditions and institutions of the southern Bantu speakers do not reveal the tendencies which are easily detectable among the Dinka and more clearly visible among the Nuer: the focusing and centering on a cosmic patriarchal spirit, the fall in stature of a multiplicity of patriarchal spirits, and the secularization and politicization of social relations. Like the other Bantu-speaking groups that have been considered, the Sotho and Nguni chiefdoms regulated cattle wealth and displaced contests and conflicts over cattle wealth from inside to outside the community. Consequently, Sotho and Nguni religiosity was largely a matter of beneficent and punitive ancestral ghosts, and sentiments of attachment to and dependency on patriarchal figures and patriarchal groupings were strong (see Krige 1936 and Schapera 1953).

7
The Northern Somali Pastoralists: Cosmic Patriarchal Spirit, Segmentary Society, Poetry of Self and Other

DINKA, NUER, AND OLD WORLD PASTORAL
TRADITIONS AND INSTITUTIONS

Since the Age of Exploration, Europeans have perceived the nonliterate, stateless peoples they encountered as representatives of what they understood to be an early phase of human history. In this way they "recognized" other peoples by locating them, more or less inappropriately, within a preexisting framework of knowledge.[1] During the last half of the nineteenth century, when Europeans began to learn more about Nilotic cattle herders (Dinka, Nuer, and Maasai) living in various parts of East Africa, they tended to understand them in just such terms. A curiosity of these European recognitions, however, is a division of opinion between anthropologists and prehistorians.

One of the first full European portraits of a Nilotic cattle-herding people is that of Merker (1910), a German military officer, whose turn-of-the-century account of the Maasai still stands in the front rank of Nilotic ethnographies. Merker faithfully recorded many features of the Maasai way of life at the time he observed it, but he was also interested in a bizarre interpretation of Maasai origins. Merker was impressed by what he called the "monotheistic" religion of the Maasai as opposed to the "polytheistic" religions of their neighbors (204). Not content with noting a few biblical parallels to Maasai myths and rites, he claimed that the Maasai were the true descendants of the Yahwistic Hebrews.

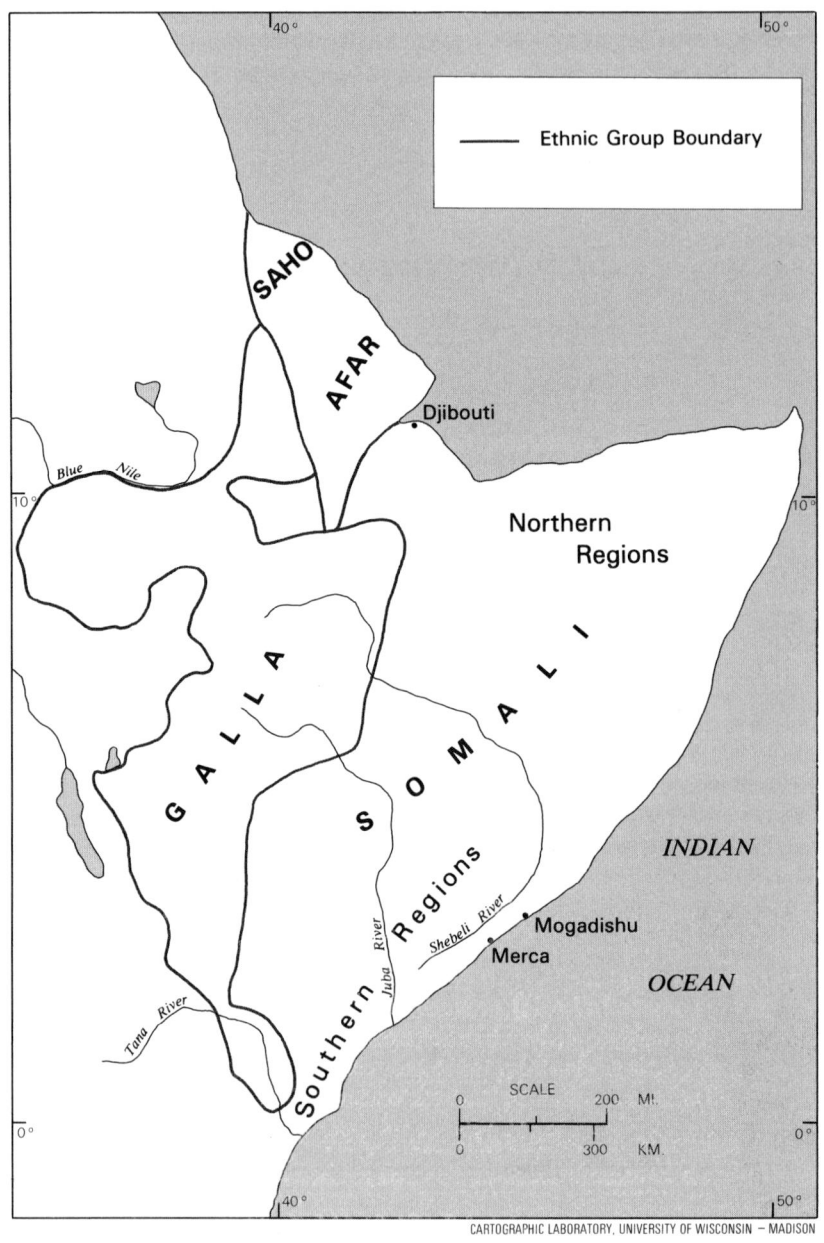

Map 7.1. East Cushitic Speakers in the Horn of Africa (after H. S. Lewis 1966)

Other Western ethnographers have been somewhat more cautious, but fascinated nonetheless with the possibility that the religions of the Dinka, Nuer, and Maasai were primitive exemplars of the monotheistic religions of the Middle East. The Seligmans (1932), Huffman (1931), Crazzolara (1953), and Evans-Pritchard (1956) all advanced a more sober version of Merker's original thesis. They saw the religions of some Nilotic peoples as featuring a monotheistic tendency quite different from the other religions of Black Africa, but resembling instead the Yahwism of the ancient Hebrews.[2]

Western prehistorians also locate the very same examples of Nilotic peoples in a preexisting scheme of history, but give them an altogether different place. The Dinka, Nuer, and Maasai are conceived as primitive exemplars of early Aryans, not early Hebrews. The most recent such statement is that of Lincoln (1981), an Indo-Europeanist. Brusquely setting aside the thesis of Nilotic monotheism as a false analogy, Lincoln cites an impressive lineage of prehistorians—Childe, Nyberg, Widengren, Piggott, Lommel, and Duchesne-Guillemin—all of whom proposed that Nilotic cattle herders bore some likeness to various peoples of early Europe (8). Lincoln goes on to show how Nilotic and Indo-Iranian myths and rites make references to an opposition between cattle-sacrificing priests and cattle-raiding warriors. He concludes that these similar features of Nilotic and Indo-Iranian tribes resulted from their similar cattle-herding ecology.

It is difficult to reconcile these two contrary reactions to the religions of the Dinka, Nuer, and Maasai and to evaluate whether they are, as ethnographers have claimed, exemplars of an early Yahwistic monotheism, or, as prehistorians have claimed, exemplars of an early cattle-herding, cattle-sacrificing paganism. Both analogies could also misleadingly obscure important differences between the Nilotic and Old World pastoral traditions.

In this and the next chapter, similarities and differences between Old World and East African stock keeping are considered, but from a perspective that does not rely on making direct analogies.[3] The conclusions reached in earlier chapters about the relationship of religion, society, and person to stock keeping follow from differences between East African pastoral traditions, rather than from the exact characteristics of any one stock-keeping people.[4] Assuming only that the effects of stock keeping on masculine identity were similar in the Old World and East Africa, these conclusions might reveal something about the history of Old World pastoral traditions and ecology. Otherwise, some aspects of Old World and East African stock keeping may differ sharply from each other.

Two Old World pastoral traditions, those of the northern Somalis (discussed below) and the early Indo-Europeans (see chap. 8), enable the evaluation of the analogies that anthropologists and prehistorians have drawn between Nilotic and Old World stock keepers.

134 *The Northern Somali Pastoralists*

DISTINCTIVE FEATURES OF NORTHERN SOMALI ECOLOGY
AND HISTORY

The Afar, Saho, Somali, and Galla are closely related peoples who speak East Cushitic languages (H. S. Lewis 1966). It is now believed that their present distribution in the Horn of Africa is the result of repeated northward and eastward movements of Cushitic speakers into the Horn of Africa from southern Ethiopia and northern Kenya, where they once made up a single speech community (see map 7.1). The Afar and Saho were the early forerunners of this movement, the Somali following them about two thousand years ago (Cassanelli 1982:4). The Galla are the latecomers, having begun their expansion at the expense of the Somali during the sixteenth century.[5]

The ecology of East-Cushitic-speaking peoples, or even of Somali-speaking peoples, is far from uniform, various groups practicing different combinations of stock keeping and grain agriculture. In his study of the East African cattle complex, Herskovits (1926) was inclined to identify some East Cushitic speakers, including certain groups of Galla, Somali, Afar, and Saho, with the East African cattle complex, but, in general, he saw the area they inhabit as a transition zone in which a camel-herding ecology came to prevail and Arabo-Islamic influences were dominant. These two factors are especially important among the northern Somalis, who herd camels, sheep, and goats in one of the more arid sections of the Horn of Africa.

Moving into that area about two millennia ago, the northern Somalis adopted a camel-herding ecology and developed an elaborate lineage system (H. S. Lewis 1966). Then, a little over a millennium ago, as Arabian peoples began to settle along the coast, trade was stimulated, town population grew, and Islamic sultanates arose. This brought the Somalis into more immediate contact with Old World religious, political, and economic systems.[6] In time, their pastoral ecology was transformed by the acquisition of horse breeding and horse riding, and their tribal religion came under the influence of Islamic belief and practice. Thus the precolonial northern Somalis must be set apart from other East African stock keepers on account of both ecological and historical factors: arid-land camel herding and early Old World contact.

At the same time, the relationship of religion, society, and person to pastoral ecology among the northern Somalis still features effects very similar to those examined in the preceding chapters. In general, those features of religion, society, and person which differentiate the Nuer from the Dinka are even more highly developed among the northern Somalis. Religiosity is focused and centered on a cosmic patriarchal spirit (originally in a non-Islamic form, later in an Islamic form).[7] Beneficent and punitive patriarchal spirits and ghosts as well as possession, divination, and fetishes are of relatively minor importance.[8] Social organization is pervasively influenced by a segmentary principle at the levels of clan-confederation, clan, maximal lineage, minimal lineage, and fraternal relations.[9] Self-representations feature a problematical relationship between self and other in which both solidarity and opposition figure prominently.[10]

These features are all the effects of a compromise of patriarchal authority by an antagonistic and oppositional individualism in a context where social cooperation and reciprocity are essential. When the implications of arid-land camel herding and Old World contacts are considered, just why these features of religion, society, and person are more highly developed among the northern Somalis than among either the Dinka or the Nuer becomes comprehensible.

ARID-LAND PASTORALISM: COLLECTIVISM
VERSUS INDIVIDUALISM

The northern Somalis inhabit a largely barren terrain of coastal plains and interior mountains in which the annual rainfall does not exceed four inches. Although at certain times of the year there are abundant pastures, the extreme aridity of the northeastern Horn of Africa precludes the possibility of the wide range of subsistence techniques that are pursued by other Somalis elsewhere in the region, such as cattle herding, fishing, or agriculture. Instead, the northern Somalis are almost exclusively herders of camels, sheep, and goats, and are obliged to organize their way of life so that they might exploit the meager pastoral resources of their homeland in as efficient a manner as possible. In his study of Somali politics and ecology, I. M. Lewis (1961) provides a concise picture of the Somali pastoral adaptation:

According to their capacity to endure arid conditions, the livestock of the northern pastoralists are divided into two herding units. Camels (collectively, *geel*) which can go without water for over twenty days in dry grazing, have greater powers of endurance and mobility than sheep and goats (collectively, *aḍi*), which, in the same conditions, need water every few days. When fresh green grazing is available watering is not required for either, so that the separation between the two stock units is least accentuated in the rainy seasons and most marked in the dry. Sheep and goats move with the nuclear family and nomadic hut (*aqal*) with a man, his wife, and young children, and sufficient burden camels for their transport. Apart from the beasts of burden required by the nuclear family and an odd milch camel, camels are in the care of boys and unmarried men. The nuclear family moves with close relatives of the husband in nomadic hamlets containing usually between two and four families. With a married woman are her un-married daughters and infant sons still too young to be out with the camels, and from time to time her husband. The latter shares his time amongst his various wives, and is often absent on expeditions to towns, or on clan affairs, or busy seeing to the needs of his camels, especially in the dry seasons when he helps with their watering. The family lives mainly on the milk and meat of the flocks herded with it, although this diet is supplemented by rice, grain, sugar and tea etc., obtained by trade, and wild berries and fruits. (32)

The striking feature of the pastoral ecology of the northern Somalis is the mobility, atomization, dispersal, and competition of herding groups. The Somali herding groups, both the family groups which herd the sheep and goats and the male youth groups which herd the camels, are relatively mobile. Throughout much of the year, they are small and widely distributed. They are not closely identified with any specific territory and must compete with other groups for scarce grazing and water resources. These characteristics of Somali pastoralism are a direct result of the irregular availability of pasture and water. Except in unusual conditions, the northern Somali are not able to gather in settlements, regularize their seasonal migrations, or even coordinate the movements of large groups.

Since the rigors of their pastoral regime require the Somalis to divide into small groups in order to seek out sparse pastoral resources, Somali families and lineages do not have a strong identification with a specific territory. These issues are complicated, but they are fully documented by I. M. Lewis's (1961) account of the details of sheep, goat, and camel husbandry.[11] His summary remarks suffice to make the essential point. The Somali pastoralist must make his own decisions in his own interests and yet is also obliged to be especially concerned about his relationships with others:

In relation to their ecology, the Somali have developed a system of grazing where no firm titles attach to pasturage except those which depend upon force. Thus the individual stock-herder has an optimum degree of freedom in his movements with his stock. As long as his water requirements are met (and titles to wells are spread widely) the only restriction placed upon his range of movement is the necessity to defend himself and his livestock against the threat of hostility. It is here, as well as in the watering of camels from deep wells, that the co-operation of kinsmen is essential. (89)

Because of economic considerations, the individual stock herder must be free to move on his own. Because of political considerations, he must join with others to defend stock and to assert his rights to water and pasture. Among the northern Somalis an arid environment enhances the two effects of a pastoral ecology: the necessity for cooperation and reciprocity and the tendency toward personal autonomy and independence. However, in the case of the northern Somali, the former effect did not precipitate centralized institutions of political authority which regulated or controlled the latter effect. The very mobility, atomization, dispersion, and competition of pastoral groups prevented the development of any such institutional alternative.

The ecology of arid-land camel herding thus favors the compromise of patriarchal authority. The place of stock raiding in northern Somali society suggests that a practico-cultural emphasis on stock raiding was also an inherent part of their camel-herding ecology.

PASTORAL CONTESTS AND CONFLICTS AMONG THE NORTHERN SOMALIS

I. M. Lewis (1961) has demonstrated how and why the northern Somali pastoralists are compelled to contest the control of pasture, water, and stock. The extreme aridity of their homeland, the variability of grazing and water resources, and the loss of stock by disease, thirst, or starvation all combine to enhance the importance of force among the Somalis. Lewis describes Somali armed conflict in the following terms:

> The pastoralists, indeed, regard fighting, whatever its circumstances, as essentially the proper pursuit of men. And war and feud occur constantly. To enumerate the number of engagements which occurred even in my twenty months in Somaliland would be difficult. Thus I frequently sought some relief from the general banter of which I was a ready target by accusing the pastoralists with whom I lived as being no better than bandits and robbers. And while such remarks were received with some show of resentment people seemed at heart flattered. For as it was often put to me, can women hold-up trade-trucks or loot and kill? But although they esteem fighting so highly, the pastoralists have no standing military organization or system of regiments. Armies and raiding parties are always *ad hoc* formations, and while feuds often last for years, and sometimes generations, they are generally waged in guerrilla campaigns. Pitched battles are rare. Spears are the traditional weapons of aggression and are still to some extent employed although they have largely been replaced by rifles. (27)

In this passage, Lewis lumps together armies and war, guerrilla campaigns and feuds, and raiding parties and looting, giving no precise account of the frequency and characteristics of the various types of conflict among the Somalis. All the same, he implies both in this and other passages (233, 242, 248ff.) that raiding parties and the plunder of stock are paradigmatic of Somali aggression, whether it takes the form of organized warfare, guerrilla campaigns, interlineage feuding, or simple looting:

> The northern Somali are essentially a warlike people who readily engage in battle or raiding to redress wrongs and injuries, to release pent-up enmities, to acquire

or maintain honour, and to gain access to natural resources or to conserve their rights over them. The aim of aggression is not so much to subjugate enemies completely as to establish political ascendancy. Somali wars are thus not properly wars of conquest, except in the limited sense of often giving the victor temporary grazing or watering rights in a particular region. While livestock are seized as booty and many raids made solely to loot camels, captives are rarely taken in battle since Somali have little use for them and do not seek to humiliate their adversaries in this fashion. (242)

Conquest is not an issue among the Somalis, since peoples, pastures, and wells cannot be surely dominated among mobile, atomized, and dispersed pastoral groups. Raiding and looting are conducted as an end in themselves or to establish political ascendancy.

Camel raiding may have been a feature of Somali pastoral ecology from its very beginnings two thousand years ago when the Somalis began to move into the Horn of Africa. But whatever the case, camel raiding became a very important feature of Somali pastoral ecology with the spread of horse breeding and horse riding in the wake of Old World contact.

I. M. Lewis's work on northern Somali politics and ecology is a classic which provides the wealth of detail absent in Evans-Pritchard's *The Nuer*. However, his relatively "synchronic" account of northern Somali social organization fails to mention the place of the horse in the earlier history of Somali pastoral traditions and institutions. When Lewis visited Somaliland in the 1950s, the horse no longer played a role in pastoral raiding and warfare. With the defeat of the Dervish anticolonial movement in the first part of this century, the independence of the Somali clans was compromised, and the functions of the horse, a political instrument, came to an end (Samatar 1982:22–23). Looking backward to the turn of the century, certain features of the pattern of religion, society, and person which Lewis observed in the 1950s can be seen as directly related to the interdependence of camel herding and horse riding which characterized Somali pastoralism for many centuries.

Understanding the implications of this interdependence requires examining Somali sentiments about livestock, sentiments which are superficially very similar to, but on closer inspection very different from, those of the Dinka and Nuer.

OLD WORLD CONTACT: THE TRIANGLE OF MAN, CAMEL, AND HORSE

Herskovits (1926:646–47) noted that camels can be regarded as taking the place of cattle in the northern transition zone of the East African cattle complex. In effect, the *bovine idiom* of the Nilotic speakers has its counterpart in the *cameloid idiom* of East Cushitic speakers. I. M. Lewis's (1961) account of the different value which the Somali placed on camels (herded by men) as opposed to sheep and goats (herded by women) seems at first to support this analogy:

The distinction between the social values of the two types of livestock can probably best be suggested by stating that the pastoralists work on a camel standard. For it is in camels that bride-wealth and blood-wealth are reckoned and ideally paid. Moreover, members of a lineage think of their joint rights in terms of camels rather than in terms of sheep and goats. And, as has been noted, the value of a man's life is phrased in camels. Their position is summed up in statements such as "camels beget children, settle blood-debts, and provide milk and transport." *After horses* [my italics] they are the most prized of Somali wealth and the pastoralist never tires of extolling the merits of his herds or of boasting of their numbers. (85-86)

Just as the Dinka and Nuer work on a "cattle standard," the Somali work on a "camel standard." But Lewis has also mentioned in passing another more prized animal, the horse, without explaining the high value which the Somali place on this beast.

In a recent study of Somali rhetoric and politics, Samatar (1982) has addressed this very issue. Samatar acknowledges a certain resemblance between the Nilotic bovine idiom and the Somali cameloid idiom. Like the Dinka and the Nuer with their oxen, the Somalis also have many names and songs for their camels (18). But this similarity can be misleading. Samatar therefore insists on a difference:

Somalis show no mystical or ritual attachment to their camels of the sort associated with other Eastern African pastoralists. Their interest in the camel and their love of it is entirely pragmatic. (12-13)

The relationship of man to cattle among Nilotes is basically different from that of man to camels among the Somalis. The first has mystical dimensions, but the second is more thoroughly pragmatic, suggesting that there is no cameloid idiom among the Somalis which exactly mirrors the bovine idiom among the Dinka and Nuer. The reasons for this are apparent when Samatar explains why the northern Somalis value their horses over their camels:

Until recently, the destinies of the horse and the camel were interlocked. The pastoral Somalis say the horse and the camel thrive on each other. . . . The observation signifies the importance the Somalis attach to the horse as an instrument in camel raiding or defending camels against raid. (21)

The horse, an instrument of pastoral raiding and warfare, has shaped the balance between stock ownership and stock expropriation in Somali pastoral ecology. Given the horse, the social significance of stock ownership is diminished while the significance of political capacities based on political instruments is enhanced. Accordingly, the romance of youth and ox among the Dinka and Nuer has become, in the Horn of Africa, a more pragmatic triangle of man, horse, and camel.

It is true that the Somalis can be said to be devoted to their horses:

> The Somalis show great kindness to their horses, rearing and caring for them with marked meticulousness. A man talks to his mount, sings to it in familiar language and will crawl on stones under a thorn bush to extract for it a bite of something to eat. (Samatar 1982:22)

But the northern Somali's adoration of his horse is essentially different from the Dinka youth's adoration of his personality ox. The horse represents power and wealth indirectly as a political instrument, rather than directly as a symbol of social status and personal identity. As Samatar points out, it is not enough to have a horse, it is also necessary to put it to use:

> The pastoral Somalis seldom ride their horses for sport, reserving the energies and services of their beloved beasts for the gravest of moments when dear life hangs on a sudden flight or pursuit. Before delivering a raid, the pastoralists will lead their horses for miles, only mounting when the object of their enterprise is in sight. The strategy is to keep the pony rested and in fit condition right up to the time of the action. Then they go into action with lightning speed, rounding up the herds and bolting away with them before the owners of the looted stock have time to launch a counter-offensive. (22)

The relationship between man and animal wealth (camel) among the Somalis is altered by the relationship of man and animal-instrument (horse). Possession of animal wealth is inseparable from political strategies and actions based on an animal-instrument. This shift had the effect of bringing the problematical relationship of self and other into the foreground of Somali experience, while resolutely pushing the mystical figure of the stock-owning, stock-exchanging, and stock-sacrificing patriarch into the background.

When the northern Somalis received the horse, perhaps sometime before the tenth century C.E., they acquired a new technical capacity. Horse riders can quickly remove camels from their rightful owners by stealth or force, camels themselves being an especially mobile form of stock wealth.[12] And while, as Samatar notes, the horse has some value for protecting camel herds, it is primarily an offensive, not a defensive, weapon.[13]

By inference, then, the dissemination of the horse among the northern Somalis would have reinforced the contradiction between authority and individualism that was already inherent in arid-land camel herding. Horse riding intensified the necessity for collective solidarity, further undermined the possibility of regulating or controlling contests and conflicts over pastoral resources by centralized political authorities, and magnified the potential of an antagonistic and oppositional individualism. The very features of the Nuer that distinguish them from the Dinka came into the foreground of pastoral tradition among arid-land, horse-riding camel herders who had Old World contacts.

POLITICIZATION OF SOCIETY AND RELIGION OF PATRIARCHAL OTHER

Both ecological and historical factors enhanced antagonism and opposition while undermining political authority among the northern Somalis. And yet, the result was not at all a state of nature, a war of all against all. On the contrary, the combination of an impressive instrument for camel raiding and the vulnerability of camel herds to expropriation brought with it a lesson in social morality. The individual Somali became all the more keenly conscious of himself as a person apart from and even opposed to others, but at the same time all the more keenly conscious that his fate and fortune were linked to those of others.

Accordingly, northern Somali representations of their lineage systems are among the best examples in the ethnographic literature of the segmentary principle.[14] A collectivity is represented so that nearness of agnatic relationship determines the priority of interpersonal loyalty; however, any agnatic relationship is qualified by a prior agnatic relationship down to the level of brothers.[15] Collectivities are conceived as fighting groups and their relationships with one another are associated with different levels of conflict: dispute, feuding, raiding, and warfare. Furthermore, the segmentary principle of division and opposition is remarkably extended to include all those peoples who could be directly or indirectly identified with the northern Somali way of life. Beyond the lineage there is the clan, which includes tens of thousands of individuals, and beyond the clan, there is the clan-confederation, which comprises hundreds of thousands of individuals. And beyond the clan-confederation, there is a sense of the Somali nation, a precolonial feature of Somali society which differentiated it from most sub-Saharan African peoples.[16]

The segmentary principle which marks Somali representations of social organization has its counterpart, or, to be more precise, its very roots, on the level of a consciousness of the problematical relationship of self and other. While the Somalis contemplate uniting with one another up to the level of what is now called a nation, they are also able to contemplate opposing one another down to the level of brothers. Proverbs recorded by Cassanelli (1982) are eloquent testimonies of this:

If you love a person, love him moderately, for you do not know whether you will hate him one day; on the other hand, if you hate someone, hate him moderately also, for you do not know whether you will love him one day. (21)

The same theme appears again in another Somali proverb recorded by Cassanelli, one which may be a Somali rendition of an Arab saying:

> I and my clan against the world.
> I and my brother against the clan.
> I against my brother.
>
> (21)

In effect, the segmentary principle of the Somali lineage system is underlaid by a general moral outlook of the problematical relationship of self and other.

These features of northern Somali social organization are correlated with the secularization and politicization of society. Northern Somali men were traditionally divided into men of warfare (*waranleh*, "spearbearers") and men of religion (*wadaad*). But until the end of the last century, when Islamic leaders of Somali religious fraternities (*tarikats*) began to play an important role in organizing resistance to the British, the tribal men of religion had a secondary and marginalized place in Somali society.[17] Men of warfare made up the large majority of the northern Somali pastoralists and the domain of secular and political action was primary and central. Men of religion were excluded from participation in secular and political actions, serving only a ceremonial role in gatherings and assemblies, which they opened and closed with prayers and blessings.[18] They frequently functioned as mediators between feuding or warring parties, but only as more or less passive go-betweens who did "not settle disputes or judge between disputants" (Lewis 1961:217). Men of religion did not supervise tribal initiation rites and age-set formations, these institutions being absent among the mobile, dispersed, and atomized Somali pastoralists.[19]

As discussed in previous chapters, the secularization and politicization of social organization is correlated with a focusing and centering of religion on a cosmic patriarchal other. This raises the possibility that Somali Islamic monotheism is a phenomenon more complex than an Arabo-Muslim influence which has incidentally seeped from the Arabian peninsula into the Horn of Africa.

It is thought that the horse reached the northern Somalis about a millennium ago, when Arabo-Muslim influences first began to be prominent in the Horn of Africa.[20] If so, the arrival of the horse in that region is correlated with a higher level of trade, the practice of new crafts, the growth of towns, the establishment of sultanates, and the spread of Islam along the coast. The integration of horse breeding and horse riding within the ecology of northern Somali pastoralism is but one dimension of a historical process by which the Horn of Africa came into closer contact with Old World religious, political, and economic systems some time around the eighth or ninth century C.E. Nevertheless, the horse sensitized the Somalis to Arabo-Muslim civilization, specifically in regard to their reception of Islamic monotheism.

By inference, the introduction of the horse into the Horn of Africa would have transformed concepts of religion, society, and person among the northern Somalis. How these concepts were transformed can be deduced from my analyses in the preceding chapters, together with the ethnography of contemporary Somali traditions and institutions. Reception of the horse would have undermined the foundations of patriarchal authority and extended the range of autonomous and independent action, resulting in a more secular and political society and a stronger focusing and centering of religion on a cosmic patriarchal spirit.[21] If this inference is correct, it means that a change in the ecology of camel herding, which was brought about by the arrival of the horse, created fertile ground for the Somali comprehension of Islamic monotheism. That is, specific political and economic consequences of Somali contact with Arabo-Muslim civilization were a crucial factor in determining its reception by the Somalis.[22]

PERSONAL POETRY AND PUBLIC ORATORY

A review of Somali oral tradition completes the picture of how the problematical relationship of self and other is intensified by arid-land pastoralism and Old World contact.[23]

Somali oral tradition is remarkably complex. Different verbal forms are associated with different social contexts, and a full understanding of the content of any specific verbal form requires an intimate knowledge of the occasion on which it was formulated and delivered. For my present purposes, however, the significant feature of Somali oral tradition is its broad division into two contrasting forms. Personal poetry is associated with individual intents and feelings, while public oratory is linked with meetings and assemblies. This division itself reflects the two sides of Somali experience which reveal a keen sense of personal autonomy and independence as well as an intense concern for social cooperation and reciprocity.

These two sides of the Somali art of the verb impressed European observers of the Somalis at the turn of the century. R. F. Burton (1894) singles out Somali personal poetry for special comment:

It is strange that a dialect which has no written character should so abound in poetry and eloquence. There are thousands of songs, some local, others general, upon all conceivable subjects, such as camel loading, drawing water, and elephant hunting; every man of education knows a variety of them. The rhyme is imperfect, being generally formed by the syllable "ay" . . . , which gives the verse a monotonous regularity; but, assisted by a tolerably regular alliteration and cadence, it can never be mistaken for prose, even without the song which invariably accompanies it. The country teems with "poets, poetasters, poetitos, poetaccios": every man has his recognized position in literature as accurately defined as though he had been reviewed in a century of magazines—the fine ear of this people* causing them to take the greatest pleasure in harmonious sounds and poetical expressions, whereas a false quantity or a prosaic phrase excite their violent indignation. (1:81–82)

While song composition and recitation are popular among many pastoral peoples in East Africa, the Somali fascination with poetry is especially intense.

Jardine (1923), who wrote two decades later—after British-Somali relations had become more complex and more tragic—is a less sympathetic observer than Burton. He is not so much struck by the esthetics of Somali speech as by what he perceives as the pernicious role in Somali politics of a vain and tedious indulgence in oratory. He points out that discourse and address are as much a Somali passion as poetry and song:

The Somalis are . . . no mean orators; and to be a man of distinction in a tribe you must have a reputation not only as a fighter and a man of many possessions, but also as a convincing spokesman. The Somali orator is extremely prolix and very histrionic; but, despite this, he is undoubtedly impressive. He possesses the first qualification of the public speaker, namely, self-confidence; and he has the utmost scorn for any rival. The consequence is that, whenever a British officer gives an audience to the leaders of a tribe to discuss any political question, he is faced by the prospect of a feast of oratory, which often lasts for a whole day. The most famous spokesman of the tribe will be the first to hold forth. Careless of repetitions and buoyed up with a sense of his own importance, he will state his tribe's case with an unceasing flow of words and gestures. This speech may extend to half an hour. The man whose reputation is only second to that of the first spokesman will then intervene. Convinced that the tribe's case is being mangled, he will himself proceed to harangue the luckless British officer in almost precisely the same terms. (Jardine 1923:33, as quoted in Samatar 1982:23)

Despite his prejudices, Jardine illustrates how argument, explanation, and persuasion figure prominently in Somali politics. But it is not, as Jardine suggests, mere pride and vanity which underlie what seemed to him endless and fruitless talk, but rather a complex and subtle politics based on a consensus of potentially autonomous and independent individuals and collectivities.[24]

In his study of northern Somali oratory and politics, Samatar (1982)

---

*Burton adds the following note to this text: "It is proved by the facility with which they pick up languages, Western as well as Eastern, by mere ear and memory" (1:82).

raises the question of why an art of the verb should be so important among the northern pastoralists. Why do they have a wide variety of prose and poetic speech patterns? Why are there a series of ranks and assemblies, each associated with a specific form of oratory (28, 31)? And why are poetic forms associated with various categories of interpersonal relationships, some antagonistic and some affectionate (74-84)? Samatar's answer is brief and to the point:

The Somali pastoral system is characterized by a marked absence of central authority and a corresponding lack of inherited offices or a hierarchy of authority of chiefs to run it. All claim to be equal and show nothing but scorn and disdain for what, in Western metaphor, may be termed "duly instituted authority." But where all are equal, anarchy is not far to seek, and that, at least at a superficial level of observation, is what seems to characterize the relations between Somali clans. On a closer look, however, it becomes fairly clear that some men in fact do wield greater power and influence in society than others and that a high proportion of these men usually have what Somalis call the "gift of speech." (24)

The northern Somalis are not like any "acephalous" or "stateless" people. "A fierce and turbulent race of Republicans" in the words of R. F. Burton, they are a people among whom a problematical relationship of self and other must be constantly mediated by person-to-person communication. "Speech is the vehicle of politics," so that "he who would lead others must persuade rather than coerce" (Samatar 1982:24-25, 27).

Thus, public oratory and assembly — not myths, rites, hymns, or ceremonies — are important features of Somali social organization and their subject matter is disputation, litigation, negotiation, agreement, and consensus. But the problematical relation of self and other not only explains the formal processes of Somali politics but also implies a sense of self apart from and opposed to others. This sense of self is confirmed by the characteristics of Somali songs, which are, from the standpoint of both their form and content, self-representations.

First, Somali songs are rigorously attributed to a specific author:

The first principle to underscore in Somali oral poetic composition is that the Somalis have a keenly developed sense of individual authorship and creativity so that a poem, once composed, becomes the property of its composer. It is regarded as a matter of great dishonor in Somali pastoral ethic — in effect, a theft liable to punitive sanctions — for anyone to claim falsely the authorship of a poem or to utilize it without giving credit to its creator. In matters of composition and publication, Somalis recognize what may be called, for want of a better term, an unwritten copyright law, no less strict than those observed in literate societies. (Samatar 1982:64)

Second, songs are identified with their authors' personal situation on some specific occasion. They represent personal dispositions or intentions which are communicated to others:

The bulk of Somali poetry is "committed" in the sense that it is composed and chanted in relation to a specific occasion for the purpose of achieving a specific end. A Somali traditional poem has a story to tell, often an argument to advance. As a rule, the occasion which prompts a poet to compose verse is socially significant: for example, reconciling two hostile clans which are on the brink of war through a poetic appeal. . . . Although a poet may also compose to give expression to a private inspiration, emotion or passion, his ultimate concern as a poet is to influence the opinions of others toward a certain vital issue. [If they were to hear a poem unknown or strange to them,] they would wait to the end and then would inevitably ask, "In what circumstances did the poet first recite the poem and what was his purpose?" (Samatar 1982:57, with question quoted from Andrzejewski and Lewis 1964:44)

Third, Somali songs are personally, rather than collectively, performed. Andrzejewski and Lewis (1964) describe the performance of the two most important genres of traditional Somali poetry, the *gabay* and the *geeraar*:

In the nomadic interior the *gabay* [and *geeraar* are] never recited with an accompaniment of music, drums, stepping, or clapping: there is in fact no participation on the part of the audience except for the occasional sporadic repetition of a particular line, hemistich, or word as a sign of delight and appreciation. (47)

The manner in which Somali poetry is composed and performed reflects its status as an expression of a self addressing others. Somali poetry thus confirms a sense of self distinct from others and yet linked to others through the art of self-representation. In this respect, it differs from the songs of East African cattle herders from Sudan to the Cape. The Somali self is revealed to others through a highly stylized, intricately constructed medium. Somali poetry features a somewhat more complex prosodic canon—rhyme, alliteration, meter—than the songs of the East African cattle herders. This poetic structure is itself the consequence of a problematical relationship of self and other: Somali poetry allows a wide range of verbal invention and expression, but only within strictly defined limits. The form and content of Somali poetry testify to both a clearer sense of self and a greater pressure of the social other on this sense of self.

SOMALI POETIC GENRES

The northern Somali pastoralists composed and recited a variety of songs. While some were performed by groups and accompanied by dancing and musical instruments (Paulitschke 1896:165; Kirk 1905:170), the two most important genres, the *geeraar* and the *gabay*, were personally composed and performed. According to Paulitschke, the *geeraar* was a man's song and associated with horse riding, while the *gabay* was a woman's song and associated with love. But Kirk (1905), who probably knew the Somali language much better than Paulitschke, describes the *geeraar* as "sung on horseback, and usually relates to raiding and fighting"; the *gabay* is "a chant of a more peaceful nature, and is often a love song" which is "usually sung round the fire in the evening" (170).

Both Paulitschke's and Kirk's accounts suggest that the two genres are broadly differentiated with respect to the theme of the problematical relationship of self and other.[25] The *geeraar* is closely associated with war and aggression, whereas the *gabay* leans toward peace and affection. A closer look at the formal properties of each genre and at specific examples of poems composed at the turn of the century confirms this.

The Somali *Geeraar*

Unfortunately, there are no thorough studies in English of Somali poetry in its traditional pastoral context. Andrzejewski and Lewis (1964), however, have provided a detailed account of the formal features of contemporary Somali genres in their introduction to their translations of classical Somali poetry. "The *geeraar*" they write,

is usually shorter than the *gabay*, and the number of syllables in the line usually varies between 6 and 8. This form also is always unaccompanied, and the chant is swifter and the melody livelier than in the *gabay*. Traditionally the *geeraar* used to be recited on horseback, but this practice has been almost completely abandoned.

War and conflict is the usual subject matter of the *geeraar*, and it is said that in the old days, when one clan declared war on another, the challenge to fight at an appointed place was usually delivered in this form. It was also chanted to pour insults and abuse on one's opponents before the battle, and to raise the morale of one's own warriors. (49)

The following *geeraar*, collected and translated by Kirk (1905), is a relatively accessible example of Somali sensibilities. It is of special interest here since it suggests that the poet's very identity is derived from the place of his horse in pastoral contests and conflicts:

> My broad-chested beast,
> how to praise him I know not.
> Like grass-covered Haud?
> Like the pattering
> rain from last evening's sky?
> Like the cubs of a
> lion roaring afar?
> Like the foals of the
> camels, Gedo [camel-name] and Lan
>   [camel-name]?

> Like my own song
> of Ged [spring wind] and Hohhad [summer
>   wind]?
> His four hoofs
> clatter over the ground,
> like a grown girl,
> who has been given her husband,
> and has received great flocks,
> who, with most costly robe,
> and silken raiment,
> and dress, has clothed herself,
> and at the time of mid-day shadows,
> to her sleeping husband,
> brings his food,
> as with the shoes of cow's hide
> she clatters?
>
>   (176–77)

The poem divides into two sections, the first raising the problem of the relationship of the poet's song to his horse and the second composing an image of the horse which suggests that the poet's song is the expressive dimension of the horse's power and energy.

The first section begins by raising the question of how the horse is to be portrayed. This question is posed in terms of the relationship of a powerful, "broad-chested beast" to the song that will be composed by the poet, who does not know "how to praise him." The verses which follow evoke natural powers that have procreative and expressive dimensions— grass-covered pastures are associated with the pattering of rain, and lion cubs are described as roaring in the wilderness. The final verses of the first section evoke a relationship of natural powers with the expressions of the poet. Here the foals of camels and the spring and summer winds are metrically named "Gedo and Lan" and "Ged and Hohhad." The significance of this naming becomes clearer in the next section.

The second section elaborates on an image of the horse. The first line describes the clatter of its four hoofs, evoking the horse's instrumental power (its mobility), which has an expressive dimension (the sound of its hoofs). In fact, the clatter of hoofs has been prefigured in preceding verses with the names "Gedo and Lan" and "Ged and Hohhad," which are metrical representations of the horse's gait. So the horse's energy has an expressive dimension which is articulated and therefore clarified by the design of the poet's song (its images and their metrical form).[26]

The eleven verses which follow then build an image of the horse as a bride coming to the poet, who is her husband. The bride is handsomely attired and brings a rich dowry. She carries her husband his supper as he lies in drowsy repose. As she comes, her leather shoes clatter. Here the relationship of horse to poet is expressed as the relationship of a natural procreative power which brings wealth and comfort to the poet, who is at ease.

I mentioned earlier that the horse is preeminently an instrumental means for contests over pastoral resources and conflict between pastoral groups. The clatter of hoofs, appearing as an image in a raiding song, is implicitly associated with the opposition of self and other in pastoral contests and conflicts. The Somali poet represents his personal identity as the expressive dimension of the natural powers of the horse and represents the horse as furnishing him with wealth, comfort, and ease. Thus, both personal identity and social circumstances are seen as directly derived from the use and value of the horse as an instrument in pastoral contests and conflicts. The poet's relationship with his horse, an instrument of expropriation and aggression, is not represented as raising a question about the poet's place in society. From the perspective of the raiding song, personal identity and social position are dimensions of the opposition of self and other.

Another *geeraar* imagines a party of youths who raid the herds of the enemy and then delight in a feast on the booty they have taken. This example shows that raiding is associated with the priority of action over talk:

> Have ye, over plains and plains,
> over (countless) plains,
> whose richness belongs to God,
> gone out to war?
> Have ye assembled the young men?
> Have ye caught Bado [a horse]?
> Have ye put on Bado the blanket and
>   trappings?
> Have ye put the toe in the stirrup iron?
> Have ye made your prayers?
> Where the enemy cut the ground,
> have ye found the tracks?
> While he is talking,
> have ye taken to the plain?
> Boys, enriched by God,
> have ye prepared the fire?
> A skin of curdled milk,
> and fat for to-night,
> have ye eaten fat?
>   (Kirk 1905:177-78)

The song begins by imagining a boundless pastoral domain ("plains and plains, over [countless] plains") being traversed by a raiding party of youths,[27] and ends by imagining the youths sitting about a fire enjoying the curdled milk and fat which God has given them as a reward. Implicitly, the camel herds of the plains ("whose richness belongs to God") are the patrimony of God rather than the property of particular groups, and are given by God to those who resort to seizing them.

Between initially riding out into God's plains and finally receiving God's reward of curdled milk and fat, a series of pragmatic actions are necessary. Men must be assembled. Horses must be caught, saddled, and mounted. Tracks must be discovered and traced through the plains. The significance of these actions is clarified by a later verse in which the poet asks: "While he [the enemy] is talking, have ye taken to the plain?" The youths are men of deeds, not words, while the enemy are just the opposite. Hence God favors the youths with a reward.

The song itself is, of course, a kind of talk, just like the talk of the enemy. But it is a special kind of talk, a raiding song recited when setting out on horseback, and it insists on the priority of action in contests and conflicts. Its implication is not unlike that of the song which depicts personal identity and social position as derived from the natural powers of the horse.[28] Here, however, the matter is formulated somewhat differently. The priority of action over words is seen as favored and rewarded by God. Curiously, the resort to the use of the horse, an instrument of expropriation and aggression, is seen as an ethical stance, not as an act of dissidence and rebellion.

Actually, something like this exists in the thinking of the Nuer, another people who have experienced the compromise of patriarchal authority. In some contexts, the Nuer also felt that raiding and warfare are the activities of men who are close to God. This outlook was understandable in that raiding and warfare were themselves an essential part of the Nuer experience of the problematical relationship of self and other, and thus closely linked with the Nuer belief in a cosmic patriarchal spirit. Similarly, at least in the context of raiding songs and raiding expeditions, the northern Somalis are able to see a link between an activity which involves aggression and expropriation and their belief in and worship of a God who stands for truth and justice.

The Somali *Gabay*

The *geeraar* is a warlike song that represents self and society in relationship to the division and opposition of self and other. In contrast, the *gabay*, a peaceful song, represents self and society in relationship to solidarity and affection between self and other.

The *gabay* usually consists of between 30 and 150 lines, though shorter ones and considerably longer ones are not unknown. The number of syllables in each line varies from 14 to 18, and in the majority of cases there is a caesura before the sixth syllable from the end. . . .

The chant of the *gabay* usually has a simple melody with great variations in the length of notes. Some are held for a considerable time, and this applies particularly to those which correspond to the end of a line in the poem: in this position they fade gradually into silence. The tempo of the chant is slow and majestic, seldom changing throughout the poem. All emotional appeal depends on the expressive power of the words, and the reciter does not especially modulate his voice or accentuate any words or lines, thus giving an impression of superb restraint and stylization. (Andrzejewski and Lewis 1964:47-48)

The following is an example of a *gabay*, titled "My Future Wife":

> It is in my mind that she whom I would marry
>   is the (daughter of) the head of the
>   Guleds.
> She is pink, and her hands are like drops of
>   rain,
> Her ankles are round, her skirt is pleated,
> Her steps are not those of a fool, she walks
>   daintily.
> She is after the fashion of an angel, a
>   virgin full of skill,
> Never yet have I seen the place of your [the
>   sweetheart's] abode, nor have I any
>   knowledge of you.
> Last night, for half the night, in my heart I
>   dreamed of you.
> We will give your aged mother a loading
>   camel,
> And to your brother one day I may present a
>   pure bay pony.
> I will divide a host of camels with your
>   father.
> Let us all take our places, come to my
>   people.
>   (Kirk 1905:181)

The poet begins with the announcement of a desire ("It is in my mind that she whom I would marry . . ."), a personal wish communicated to and therefore shared with others. The four lines that follow portray the girl as an angel and a delight. Then the poet reveals that he does not know the girl and has never seen her home, but that she fills his thoughts and dreams. The last four lines, addressed to the girl herself, compose a little society as representative of these thoughts and dreams. The poet says that he will come to terms with her mother, her brother, and her father by presenting them with the stock of their heart's desire. Then he calls upon all to "take their places" as he asks the girl to come as a bride to his people.

This love song reveals a side of Somali tradition and experience that is the complete opposite of what is seen in the raiding song. The subject is not hostility but affection between self and other. The man announces his dream of marrying a girl, an anonymous other whom he does not know. He foresees the realization of his wish by means of a series of dyadic contracts with individuals who have no existing relationship to him. As a consequence of these contracts, an affinal society is constituted among unrelated individuals. This done, the loved one is able to come to her lover.

The warp and woof of the poem is the problematical relationship of self and other: The individual speaks for himself, but to others. There is personal desire, but it is to possess another. There are unknown individuals, but they can come to agreement. The society which results is composed by dyadic contractual agreements and the individual's private wish moves toward an image of everyone taking their proper stations. The thrust of the poem is toward solidarity rather than opposition. If the Somalis are able to see antagonism and opposition in all their relationships, they are nonetheless able to imagine harmony and love among total strangers.

CAMEL-HERDING SOMALIS AND CAMEL-HERDING BEDOUINS

The camel-herding Somalis are in many ways an unusual, even a unique people. Nevertheless, those dimensions of their pastoral traditions and ecology which have been considered in the preceding analysis are also more or less characteristic of the camel-herding Bedouin of North Arabia. These include arid-land camel herding, a practico-cultural emphasis on camel raiding, the presence of mounts (camels as well as horses), a cosmic patriarchal other (first non-Islamic and then Islamic), the relative absence of punitive and beneficent patriarchal spirits and ghosts, a segmentary principle of social organization, the problematical relationship of self and other, and public oratory and personal poetry.[29] In other words, the same features of religion, society, and person are to be found among two separate instances of arid-land camel herders.

Given the similarities between the northern Somali and North Arabian traditions, however, certain differences are all the more interesting. Unlike the northern Somalis, the North Arabian Bedouins have used their camels as mounts from a very early date. Furthermore, as the North Arabian Bedouins came into contact with horse riders about the middle of the first millennium B.C.E., camel riding was increasingly adapted to use in raiding and warfare while horse riding gradually spread among camel-herding peoples in many parts of Arabia (Dostal 1959).

The relatively early use of mounts for raiding and warfare by the

Bedouins is significant in the light of another contrast between Arabia and the Horn of Africa. Sometime around the third century C.E., Bedouin society and culture became more influential in northern Arabia as trade declined and town population decreased. Then, as trade increased and towns recovered toward the end of the sixth century C.E., the way of life of Arabian townsmen, settlers, and nomads was subjected to the strain of social changes and foreign influences. At this time, early Islam appeared among Hijaz farmers and merchants, first as a religious movement and then as a political movement aimed at unification of Arabian townsmen, settlers, and tribes.

Early Islam is usually seen as inspired by Judaic and Christian influences in pre-Islamic Arabia. But they were clearly not decisive influences, since the Arabians did not elect to adopt either Judaism or Christianity as their religion. Instead, they turned to a monotheistic cult which arose more directly out of Arabian tradition and experience. The origins of an Arabian monotheism lie not so much in the religious beliefs and practices of the Arabian settlements which were differentially influenced by foreign cults, some monotheistic and some polytheistic, but in the more purely Arabian religiosity of the tribal periphery.

Among arid-land, mounted camel herders, the problematical relationship of self and other was associated with a religiosity of a cosmic patriarchal spirit. With the collapse of trade sometime during the third century C.E., this religiosity became a more important factor in the religiosity of townsmen and settlers as a consequence of nomadic cultural and social influence which accompanied tribal hegemony during this period. Then, centuries later, this Arabian monotheistic religiosity, which had become common to townsman, settler, and nomad, served as the seed of a unifying cult of Arabian, rather than foreign, origin.

The monotheistic cult which appeared among settlers and townsmen in the seventh century C.E. was, of course, in various ways quite different from the monotheistic religiosity of the tribal pastoral periphery, even though the latter inspired the former. Among the settlers and townsmen, the monotheistic cult first took the form of a more or less vague religiosity, but was rapidly developed as a system of canonical ritual and belief. In effect, the destabilization of camel-herding ecology by the use of mounts for raiding and warfare together with the Bedouinization of Arabian society and culture were preconditions for the formulation of a monotheistic cult in Arabian towns and settlements during the seventh century.

In the Horn of Africa, there was not the same sequence of pastoral cause and religious effect. Both the horse and Islam seem to have arrived there more or less at the same time. Thus, the destabilization of pastoral ecology among the tribesmen of the interior coincided with the spread of a monotheistic cult among the coastal settlers. A pastoral "effect" therefore accompanied, rather than preceded, the adoption of a monotheistic cult. On the other hand, it was not until the late nineteenth century that Islam began to be especially important among the camel-herding Somalis as a religious movement. This was a period when contact with colonial powers was strongly affecting the way of life of all the Somalis, both tribesmen and townsmen. At this time, Islamic leaders who had received their training in Islamic schools began to organize the Somali tribesmen by founding religious brotherhoods (*tarikats*), which were an alternative to the Somali lineage system and which eventually played a central role in resistance to European colonial intrusions.[30] There is, then, a parallel between Islam in seventh-century Arabia and Islam in nineteenth-century Somaliland.

With this parallel in mind, Evans-Pritchard's impression of a similarity between early Hebraic and Nuer religion can be reconsidered. The Dinka, Nuer, Somalis, and Bedouins are all very different peoples with very different pastoral ecologies. However, the pastoral way of life of each is associated in varying degrees with compromise of patriarchal authority and a problematical relationship of self and other. The result is a similar coloring of religion, society, and person among peoples who are in other respects very different from one another. From what is known of the ancient Hebrews, it is clear that they were not at all like the Dinka, Nuer, Somalis, or Bedouins. Still, they were an early (first millennium B.C.E.) tribal people of the Old World who had had some connection with arid-land pastoral ecology, and their religiosity may have featured a compromise of patriarchal authority and a problematical relationship of self and other.[31] If so, the cult of Yahweh is in some sense an early forerunner of the cult of Allah. In ancient Israel, as in medieval Arabia, a monotheistic cult appeared, not among pastoralists, but among settlers and townsmen who had historical connections with an arid-land pastoral ecology.[32] The fixing of the cult of Yahweh at Jerusalem played a role in unifying the tribes of Israel, just as the fixing of the cult of Allah at Mecca played a role in unifying the tribes of Arabia. This came about among the Hebrew tribes, as among the Arab tribes, following a period during which the weakening of an intrusive foreign rule had permitted tribal peoples to assert their autonomy and independence. The monotheism of the early Hebrews, like that of the early Arabs, may therefore have exhibited a pastoral "effect," even though neither of these peoples were exclusively or even largely pastoral nomads or seminomads. If Yahwism does feature a pastoral "effect," this would explain why Evans-Pritchard was able to persuade himself that he could perceive some likeness between Nuer religion and Old Testament religion.

8
Early Indo-Europeans: Socio-Cosmic Patriarchal Spirits, Community of Production, Divided Self

THE DEEP STRUCTURE OF INDO-EUROPEAN
MYTHOLOGICAL TRADITIONS

Prehistorians generally agree that cattle herding was an important subsistence technique for many early Indo-European peoples and that this had considerable influence on their traditions and institutions (Lincoln 1981).[1] But was there a specific configuration of pastoral tradition and ecology among early Indo-European peoples in general? The ethnography of East African cattle herders raises doubts about such a possibility.

Cattle herding among different East African peoples is consistently associated with two contradictory effects: the enhancement of concepts of authority (since stock keeping is dependent on cooperation and reciprocity) and the enhancement of an antagonistic and oppositional individualism (since stock keeping provides opportunities for self-assertion). Despite these uniform effects of cattle herding, however, the configuration of pastoral traditions varies widely from people to people and from period to period, because the way in which tension between authority and individualism is resolved in a pastoral tradition is acutely sensitive to historical and ecological factors.

Presumably the pastoral traditions of early Indo-European cattle herders were no less variable and no less subject to change than those of East African cattle herders. In fact, one would expect the former to be even more variable and changeable, given the involvement of early Indo-European cattle herders with other Old World states and societies. If this is the case, it would be unlikely that the configuration of pastoral traditions among early Indo-European peoples assumed one specific form, such as the opposition of a class of cattle-sacrificing priests to a class of cattle-raiding warriors. But it might still be possible to evaluate the effects of a pastoral phase of early Indo-European social history at a higher level of abstraction.

Georges Dumézil has argued that the mythological traditions of different early Indo-European peoples have the same underlying structure, one that is not characteristic of the mythological traditions of other Old World peoples. This structure can be understood as representing a general framework within which early Indo-European concepts of religion, society, and person tended to vary.

In this chapter, Dumézil's reconstruction of the framework of early Indo-European mythological traditions is examined with the following two questions in mind: Does the framework feature traces of the effects of a pastoral phase of social history (authority opposed to individualism)? And if it does, do these effects bear any resemblance to the configurations of pastoral tradition and ecology considered earlier?

THE TRIPARTITE IDEOLOGY: PRIEST, WARRIOR, AND PRODUCER

In numerous books and articles published over a span of fifty years, Dumézil argued that the mythological traditions of early Indo-European peoples have in common a tripartite ideology consisting of a hierarchy of a priestly function, a warrior function, and a productive function.[2] Dumézil reached this conclusion by means of a unique method, one that involved translating the techniques of comparative linguistics from the level of language structure to the level of myth structure.

By comparing the similarities and differences of the languages of Europe and India, linguists were able to account for the way in which Indo-European languages had been differentiated from a hypothetical and unattested mother language, Proto-Indo-European. Dumézil devised a comparative Indo-European mythology that was more or less analogous to this project. Examining the similarities and differences of early Celtic, Italic, Greek, Iranian, and Indian religion, he reconstructed a tripartite ideology. By analogy with the reconstruction of Proto-Indo-European, Dumézil proposed that this tripartite ideology, which was itself hypothetical and unattested, indicated the original form of early Indo-European mythological traditions.

While Dumézil's method and theory have been the focus of heated controversy in Indo-European studies in the past, their contribution has now come to be accepted. Indo-Europeanists disagree as to whether the tripartite ideology could be considered an original Indo-European protomyth, but they have been more inclined to accept other implications of Dumézil's work. For example, it is now generally agreed that there are systematic correspondences between the mythological traditions of different Indo-European peoples, and as a consequence of this, early Indo-European pantheons are now viewed as an integrated structure rather than as the result of a piecemeal, historical accretion of divinities (Littleton 1973).

If the tripartite ideology is the best possible account of the general pattern of early Indo-European mythological traditions, does this pattern indicate in any way that it originated in a specific form of early society? Dumézil gives two different answers to this question. Since the tripartite ideology depicts systematic correspondences between different Indo-European mythological traditions, he sometimes sees it as a fixed and invariant philosophy or outlook which transcends historical change. At the same time, since the tripartite ideology also points toward an earlier time and place when differentiated mythological traditions were more similar, he sometimes sees it as reflecting the values of a specific form of early society.

In a summary of his work (Dumézil 1958), for example, he presents two inconsistent arguments one after the other. In one place, he claims that the tripartite ideology is an early Indo-European formulation of functions which are aspects of social life in all times and places. In every community, he argues, there are three requirements: (1) a religion guaranteeing an administration based on a law and a stable morality, (2) a protective and conquering force, and (3) a means of production as the basis of nourishment and enjoyment. However, the implications of these functional necessities have not been fully recognized by peoples other than the Indo-Europeans:

For a society to respond to and to fulfill over-riding necessities is one thing; to bring them into full consciousness, reflect on them, make of them an intellectual structure, a matrix of thought, is another thing. In the ancient world, only the Indo-Europeans have accomplished this philosophical project [my translation]. (23)

This explanation of the tripartite ideology is not very satisfying. Even if the three functions are essential features of all societies, it is not clear why their formulation in the mythological traditions of early Indo-Europeans should be privileged in some special way.

While Dumézil's first explanation of the tripartite ideology sidesteps its historicity by asserting its universality, his second explanation directly addresses its specialized social origins. Referring to Wikander's (1938) study of the Aryan *Männerbund*, Dumézil proposes that the distinctive feature of early Indo-European society was the existence of mobile "warrior bands" whose members were ascribed a unique "moral status." He then cites the second-millennium B.C.E. expansion of certain Indo-European-speaking peoples as evidence of the social importance of these warrior bands:

> It appears that it is indeed the differentiation of a class of warriors, with its peculiar "moral" status, joined by a kind of supple alliance to an equally differentiated class of priests, which has been the originality and novelty of the Indo-Europeans and, with the support of the horse and chariot, the reason and means of their expansion [my translation]. (Dumézil 1958:17)

This second explanation pictures early Indo-European society as taking a very specialized form because of the peculiar importance of the early Indo-European warrior identity in conjunction with a priestly role. This comes close to the issue of the relationship of warrior identity to religious authority as a key feature of pastoral traditions.

Assuming that mythological traditions are collective representations which directly or indirectly reflect social traditions, the tripartite ideology can be examined to determine whether it bears traces of the effects of a pastoral ecology (authority contradicted by individualism).[3]

THE TRIPARTITE IDEOLOGY AND THE WARRIOR IDENTITY

Figure 8.1 illustrates Dumézil's reconstruction of the hierarchy of the three functions.[4] The gods of early Indo-Iranian mythological tradition are cited as representative of each function, since, according to Dumézil, the tripartite ideology is more complete and explicit there than in other early Indo-European mythological traditions. Along the vertical axis, the three functions are labeled, not by the social roles of priest, warrior, and producer, but by the terms *magico-juridical power*, *physical force*, and *production, community, and enjoyment*. The latter terms are in closer accord with Dumézil's later development of his approach, which stresses that each function is to be seen as a dimension of an ideological construction rather than as primarily a designation of a social class.

The three functions are in a hierarchical relationship, first over second, second over third. Each of the three functions also features a duality. Along the horizontal axis, the first function divides into magical powers and juridical authority, which are united with one another. The second function divides into brute force and chivalrous force, which are opposed to one another. The third function, which refers amorphously and eclectically to various dimensions of social life, does not have two separate aspects, but is nonetheless represented by a "twin" divinity.

The problem of an individualistic self is apparent in the tripartite ideology. The second function contrasts two warrior divinities, one a sociable leader and the other a solitary adventurer. As Dumézil has shown, the

First Function: Magico-Juridical Power	
Cosmic	Social
(Varuna)	(Mitra)
merciless, sudden, demonic	progressive, reassuring
terrible, disturbing	benevolent, friendly
CREATIVE FORM	**CONTRACTS**
"binder"	alliances & treaties
knots, nets	honest relations
	stranger to violence
cosmic, other world	near to man, this world
more god	more priest
closer to second function	closer to third function

Second Function: Physical Force	
Asocial	Social
(Vayu)	(Indra)
physical vigor, blind fury	harmonious force
HUMAN BEAST	**CHIVALROUS KNIGHT**
solitary adventurer	sociable
not brilliant	
not intelligent	leader
not beautiful	
brute force	uses "developed" weapons

Third Function: Production, Community, and Enjoyment			
(the Nasatya twins)			
many diverse gods and goddesses			
health	commerce	peace	abundance
youth	herding	stability	nourishment
fertility	fishing	maternity	social masses
sexuality	agriculture	affection	riches
beauty	earth	water	piety

Fig. 8.1: The Three Functions in Indo-Iranian Mythology

warrior function is the key problem addressed by the mythical and ritual hierarchy which is represented by the tripartite ideology.[5] In what follows I will illustrate this point by showing how the relationship of the warrior identity to society is the problem behind the structure of the tripartite ideology.

In the tripartite ideology, "opposed" warrior divinities (second function) are set over and above "twin" communal divinities (third function), which represent multitudinous facets of social relations based on reciprocity, cooperation, attachment, and dependency. These facets include procreation, nurturing, production, commerce, affection, enjoyment, and so forth. While this indicates that the warrior divinities somehow transcend communal divinities, it also insists on a differentiation of the warrior divinities from social relations based on communal life. In other words, the tripartite ideology not only gives special prominence to the warrior identity but also raises the question of the relationship of the warrior identity to communal life.

The opposition of warrior divinities (second function) confirms that this is a question of whether the warrior identity is compatible or incompatible with communal life. As a representative of chivalrous convention, military leadership, harmonious force, and developed weapons, one warrior divinity (Indra) takes a form which highlights the social qualities of the warrior: leadership, companionship, organization, intelligence, and beauty. As a representative of solitary adventures, brute force, and blind fury, the other warrior divinity (Vayu) takes the form of a raw and wild animal nature which is entirely lacking in social qualities.

Thus, both warrior divinities are set apart from communal divinities, but the first specifically represents the warrior identity as having social qualities, whereas the second represents the warrior identity as wholly lacking in social qualities. Such a double representation articulates the problem of what features of the warrior identity are compatible or incompatible with communal life. This problem is then addressed by transcendent socio-cosmic divinities (first function).

The two socio-cosmic divinities represent an order to which the warrior is subject. This order comprises both the world outside society (a cosmic order) and the world inside society (a social order). According to Dumézil, the two Vedic gods which represent the first function, Varuna and Mitra, are identified with each other and invoked in concert (VarunaMitra). Taken together as a unity, they are the preservers of a socio-cosmic order ($ṛta$) that is "right" and "true."[6]

Thus the effects of a pastoral ecology, an individualism that has a problematical relationship with society and a socio-cosmic patriarchal authority which addresses this problematical relationship, are present in the tripartite ideology. Since it is known that early Indo-European peoples did practice cattle herding, cattle raiding, and cattle sacrifice (Lincoln 1981), it is plausible that the structure of the tripartite ideology has some intimate connection with a pastoral phase of early Indo-European social history.[7] But the structure of the tripartite ideology is not at all consistent with the pattern of traditions and institutions that result from the compromise of patriarchal authority among some types of stock keepers. From the controlled comparison of the Dinka and the Nuer, it is apparent that this pattern involves the focusing and centering of religiosity on a cosmic patriarchal other, the fall in stature of all other spirits, ghosts, and fetishes, the marginalization of religious ceremonies and offices, and the secularization of the warrior identity. The tripartite ideology does not feature such a pattern, but instead a complex system of socio-cosmic, warrior, and communal divinities. A logical conclusion would be that pastoral contests and conflicts were displaced from inside to outside early Indo-European society. This would presuppose some form of politico-religious authority that regulated the distribution of cattle wealth inside society and organized raiding of and warfare over pastoral resources outside society.

The form of the tripartite ideology is consistent with this conclusion. First, it confirms that a warrior identity is not just a dimension of society, but a crucial problem which determines the overall design of a mythical and ritual hierarchy. Second, it confirms that the warrior identity itself is associated with military leadership, convention, and organization, even though it also features an individualistic dimension which has a problematical relationship with social life. An example of a regime that is at least reminiscent of this pattern is the Kingdom of Nkore, in which king and court controlled and regulated contests and conflicts among the members of a pastoral caste on the inside of a state society while organizing them for the purpose of military conquest and expansion. The Hima warrior identity, as represented in Hima self-representations, featured exaggerated images of an antagonistic and oppositional individualism; however, such heroic exploits were normally performed in the context of state military service and state military expeditions.

This parallel is not intended to suggest that early Indo-European societies generally had the same, or even a similar, form as the state system in Nkore. It only indicates that the broad pattern of pastoral tradition and ecology among early Indo-European cattle herders involved a relationship of authority and individualism where the former was not compromised by the latter. It is doubtful whether any other parallel could be drawn between the Kingdom of Nkore and early Indo-European society. The early Indo-Europeans were Old World peoples with highly developed military instruments which were not to be found in precolonial East Africa. These military instruments, which included horses and chariots, seem to have intensified the question of the place of the warrior identity in communal life, so much so that the two sides of the warrior identity, one representing organized military force, the other representing a solitary human beast, are a key feature of the structure of Indo-European mythical and ritual systems.

This implies that participation in Old World religious, political, and economic systems, which brought with it advanced military instruments, had the same consequences for northern wetland Indo-European stock keepers as it did for southern dry-land Afro-Asiatic stock keepers like the northern Somalis and the North Arabian Bedouins. It intensified the contradiction between authority and individualism, the two effects of a pastoral ecology.

Notes
References
Index

Notes

PREFACE

1. The term "East Africa" is used in the literal sense of the eastern half of the continent from the Sudan to the Cape.

CHAPTER ONE. YOUTHS, SONGS, AND PERSONALITY OXEN

1. The relationship of youths and oxen among various East African peoples has received considerable attention. The "identification" of youths with oxen has been mentioned or debated by the Seligmans (1932:249), Evans-Pritchard (1956:254), Lienhardt (1961:16–17), Beidelman (1966), Deng (1973:96–98), Rigby (1971), and Gourlay (1972). Taking a psychoanalytic perspective, Beidelman (1966:246) presents the most forceful case that the young man sees a symbol of himself in his castrated personality ox. Gourlay (1972:245–46) has criticized Beidelman's psychoanalytic interpretation, citing specific excerpts from Karimojong songs.
2. I am especially indebted to the work of Gourlay (1972) on this point. His study of the content of Karimojong songs includes the first extended criticism of the notion that young men identified themselves with their oxen among East African cattle-herding peoples.
3. There are age and sex distinctions regarding the consumption of the milk, blood, and meat of cattle.
4. See Kelly (1985) for an analysis of the significance of bridewealth among the Dinka and Nuer.
5. I use the term "son-father relationship," rather than "father-son relationship," as another reminder that the Dinka father should not be thought of as determining the character of the Dinka son. The issue here is how the relationship of the two is affected by Dinka pastoral ecology.
6. For the comments of ethnographers on tension in son-father relationships among the Dinka, see Lienhardt (1961:44–45) and Deng (1973:xxxii–xxxiii, 123–26). Also see Beidelman (1966), who reviews the sexual symbolism of spears and cattle among the Nuer, a people who resemble the Dinka in many ways.

7. The age-sets are not military organizations among Nilotic peoples, but they are associated with ritualized contests and conflicts among young men.

8. Herskovits studied what he called a "cattle complex," a group of traits which tended to be associated with cattle herding all over East Africa. He rejected the possibility that these traits were the result of a contingent historical connection, arguing instead that they followed from the psychological and institutional implications of placing a high social value on cattle wealth. For a recent discussion of social traits correlated with the presence and absence of stock, see Meeker, Barlow, and Lipset (1986).

CHAPTER TWO. ELDERS, CREATION MYTHS, AND THE COSMIC PATRIARCHAL SPIRIT

1. Not all Dinka religion is appropriately termed "patriarchal," but by and large it is a religion of fathers. Lienhardt (1961), however, describes a "mother goddess" or "woman goddess" (see chap. 3).

2. See, for example, Merker (1910) on the Maasai; Azaïs (1926) on the Galla; and Seligman and Seligman (1932) on the Nuer and Dinka. Following the Seligmans, Evans-Pritchard (1956:vii) notes a similarity between, on the one hand, the Dinka and Nuer concept of a Supreme Being and, on the other, the concept of Yahweh among the ancient Hebrews. In one place, he goes so far as to write of the "markedly monotheistic tendency" of Nuer religious thought (49). Like Lienhardt (1961) in the case of Dinka religion, Crazzolara (1953) describes the Nuer as believing in the oneness of a Supreme Being, but does not argue that Nuer religion has some connection with "monotheism." The concept of the oneness of a cosmic patriarchal spirit is linked with cattle herding among the Nuer and Dinka, but not among Bantu-speaking cattle herders (see chap. 6).

3. Here a complication is being intentionally avoided. There are two types of clans and elders among the Dinka, priestly and warrior, or as I prefer to phrase it, religious elder and secular elder. Strictly speaking, the priestly elder stands to secular elder as father stands to son. The opposition of father and son appears as an opposition of social role in Dinka society; tension between son and father is also tension between two sides of Dinka society as represented by chief and priest. Treatment of this additional feature of Dinka society would complicate and lengthen my analysis, but not substantially change my conclusion.

4. As his discussion develops, however, Lienhardt begins to give special weight to the experiential relationship of fathers and sons, failing to mention even once the special case of fathers and daughters.

5. Where Lienhardt glosses *muk* as "bringing up, which involves caring for, feeding, protecting, and instructing," he mixes references to the father-son relationship with references to the parent-child relationship. This suggests that the Dinka are more conscious than Lienhardt that Divinity is not like a real father but has qualities that children experience in both parents. This does not mean,

however, that the Dinka myth of Divinity and man is actually modeled on experience of the parent-child relationship. Lienhardt makes a strong case that Divinity is a patriarchal spirit that is most closely associated with tension in the father-son relationship in particular.

6. In the original text, Lienhardt here remarks: "In fact, what was probably intended was the free-divinity Deng." The Dinka see Deng, like the other free-divinities, as a particular manifestation of Divinity. However, he is the one free-divinity who is most closely identified with Divinity.

7. Deng elects to translate the Dinka word for the cosmic patriarchal spirit, *nhialic*, as "God."

8. Of course, a song is not really the original or innovative "composition" of a youth any more than the hymn is a really timeless and authoritative "tradition." Songs can be formulaic and derivative and hymns can represent original and individual points of view. The point is that the song rests on the rhetoric of a present creativity, whereas the hymn rests on the rhetoric of timeless tradition.

9. The possibility that hymn and song can be opposed as the rhetoric of father and the rhetoric of son does not mean that these two generic expressions are mechanical and inflexible: "On whatever occasion hymns are presented, they are generally a means of communication between the ancestors and spirits and their representatives in this world, usually elders. During war, when young warriors sing in prayer for victory, their hymns take the form of war songs" (Deng 1973:238). Deng is quite explicit here. Hymns are the songs of elders, not youths; of fathers, not sons. Although some exceptional hymns are identified with youths, their character confirms the rule. When youths supplicate Divinity, they do so at the margins of the community in the absence of elders, praying for divine sponsorship of their man-slaying and cattle-seizing activities.

10. The contrast between representations of the father and representations of the son also goes beyond the domain of words. Consider, for example, the contrast between the father's cattle sacrifices and the sons' cattle raids. The desire to assert oneself through cattle wealth leads to dissension and hostility, just as the ability to overcome this desire by giving up cattle wealth leads to the possibility of solidarity and cooperation. In the song, the desires of the self are associated with an inordinate love of cattle; in the hymn, a denial of self is associated with the ability to give up cattle. Evidence supporting this revision of Lienhardt's argument may be found in Deng's (1973) discussion of Dinka hymns (cf. Lincoln 1981).

CHAPTER THREE. THE MULTIPLICITY OF PATRIARCHAL SPIRITS
AND THE POWER OF CATTLE-OWNING FATHERS

1. Lienhardt (1961) notes the Dinka view that "the effects of the free-divinities on individuals have been the more widely and deeply felt as their own political autonomy as been undermined," and observes that "the rise of the free-divinities,

potentially equally affecting all Dinka as individuals and families, corresponds to their recognition of increasing individualism in their life and intimations of changes in the basic structure of their society" (169). By "individualism" Lienhardt means not the traditional tension between son and father but the very breakdown of patriarchal authority, and hence the breakdown of the son-father complex in Dinka society and culture. So the recent proliferation of free-divinities like Garang and Abuk seems to be associated with certain strains and pressures on the Dinka which have raised questions about patriarchal ideals and values, the very foundation of Dinka communal traditions and institutions. At the same time, these free-divinities are not entirely new but have risen in prominence.

2. I have already cited several examples of how the Dinka thesis of the oneness of Divinity is contradicted by various Dinka beliefs and practices. There are many others. Lienhardt (1961) documents a Dinka tendency to see the free-divinities Deng, Garang, and Abuk as related to one another much like the members of a family. The free-divinities Garang and Abuk are associated with the first man and woman in Dinka myth (89, 161, but contradicted on 84) and sometimes they are called "husband of Abuk" or "wife of Garang," respectively. Deng, who is sometimes called "son of Divinity," is also addressed as "father of Garang." On the other hand, Garang and Abuk are sometimes called "father of Deng" and "mother of Deng," respectively. All of these expressions qualify the idiom of the unique and singular "creator" that is so clear a feature of Divinity or *nhialic;* for insofar as religiosity shifts toward the familial relationships of father/son, husband/wife, mother/son, and mother/daughter, the "creator" must go slightly out of focus. Therefore, the free-divinities are not exactly, as Lienhardt argues, the "multiplicity" to be subsumed under a universal and singular Divinity, *nhialic,* but point toward dimensions of Dinka experience that bring into question the cosmic patriarchal spirit as center. See Lienhardt's final attempt to establish his argument, where he explains Deng, Garang, and Abuk in terms of Dinka ecology (160).

3. It is true that Lienhardt does discuss at some length the relationship between Divinity and two particular clan-divinities, Flesh and Hedgehog. Flesh and Hedgehog are the clan-divinities of spearmaster clans. These are priestly clans which, in contrast with warrior clans, are distinctive patrilines precisely because their members represent Divinity among the Dinka (108, 165). So it is not too surprising that Flesh and Hedgehog are intertwined with their special relationship with Divinity, and this is probably a feature of these particular patrilines and not of clan-divinities in general. When Lienhardt made the statement that clan-divinities are mediators between Divinity and actual fathers, he may have been thinking of the special case of the spearmaster clans.

4. Lienhardt (1961) cites Fr. P. A. Nebel (1936): "*'ram,* p.t. *rom,* to meet, to do or have in common; . . . *og a ram* (greeting on the road); *rom thok,* to join in conversation; . . . *ram akeuic,* to abut . . . *koc ram nhim,* capricious'" (1961:134 n. 2).

5. These Dinka "totems" are totally inconsistent with Lévi-Strauss's analysis of the use of animals and plants to represent social groupings. For Lévi-Strauss, the animals and plants refer to differences, not similarities.

6. According to Lienhardt (1961), the opinion that the free-divinities came

to the Dinka from elsewhere should not be taken as fact, for he could not find any firm evidence to support it. He is certain that Deng, who is closely identified with Divinity, does indeed have a long and complex history among the Dinka (90-91).

CHAPTER FOUR. THE NUER WARRIOR IDENTITY AND THE SEGMENTARY PRINCIPLE

1. See Evans-Pritchard (1940:3), Lienhardt (1961:1), and Southall (1976:466).
2. Henceforth, the term "Nuer" refers specifically to the eastern Nuer, the segment of the Nuer who were most involved in cattle raiding among the Dinka and who were most closely studied by Evans-Pritchard in the 1930s.
3. For other comments on Nuer character, see Howell (1947:133, 1954:7), Huntington (1983:494), and Kelly (1985). Johnson (1981) has recently criticized European accounts of the Nuer as being influenced by a stereotype of the "fighting Nuer." Since cattle raiding was only one dimension of Nuer identity and society, this point is well taken. Nonetheless, Johnson does not offer evidence that seriously challenges the view that the Nuer, far more than the Dinka, saw themselves as cattle raiders and regularly engaged in cattle raiding. In a still more recent study, Kelly (1985:36-45) documents specific instances of the greater success and frequency of Nuer cattle raids against the Dinka in comparison with Dinka cattle raids against the Nuer.
4. See Jackson (1923), cited by Glickman (1972:586); Evans-Pritchard (1940a:3-4, 125); and Howell (1954:7).
5. See Sahlins (1965), Newcomer (1972), Glickman (1972), Southall (1976), and Kelly (1985). Each author has a different position on this problem.
6. Southall (1976:467) cites McLaughlin's (1967:27) glottochronological analysis as yielding a date of 85 C.E. for the separation of the Dinka and Nuer languages, but suggests that the analysis in question should be regarded as erring on the shallow side. If he is right, the Nuer and Dinka have been "different" for at least two millennia (cf. Kelly 1985:11).
7. If the Nuer and Dinka are to be considered one people, it would seem to hinge on whether they themselves wanted this to be the case.
8. Kelly (1985) focuses on institutional differences, especially bridewealth payments. He does acknowledge the importance of the Nuer warrior identity as a factor in determining these institutional differences.
9. I have retained the terms "Nuer" and "Dinka," since, so far as I am aware, their usage has not yet been challenged by the Nuer and Dinka themselves.
10. Southall (1976) provides a somewhat better documentation of Nuer images and claims than of the actual facts and events of Nuer cattle raiding. For the latter, see Kelly (1985:36-45).
11. The contrast between Nuer and Dinka is, of course, a relative one. Among the Nuer, as among the Dinka, fathers/elders were more closely associated with

cattle owning and cattle exchanging, while sons/youths were most closely associated with cattle raiding. Evans-Pritchard (1936) observes that "in the many situations that arise in the daily life of cattle-camps, one has opportunity to see how the young give way to the old and listen without interrupting to their advice and admonition in disputes and discussions of all kinds. They will order the younger men to perform services for them and will lecture them upon shortcomings; and the extraordinary pride of a Nuer, the object of ceaseless astonishment of Europeans, no matter how long they have resided in the country, is not injured by orders and admonitions from a man of a senior age-set" (267). The Nuer and Dinka were similar, but the important point for the purpose of this study is how they were different.

12. Nuer songs might be "predicted" to have the following features as a consequence of the Nuer emphasis on cattle raiding: Songs might be composed by both younger and older men, reflecting the emphasis on the individualistic side of personal identity for both of these groups. Songs might be oriented less toward the son-father relationship and more toward the problematical side of social relations. Song genres might be more nearly concerned with solidarity and opposition in social relations (love and war) rather than with dependence and independence in the son-father relationship.

13. See Evans-Pritchard (1950:10, 1936:256), Deng (1973:311), and Lienhardt (1961:36).

14. Evans-Pritchard's impressions of the "fighting" Nuer were influenced by the particular setting in which he met them (see Johnson 1981). He had arrived in Nuerland shortly after the imposition of a Pax Britannica. Since the Nuer had not greeted this imposed regime with enthusiasm, they would not have been inclined to respond to the British ethnographer with perfect civility and affection.

15. My own view of the segmentary principle is closest to Bonte's (1979). He attributes segmentation to an inability to achieve a stable political hierarchy and to an attempt to assert private rights while also maintaining communal solidarity. This is very close to my own analysis, which, however, attempts to explicate this conflict more fully. Bonte's perspective is Marxist in the sense that he focuses on problems in the pastoral mode of production (see also Bonte 1981). I have arrived at a similar conclusion by attempting to explain how cattle are a form of wealth that becomes a vehicle for masculine identity.

16. There are in fact two dissenters. While Kelly reads Evans-Pritchard's study as a literal account of a lineage-based social organization, Kuper (1982) has argued that the references to lineage segmentation in *The Nuer* do not refer to any ideological or experiential reality whatsoever. Both Kelly and Kuper have overlooked the more important side of Evans-Pritchard's study by identifying it with "segmentary lineage theory," an "acultural" anthropological approach that it inspired (see the discussion of segmentary lineage theory which follows; see also n. 22 for a further comment on Kuper's criticisms).

17. Cf. Evans-Pritchard (1940a:126), Howell (1947:133), Southall (1976:485), Huntington (1983:494), and Kelly (1985).

18. Southall (1976), citing Gough's analysis, observes: "She argues convincingly that the more consistent and unitary agnatic framework of Naath group struc-

ture, which has been taken by Sahlins and Lienhardt as the basis of Naath military superiority over the Jieng, was result rather than cause, or at least an accompanying cumulative process of accentuation" (472).

19. It is interesting that the criticism of Evans-Pritchard's account of a political system based on a segmentary principle has followed a parallel course in Middle Eastern and North African studies. His 1940 work is the charter for segmentary theory in sub-Saharan Africa; *The Sanusi of Cyrenaica* (Evans-Pritchard 1949a) is its charter in Middle Eastern and North African studies. At first, his account of the segmentary principle of the lineage system of the Cyrenaican Bedouin was accepted at face value by Peters (1960), Lewis (1961), and Gellner (1969). Later the criticism that lineage segments are "representations" of groups, not actual political groups, is made by Peters (1967), Salzman (1978), and Seddon (1979). (For sub-Saharan Africa, cf. Holy 1979a, 1979b). Alternative modes of political organization which do not follow a segmentary principle are demonstrated by Eickelman (1976). (For sub-Saharan Africa, cf. Holy 1979a, 1979b). Meeker (1979, chap. 10) makes the point that segmentation is the reflection of an instability in social relations which is correlated with a history of stock keeping. (For sub-Saharan Africa, cf. Bonte 1979).

20. Evans-Pritchard's work on the Nuer has probably become the subject of so much controversy precisely because his ethnographic portraiture is powerful at the same time as his documentation of Nuer viewpoint and argument is skimpy. His work is provocative and yet at a distance from its object. This fault is not to be found, at least not to the same degree, in his study of Azande magic and witchcraft, which is more deeply textured as ethnography.

21. For an especially good illustration of this approach, see Lewis (1965a). In explaining his method, Lewis quotes the "dictum" of Fortes and Evans-Pritchard (1940): "Comparative study . . . has to be on an abstract plane where social processes are stripped of their cultural idiom and are reduced to functional terms" (Lewis 1965a: 106). In other words, the sociological method involves suppressing the indigenous meanings of institutions and conceiving them according to the programs of social anthropology. Lewis enjoins the method by warning that "otherwise the criteria of our classification are little more than superficial cultural features which may have very limited functional significance" (106). I suggest that cultural features are judged to be superficial by Lewis only because they deviate from an anthropological interpretation that he erroneously imposes on social behavior.

22. Kuper (1982) has recently condemned segmentary lineage theory *in toto* as a figment of the imagination of anthropologists that has no referent in the ideology or experience of any people anywhere. While Kuper's criticisms of segmentary lineage theory are to my mind compelling, they do not apply, in my opinion, to Evans-Pritchard's concept of a segmentary principle as a culture-specific way of thinking and experiencing social relations (rather than a model of social organization). Kuper does not consider instances of Afro-Asiatic-speaking peoples, such as the Berbers, Bedouins, Yemenis, Somalis, or Gallas. The ethnography of these peoples is replete with detailed examples of the segmentary principle in the sense that this term is used in my study (see n. 19 above). Furthermore, Kuper groups the Nuer with peoples in sub-Saharan Africa and Oceania, among whom

such a segmentary principle is probably nonexistent, but the Nuer may well have more in common with Afro-Asiatic-speaking peoples than with sub-Saharan and Oceanian peoples.

23. Kelly (1985, chap. 4) sums up the evidence for and provides a graphic illustration of this point.

24. This does not mean that the Nuer were higher than the Dinka on some scale of social evolution as suggested by Sahlins (1961), Newcomer (1972), and Kelly (1985). That the Nuer were better than the Dinka in pastoral raiding and warfare is hardly a measure of their historical adaptability. Perhaps the Dinka did not fare so well in a world which involved contests and conflicts over cattle, but history does not begin and end with this issue.

25. Nevertheless, even though the social functions of religion are diminished, the Nuer are not less religious than the Dinka. Evans-Pritchard (1956) confirms the importance of Nuer religious convictions.

26. On some occasions, it is true, great prophets arose and became important charismatic leaders among the Nuer (Beidelman 1971). But they are exceptional and irregular religious leaders and not to be compared with the Dinka masters of the fishing spear.

27. Evans-Pritchard (1940) cites a Nuer remark which indicates that Nuer lineages and tribes do not conceive themselves as submitting to leopard-skin chiefs: "We took hold of them and gave them leopard skins and made them our chiefs to do the talking at sacrifices for homicide" (173).

28. Evans-Pritchard (1940:263–64) seems to qualify his study in precisely this way.

CHAPTER FIVE. THE COMPROMISE OF PATRIARCHAL AUTHORITY AND NUER "MONOTHEISM"

1. See the acknowledgement of Lienhardt in Evans-Pritchard's (1956) study (viii–ix) and the acknowledgement of Evans-Pritchard in Lienhardt's (1961) study (viii). Lienhardt was a student of Evans-Pritchard who visited the Dinka about fifteen years after his mentor had visited the Nuer. Evans-Pritchard completed his study, *Nuer Religion*, several years after his student had returned from the field and completed his dissertation, and then some years later Lienhardt published his own study, *Divinity and Experience: The Religion of the Dinka*. Lienhardt was also directed by Evans-Pritchard to undertake fieldwork among the Nuer regarding certain problems that Evans-Pritchard had been unable to resolve during his own sojourns in Nuerland.

2. I have for the most part followed the presentation in Evans-Pritchard (1956), but see also Evans-Pritchard (1951b, 1953a). See also Crazzolara (1953:61–64), whose description of the Nuer *kwoth nhial* is consistent with that of Evans-Pritchard.

3. Evans-Pritchard (1956:vii, 315) notes that Dinka and Nuer religion are

similar insofar as they resemble the religion of the Old Testament, but that they are in this respect not typical of the religions of Black Africa and indeed not typical of the religions of other Nilotic peoples such as the Alur, Acholi, Anuak, Shilluk, and Kenya Luo. Schneider (1979:48–52) agrees with this assessment and adds that the Dinka and Nuer religious traditions are unlike those of their western Nilotic neighbors but similar to those of eastern Nilotic peoples, such as the Maasai. Schneider also remarks that the Dinka and Nuer religions are similar to the religions of Cushitic peoples of Ethiopia and the Horn of Africa, such as the Galla and Somali, but very different from the religions of cattle-herding Bantu speakers in sub-Saharan Africa, among whom ancestor worship and witchcraft are more prevalent. He claims that the religions of Cushitic peoples are more like "Middle Eastern" religions (he has in mind Islamic and Christian peoples) and that the Dinka and Nuer religions are therefore more like "Middle Eastern" religions than the religions of sub-Saharan Africa.

4. See Merker (1910:203–4) on the Maasai; Azaïs (1926:113) on the Galla; Seligman and Seligman (1932, chaps. 4–6, quoted by Evans-Pritchard 1956:vii) on the Dinka and Nuer; Huffman (1931:56–57, quoted by Evans-Pritchard 1956:vii) on the Nuer; Crazzolara (1953:59–64, quoted by Evans-Pritchard 1956:vii) on the Nuer; Pettazzoni (1956:38–42) on the Nilotes and Cushites; Schneider (1979:48–52) on some Nilotic speakers and some Cushitic speakers, as opposed to all Bantu speakers. See also Kesby (1977, chap. 9), who proposes that East African religions can be placed on a spectrum ranging from the Nilotic-speaking Maasai among whom a Supreme Being is important, but ancestors and spirits of the bush are not, to the Bantu-speaking Gand who recognize, besides a Supreme Being, a plurality of divinities, ancestors, spirits of the bush, and witches. These observations should be differentiated from Schmidt's (1935) dubious theory of a more or less universal "primitive monotheism." Schmidt and his followers attempted to confirm the existence of an *urmonotheismus* among various tribal peoples all over the world. This primitive monotheism, which Schmidt attributed to a logical principle, was supposed to take the form of a Supreme Being who was conceived as a creator. These views have not agained acceptance among either anthropologists or historians of religion. Pettazzoni (1967, 1956:38–42), a historian of monotheism and a critic of the theory of *urmonotheismus*, by and large accepts the accuracy of the ethnographic accounts of the peculiar "oneness" of the Nilotic and Cushitic high god. Pettazzoni (1956) has surveyed the high gods of "primitive" peoples precisely to show that they are not consistent with the notion of *urmonotheismus*. His point is that the representation of high gods, and in particular the stress placed upon high gods, varies considerably, especially with changing subsistence techniques, such as agriculture, pastoralism, hunting and gathering, and so forth. But while rejecting Schmidt's notion of an *urmonotheismus*, Pettazzoni (1956:436–39) does propose that the high god of certain kinds of pastoral peoples, including principally Semitic, Hamitic (Nilotic and Cushitic), Ugro-Finnic, Ural-Altaic, and Indo-European speakers, was a forerunner of the concept of divinity that was eventually developed into monotheism. Pettazzoni does not explain why such a concept would be favored by pastoralism or why it is not an important feature of the religious traditions of all pastoralists, such as the Bantu speakers.

5. At the close of this book, he notes that Nuer religion may be regarded at one level as "monotheistic, at another level as polytheistic; and it can also be regarded at other levels as totemistic or fetishistic" (Evans-Pritchard 1956:316). Perhaps it was this "mixed" character of Nuer religion which led Evans-Pritchard to conclude a few pages later that *kwoth nhial* was an intuitive apprehension of the divine (321-22). Such a lofty religious concept may have seemed to him too much at odds with other dimensions of Nuer religious experience to be sociologically explained.

6. See Lienhardt (1961:219). See Evans-Pritchard (1956:21-27) for an account of Nuer prayer and Evans-Pritchard (1956:289, 300) for comments on the relative unimportance of a priesthood. It must be remembered that the Nuer do have religious offices and ceremonies (Evans-Pritchard 1956:21-27, 287-310). At issue are relative, not absolute, differences between the Nuer and Dinka. See, for example, Beidelman's (1971) analysis of Nuer priests and prophets. Beidelman argues that Evans-Pritchard was wrong in considering the Nuer prophet as a recent introduction and demonstrates that the Nuer priest, who speaks for the Nuer to God, and the Nuer prophet, who speaks for God to the Nuer, are two modalities of Nuer religious leadership. His article does not challenge the generalization of Lienhardt and Evans-Pritchard that religious leadership is more highly developed among the Dinka than among the Nuer.

7. Significantly, the Nuer also contrast themselves as guileless in their relationships with the Dinka, whom they regard as "cleverer and more cunning" (Evans-Pritchard 1956:11).

8. Cf. Evans-Pritchard (1940:171). Deng (1973:71-73) has noted that Evans-Pritchard's concept of "ordered anarchy" seriously underestimates the role of law in Nuer society. See also Howell (1954).

9. Evans-Pritchard (1956:28-29) acknowledges that the Nuer were reluctant to discuss the spirits of the air with him, since the government was hostile toward the prophets of such spirits at the time of his visit. The important point is that his assessment of these spirits takes into account Nuer reluctance to discuss them (see also Evans-Pritchard 1953b).

10. Even if a man were not directly descended from a Dinka father in eastern Nuerland, he was likely to be related to people of Dinka origins through his mother. Nuer explain the spread of Dinka belief and practices among them by intermarriages (Evans-Pritchard 1956:82-83).

11. Cf. the Dinka attitude: "Those killed by lightning are described sometimes as 'whom Divinity has seen' or 'whom Deng has seen,' or Divinity is said to have struck them on the head. They are not mourned" (Lienhardt 1961:92-93).

12. Evans-Pritchard (1956) and Crazzolara (1953) are not in full agreement with regard to the hierarchical structure of Nuer religious thought. They differ, for example, on the details of certain spirits of the air and earth (Evans-Pritchard 1956:32). However, the Nuer are consistent only in their concern with asserting some form of spiritual hierarchy, not in the pecise manner in which they assert it. The disagreements between Evans-Pritchard and Crazzolara probably reflect this variability.

13. The Nuer notion of a spiritual hierarchy also extends beyond the issue

of spirits of the air and earth to their classification of natural species. The Nuer take a special interest in and have a high regard for birds, which they conceive as near to God (*kwoth*). In their classification of birds, they take some pains to differentiate those species which are "higher" and more respected from those which are "lower" and less respected. Some are classed as *gath kwoth*, the children of God (speckled vultures, hooded vultures, white pelicans, pied crows, black crows, glossy ibis, sacred ibis, crested cranes, goshawks, and doves) and others are classed as *gaat nya kwoth*, sons of daughter(s) of God (guineafowl, francolin, finches, swallows, weaver-birds, wagtails, bats, etc.). The difference between the two classes is influenced by the tendency to correlate highness and lowness with proximity to the heavenly spirit (*kwoth*) and also with being Nuer and not being Nuer: "Birds of which Nuer think little, such as guineafowl, the francolin, and some of the marsh bird — the most earth-bound birds — are described by them as being *jaang*, Dinka or Dinka descent" (Evans-Pritchard 1956:90).

14. See Evans-Pritchard (1956:45-48, 51). Cf. the invocation of the free-divinities in a war song (Lienhardt 1961:88-89).

15. *Dil* signifies an aristocrat as opposed to a commoner in some contexts. In others, *dil* signifies a person of Nuer descent as opposed to a person of Dinka descent (Evans-Pritchard 1949b:246).

16. Attributing the Nuer belief in fetishes to foreign influences (especially the Sudanic *jur* peoples), Evans-Pritchard (1956) observes that "the Nuer have tried, not entirely successfully, to assimilate these Sudanic medicines [fetishes], which represent something quite alien to their traditional way of thinking, to their conception of Spirit [*kwoth*]" (99-100).

CHAPTER SIX. AUTHORITY AND INDIVIDUALITY AMONG BANTU-SPEAKING CATTLE HERDERS

1. See Karugire (1977), Morris (1964:2), Oberg (1940), and Roscoe (1923:15-17, 160). Also cf. Maquet (1961:109-16) for comments on the relationship of the state and cattle wealth in precolonial Rwanda.

2. Karugire (1977, chap. 5) tells us that the late nineteenth century was a period in which Nkore militarism was of unusual importance. Of the seven heroic recitations that Morris recorded and translated, five date from the late nineteenth and early twentieth centuries.

3. The two genres of heroic recitations are not the only categories of poetry in Nkore. Karugire (1977:8) distinguishes what he calls "plain song" from "heroic recitations." Both plain song and heroic recitations, he says in passing, deal with "war, natural calamities, cattle, and women."

4. The passage omitted from the quotation comments on what happened to the recitations after raiding and warfare were suppressed: "Although today warfare can no longer provide a source of inspiration for these poems, the traditional form

is preserved and the incidents which provide the composer with his inspiration are treated as though they were military engagements. An incident, which may have been no more than a scuffle at a watering place with the inmates of a rival kraal, is described as an encounter in which the *omwevugi* defies the spears of the enemy and silences their rifles" (Morris 1964:14).

5. Morris (1964) puts it this way: "[The] poems are basically factual, but, although the incident which has given the composer his motif will have actually taken place, the poem will not make any attempt to give an accurate account of what occurred. The poet's intention is not to describe events, but to use them as a pretext for boasting of his own and his companions' valour. Exaggeration, invention of detail, and the transposing of chronological sequence are carried to such an extent that it would be profitless to try to treat these poems as factual records" (13).

6. In their study of Tutsi court poetry, Coupez and Kamanzi (1970) describe various poetic genres, including a "warrior poem" and a "pastoral poem" which are very similar to the popular Hima *ekyevugo* and *ekirahiro*, respectively. Coupez and Kamanzi note that the Tutsi term for the "warrior poem," which seems to be a cognate of the Hima term *ekyevugo*, can be literally translated as "a piece in which one speaks of oneself" (96).

7. It is my impression that Hima heroic recitations have more in common with the praise poetry found among many Bantu-speaking peoples of Africa than with the songs of Nilotic peoples like the Dinka and Nuer. The praise poetry of Bantu speakers is not always associated with stock keeping or with the pastoral warrior identity. Perhaps the Hima heroic recitations might be described as "heroicized" praise poetry. This issue receives more attention in the last part of this chapter, where Nguni and Sotho praise poems are considered.

8. In his ethnography of caste in Rwanda, Maquet (1961) describes how in the nineteenth century young Tutsi men were trained in companies in which they held lifelong membership. This training instilled "heroic" ideals and values: "The young men (*intore*, the chosen ones) lived at the court of the king or of the chief who had been allowed to recruit an army. Under the direction of an officer called the chief of the king's residence . . . or of its counterpart at a chief's court, they were trained for several years in military skills such as bow and arrow shooting, the use of the sword, spear, and javelin. They learned warlike dances, and to memorize and to recite the poems in which the high deeds of extraordinary bravery and boldness of the past warriors were exalted. They were also taught how to compose poems in imitation of these great models. They attended evening sessions near the fire, in the kraal, where by sarcasm and humiliation, their capacity for self control was put to the test" (109–10).

9. The role of the king as sponsor of foreign cattle raids and wars was especially developed in Rwanda. Maquet (1961) describes how the Tutsi king pursued an external policy of "looting and imperialism," which included raiding border peoples for captives and cattle, assassination of their kings and chiefs, and outright annexation of their territory by threat of force or open warfare: "Permanent encampments established not far from the borders were defensive indeed, but they were also bases for expeditions into neighboring territories. Whatever their frequency,

it is certain that they were foci for strong feelings of admiration, pride, and emulation. Many features of these events exalted the spirit of conquest: the procession of the victorious warriors, and the recitation of poems telling of the achievements of heroes. The whole country was mystically committed in the expedition through the king, the country's personification, who was magically taking part in it. The king and the queen-mother had (as the expedition leader) to sit motionless during the day of the battle (the army-chief in the field when deciding when to attack had to take into account the pace of time necessary for a messenger to reach the court). The secrecy about the expeditions stressed their importance. Even after the battle was over, a messenger was sent to the court who could not tell anything about the expedition except that it was over. Then a few warriors were chosen by the army-chief to go and tell the king—and the king only—the story of the battle" (115–16).

10. Since East African pastoral peoples who are not part of state systems are generally egalitarian, the caste hierarchies of Nkore, Rwanda, and Burundi have sometimes been attributed to the more hierarchical social systems of the agricultural Bantu speakers, but this is an oversimplification. Pastoral societies, like those of the Dinka and Nuer, are stateless and egalitarian because it is so difficult for any person or any class to become dominant where the resource on which social prestige rests can be contested and challenged. Kingship resolved this problem in Nkore, Rwanda, and Burundi by regulating cattle raiding and warfare, thereby making it possible for certain classes to monopolize stock wealth. But once the institutions of authority (which originated among the Bantu speakers) resolved the problem of contests and conflicts over cattle, the pastoral "will to power," that is, the desire to accumulate cattle wealth, resulted in the exaggerated importance of rank and status. So the hierarchical systems of Rwanda, Burundi, and Nkore are neither "Bantu" nor "Hamitic" in origin but a result of the coincidental merging of the two.

11. While the Kikuyu are Bantu speakers, their ethnic origins are complex. They are thought to be the result of a merging of a Paranilotic hunting, stock-keeping people (Athi) and a Bantu iron-working, agricultural people (Gumbi). See Muriuki (1974, chaps. 2 and 3) and Oliver (1977:658).

12. See also Kenyatta (1938:64) and Leakey (1977:168, 207).

13. For an account of Kikuyu raiding and warfare, including a description of the structure of military leadership and organization, see Leakey (1977, chap. 24). For an evaluation of the accounts of the Kikuyu age-set organization and its military functions, see Muriuki (1974, chap. 5). The Maasai also forayed in return among the Kikuyu, and on their southern borders Kikuyu settlements were sometimes fortified against Maasai raids (Leakey 1977:7, 8). Muriuki (1974) argues that Kikuyu and Maasai were not as hostile as has been supposed. He notes many examples of intertribal relationships, including trade, economic cooperation, intermarriage, and the absorption of Maasai groups by the Kikuyu. At the same time he acknowledges that the Kikuyu and Maasai did more or less regularly engage in raiding one another.

14. Jomo Kenyatta, the Kenyan nationalist, participated in discussion classes conducted by Malinowski at the London School of Economics, at which time he

wrote an ethnography of his people, the Kikuyu. I have found his summary account of the life experiences of youths especially relevant to the problems of a youthful masculine identity. See also Routledge and Routledge (1910), Hobley (1922), Cagnolo (1933), Cavicchi (1977), and Leakey (1977).

15. The "praise poems" of the Kikuyu—the lauding of a person, symbol, or object—are a common feature of Bantu-speaking peoples all over Africa, and elsewhere have no necessary relationship to cattle at all. For a general review of the characteristics of "praise poetry" in Africa, see Finnegan (1970, chap. 5). The praise songs of Bantu-speaking peoples in Africa frequently, but not always, take the form of a poem in which the poet describes not himself but another person or object. Among cattle-herding Bantu speakers, however, such as the Nguni and Sotho peoples, praise poetry is sometimes transformed into a self-representation that is associated with cattle raiding (see also n. 7 above).

16. Routledge and Routledge (1910) make the comment that "Kikuyu polity is local government run mad" (195), which does not necessarily imply an absence of leadership, perhaps, so much as an excess of it. See also Cagnolo (1933:24) and Leakey (1977:14–15), but cf. Cavicchi (1977:215–23), who argues that other observers have gone too far in suggesting that the Kikuyu had no chiefs. Whatever the case, they certainly had a very keen sense of social rank and were extremely sensitive to the relative prestige and influence of different individuals. Lambert (1956:100–110), who studied contemporary Kikuyu institutions in detail, provides an extensive account of the important place of leadership among the Kikuyu, noting that it is a characteristic that first emerges informally among youths and is later institutionalized in the form of judicial offices and councils.

17. See Cavicchi (1977:83, 94, 218–23), but see also the example of a man who became rich through trade (Cavicchi 1977:219).

18. See, however, Leakey's (1977:1069–70) description of minor raids, which were carried out by only a few individuals.

19. To what extent Kikuyu and Maasai military raiding practices were different is not clear from the ethnographic record. Some observers remark that Kikuyu military tactics were adopted from the Maasai (Muriuki 1974:98), but they do not specify exactly which military tactics they have in mind. Leakey (1977:1071–72) notes that the Kikuyu engaged in organized daytime raids on the Maasai, but that the Maasai could not make such raids on the Kikuyu except when the armies of the latter were disorganized. As a result, most of the Maasai raids were brief nighttime activities. Jacobs (1977:49) has shown that most Maasai raiding was on a small scale and practiced as a kind of sport. He cites evidence that the agricultural Kikuyu and Sukuma, not the pastoral Maasai, were the most inveterate livestock raiders.

20. Cf. Leakey (1977:27–28, 432–33, 1058–61).

21. Muriuki (1974, chap. 5) rejects the prevailing view that Kikuyu age-sets were adopted from the Maasai and argues that they have older Paranilotic origins and predate Kikuyu-Maasai contact. Still, he acknowledges that Kikuyu age-set formations and military organization were strongly influenced by Maasai models. On Maasai influences on Kikuyu raiding and warfare, see also Leakey (1977, chap. 24). On the Maasai origins of the Kikuyu concept of God, see Leakey (1977:1075) and Routledge and Routledge (1910:225–26).

22. See Routledge and Routledge (1910:213, 272-77) and Leakey (1977, chap. 27).

23. See Oliver (1977), Crazzolara (1950), Ogot (1967), and Ehret (1971).

24. Ehret (1974) argues that grain-cultivating, cattle-herding Central Sudanic peoples carried these subsistence techniques to the Bantu-speaking peoples of Central Africa during the first millennium B.C.E. and that from there grain-cultivating, cattle-herding Bantu-speaking peoples moved into southeastern Africa during the first centuries C.E. This is a much less direct connection than that between forest-dwelling Bantu speakers and northern grasslands pastoralists in the interlacustrine area. On the other hand, it has also been argued that the Bantu speakers of southeastern Africa learned their more productive cattle-herding techniques from Khoisian peoples (Birmingham and Marks 1977:606) during the first part of the second millennium C.E., but this has since been discounted by Oliver (1978:396-97).

25. See also Marks and Gray (1975:426-27) for a similar assessment by historians.

26. See also Marks and Gray (1975:417-19) for a similar assessment by historians.

27. Surviving praise poetry is largely drawn from the praise poems of chiefs rather than from those composed and performed by more ordinary people. This may distort our picture of earlier praise poems.

28. See, for example, the collection of Shona praise poems translated by Fortune and Hodza (1979).

29. See Damane and Sanders (1974:1-6, 13-14) and Marks and Gray (1975:433) for some indication of the importance of cattle raiding and warfare among the Sotho and Zulu chiefdoms, respectively. See Omer-Cooper (1976:322-26) for comments on the emergence of military regiments under the leadership of Zulu chiefs and the abandonment of initiation rites and age-set formations.

30. A brother of Moshoeshoe, Makhabane was killed in a raid on the Thembu.

31. Damane and Sanders (1974) mention that if the chief is referred to in the first person singular, he himself is the poet. They also note, however, that the chief's own poet, his *seroki*, may sometimes quote the chief in his poems and that the chief in turn sometimes inserts lines composed by his *seroki* into his poems.

CHAPTER SEVEN. THE NORTHERN SOMALI PASTORALISTS

1. This is not necessarily a failing. It is the first step in humanizing the "other," a step which lays a foundation, however imperfect, for a dialogue.

2. These impressions still shape Western perceptions of Nilotic society and culture. In a recent comparative study of East African pastoralism, for example, Schneider (1979) has proposed that some Nilotic religions, such as those of the Nuer and Dinka, are generally closer to the religions of the Middle East than to those of sub-Saharan Africa.

3. The term "Old World" (in the sense of Europe) is usually contrasted with the "New World" (in the sense of the Americas). Here, however, the "Old World"

is intended to signify those world regions which were strongly interconnected throughout the historical period, as opposed to much of the interior of East Africa, which was more weakly interconnected with other world regions until the last one or two centuries.

4. This method is basically a Weberian one. The analysis of different cases leads to the formulation of "ideal types" which do not exist anywhere in a pristine form, since they isolate only certain dimensions of tradition and experience. In *The Protestant Ethic and the Spirit of Capitalism*, Weber sometimes states that he wishes to determine how religious ideals affect day-to-day life; however, he constantly analyzes the interaction of the two, not the way one determines the other. In my study of the correlation of religion, person, and society with stock keeping, I aim at analyzing the interaction of ideal and action as it is affected by a pastoral ecology, not the way in which either ideal or action determine one another.

5. See H. S. Lewis (1966:42). See also the summary of recent scholarly opinion on this matter in Cassanelli (1982, chap. 1). Recent views based on new work have discounted I. M. Lewis's (1960) earlier belief that the Somalis were originally a people of the Horn of Africa who had expanded at the expense of the Galla.

6. See Cerulli (1957–64), Lewis (1961:16–18), and Cassanelli (1982, chap. 4). Cassanelli (1982:46) believes that the Somalis raised livestock primarily for their own subsistence and were never large-scale traders in livestock before the arrival of the British in the nineteenth century. Even if this is correct, it is best assumed, in the absence of contrary evidence, that the Somali pastoralists had some sort of trading relationship with the coastal towns during the medieval period, since this is the typical pattern among nomadic pastoralists who are in contact with sedentary villagers and townsmen. See Khazanov's (1978:121–22, 1981:142–43) comments on nomadism and on this feature of Eurasian nomadism in particular.

7. For references to the prominence of a cosmic patriarchal spirit in the pre-Islamic religions of East Cushitic peoples, see chap. 5, n. 4.

8. Lewis (1961:26, 248ff.). The curses and blessings of patriarchs and men of religion are important among the Somalis, and patriarchal ancestors and deceased men of religion are revered as saints. However, anxiety over punitive and beneficent spirits and ghosts is of much less importance than among the Dinka and Nuer. Cf. I. M. Lewis (1955–56, 1961, 1965b, 1966).

9. Lewis (1961:7–8, 30, 128, 132, 296–97).

10. See Samatar (1982) and in particular the remainder of this chapter.

11. See Lewis (1961, chaps. 2 and 3), especially pp. 47, 49, 53, 62, 63, 64, 66, 72, 73, 74, 77, and 82. Cf. Samatar (1982:17). Cf. Evans-Pritchard (1940:114–17) and Lienhardt (1961:6–10).

12. The Somalis of the Horn of Africa did not ride their camels as did the camel-herding Bedouins of Arabia. When the camel-herding Bedouins came into contact with horse riders during the late first millennium B.C.E., it intensified the aggressive side of their pastoral ecology, but did not add a new dimension to it. See Dostal (1959) and Meeker (1979, 1988).

13. Cf. Meeker (1979) for an analysis of mounts as offensive instruments in camel raiding among the North Arabian Bedouins.

14. Recall that the segmentary principle is a culture-specific phenomenon which does not uniquely refer to lineages but to various patterns of social organization. In general, however, lineage systems which feature a segmentary principle are common among nomadic and seminomadic arid-land stock keepers, primarily in North Africa and the Middle East.

15. As in the case of the Nuer, it cannot be assumed that the Somali lineage system represents the actual political organization of the Somalis. A close reading of Lewis's (1961) ethnography reveals that the definition of collectivities by the Somali lineage system is constantly violated in practice. See chap. 4, n. 19, for comments on the parallel criticisms of the segmentary lineage theory in sub-Saharan African studies and in North African and Middle Eastern studies.

16. The Somalis have been designated as the one instance of a sub-Saharan African people among whom there existed premodern foundations for a national identity and national territory (Laitin 1977). From the point of view of comparative sociology, however, the precolonial Somali concept of a Somali nation is somewhat like the Nuer concept of themselves as a people who are united not by ethnicity but by a moral outlook, "those who raid" (*naath*) as opposed to "those who are raided" (*jaang*).

17. Men of religion, specifically leaders of Muslim *tarikats*, became more prominent toward the end of the nineteenth century when the Somalis began to organize to resist the British (Samatar 1982). However, Samatar believes that men of religion were not important figures in tribal society earlier in the nineteenth century (96–97). There is a parallel here between the Somali and the Nuer responses to British intrusion. Evans-Pritchard (1940:172, 185–89; 1956:310) observes that prophets were not normally important figures in Nuer society but rose to prominence as the Nuer came under pressure from the British.

18. Lewis (1961:28, 176, 199, but cf. 196–97, 225, 241).

19. The northern Somali do have an initiation rite (circumcision). It is not organized as a lineage or tribal ceremony, but consists of "an individual act," usually carried out "about the age of puberty" (Lewis 1961:75). Lewis implies that the Somalis see it as an Islamic rite, not associated with assumption of the warrior identity (75).

20. Samatar (1982:21) cites Drake-Brockman (1912), who claims that the best Somali ponies are of Arabian stock, but presents no evidence of this.

21. Pagan Cushitic-speaking pastoralists in Ethiopia, some of them horse riders, were among those peoples whom ethnographers identified as "monotheists" and contrasted with other "polytheists." Since Cushitic-speaking pastoralists usually inhabit the more arid zones of East Africa, this suggests that the problematical relationship of person and society, and hence the focusing and centering of religion on a cosmic patriarchal spirit, are generally correlated with arid-land pastoralism (see chap. 5, nn. 4, 5).

22. The very "birth" of Islam in Arabia itself followed a long period of gestation in which the ecology of camel-herding pastoralism was transformed by increasing use of mounts (both camels and horses) by the Arabian Bedouin. In this sense, early Islamic history is itself preceded by a drastic change in the ecology of Arabian pastoralism. See Dostal (1959) and Meeker (1979, 1988).

23. This review is of special interest since the controlled comparison of the Dinka and Nuer in the first few chapters could not be extended to Dinka and Nuer oral tradition.

24. To see how this is so, see Samatar's (1982:36–54) analysis of a case study in Somali oratory and politics. Samatar argues that the British-Somali war may have directly resulted from the failure of British officers to appreciate the implications of both Somali oratory and politics.

25. This is also suggested in yet a different way by Samatar's (1982) quotations of northern Somali opinions regarding their poetry. Poetry, the northern pastoralists say, is the means of "violating or ennobling the soul" (4) and "brings evil and dishonor as well as fame and respect" (26).

26. Such metrical evocations of camel gaits or horse gaits are also very common in the poetry of the North Arabian Bedouins (see Meeker 1979).

27. Here it is very likely that the words "plains and plains, over (countless) plains" feature a meter intended to evoke the beat of horses' hoofs. This device appears in the first raiding poem considered and is appropriate since the poems are assumed to be fit for singing on horseback.

28. For examples of the poetry of other arid-land camel herders in which the priority of deeds over words is emphasized, see my analysis of North Arabian Bedouin stories and poems (Meeker 1979).

29. See Meeker (1979, 1988). On the particular issue of Bedouin poetry, cf. Abu-Lughod (1985).

30. See Samatar (1982) for an account of the Somali resistance to European powers; see I. M. Lewis (1955, 1956, 1961, 1965b, 1966) for an account of the Somali religious brotherhoods.

31. De Vaux (1961) describes the Hebrew tribes as nomadic or seminomadic pastoralists, but Gottwald (1979) has contended that at best only a small minority of the Hebrew tribes were nomadic or seminomadic. However, the cult of Yahweh might feature a pastoral "effect" even though few, if any, of the Hebrew tribes were actually nomadic or seminomadic pastoralists at the time of their unification. The earliest followers of Muhammad were farmers and merchants, not camel-herding nomads, and yet the traditions of the former group were strongly shaped by past and present relationships with the latter. The question of whether the cult of Yahweh is historically related to arid-land pastoral ecology would have to be examined from the perspective of the long-term role of such an ecology in the history of the Hebrew tribes.

32. Seale (1974) illustrates how various Old Testament passages closely resemble the oral traditions of arid-land pastoralists.

CHAPTER EIGHT. EARLY INDO-EUROPEANS

1. In the case of the early Indo-Iranians, in particular, Lincoln has shown that references to cattle sacrifice and cattle raiding are prominent features of the

earliest Indo-Iranian myths and rites. He has also shown that these features are not inconsistent with archaeological evidence that cattle herding was an important subsistence technique among peoples in early eastern Europe and central Asia, the hypothetical homelands of early Indo-European peoples.

2. For a sympathetic, but critical, account of Dumézil's comparative mythology as well as some discussion of its critics, see Littleton (1973).

3. Dumézil (1970) has himself taken this view of early Indo-European mythological traditions: "The function of that particular class of legends known as myths is to express dramatically the ideology under which a society lives; not only to hold out to its conscience the values it recognizes and the ideals it pursues from generation to generation, but above all to express its very being and structure, the elements, the connections, the balances, the tensions that constitute it; to justify the rules and traditional practices without which everything within a society would disintegrate" (3).

4. For the most part, I have used Dumézil's (1958) synthesis of his arguments regarding the tripartite ideology. Littleton (1973:130) describes this work as "in many ways [the] most important general synthesis yet to be published by Dumézil." Also see Dumézil (1968, 1971).

5. For an extensive analysis of the "problematical" relationship of the early Indo-European warrior identity to society, see Dumézil (1970).

6. See Dumézil (1977:45 n. 1, 60) as well as Dumézil's fuller response to Gonda's (1972) criticisms of his views of Varuna and Mitra (Dumézil 1977:55–85). Gonda describes ṛta somewhat differently as "that untranslatable term which may be approximately described as the supreme and fundamental order-and-reality conditioning the normal and right, natural and true structure of cosmos, ritual and human conduct" (109).

7. The Indo-Iranian mythological tradition makes more than a few explicit references to cattle sacrificing and cattle raiding (Lincoln 1981). In particular, the warrior god Indra is directly associated with cattle raiding: "When it would be necessary that the generous Indra should favor two peoples, rich in boons, who fight each other with their entire warrior bands for the stake of beautiful cows, he, the terrible one, joins with the one, and, with the rumbling warriors, he drives forth the cattle [of the other] out [from the pen]" (Rig Veda 5.34.8, as quoted by Dumézil 1970:61).

References

Abu-Lughod, L. 1985. Honor and the sentiment of loss in Bedouin society. *American Ethnologist* 12:245-61.
Andrzejewski, B. W., and I. M. Lewis. 1964. *Somali Poetry*. Oxford: Clarendon Press.
Azaïs, F. 1926. Étude sur la religion du peuple Galla. *Revue d'éthnographie et des traditions populaires* 7:113-20.
Beidelman, T. O. 1966. The ox and Nuer sacrifice: Some Freudian hypotheses about Nuer symbolism. *Man*, n.s. 1:453-67.
Beidelman, T. O. 1971. Nuer priests and prophets: Charisma, authority, and power among the Nuer. In *The translation of culture: Essays to E. E. Evans-Pritchard*, ed. T. O. Beidelman. London: Tavistock Publications.
Birmingham, D., and S. Marks. 1977. Southern Africa. In *The Cambridge history of Africa, from c. 1050 to c. 1600*, ed. R. Oliver. Cambridge: Cambridge University Press.
Bonte, P. 1979. Pastoral production, territorial organisation and kinship in segmentary lineage societies. In *Social and ecological systems*, ed. P. C. Burnham and R. F. Ellen. London: Academic Press.
Bonte, P. 1981. Marxist theory and anthropological analysis: The study of nomadic pastoralist societies. In *The anthropology of pre-capitalist societies*, ed. J. S. Kahn and J. R. Llobera. London: Macmillan.
Burton, R. 1894. *First footsteps in East Africa*. 2 vols. London: Tylston and Edwards.
Cagnolo, C. 1933. *The Akikuyu: Their customs, traditions and folklore*. Nyeri: Mission Printing School.
Casalis, E. [1861] 1965. *The Basutos; or, twenty-three years in South Africa*. Reprint. Cape Town: C. Struik.
Cassanelli, L. V. 1982. *The shaping of Somali society: Reconstructing the history of a pastoral people, 1600-1900*. Philadelphia: University of Pennsylvania Press.
Cavicchi, E. 1977. *Problems of change in Kikuyu tribal society*. Bologna: EMI.
Cerulli, E. 1957-64. *Somalia: Scritti vari editi ed inediti*. 3 vols. Rome: Instituto Poligrafico dello Stato.
Coupez, A., and Th. Kamanzi. 1970. *Littérature de cour au Rwanda*. Oxford: Clarendon Press.
Crazzolara, J. P. 1950. *The Lwoo*. Part 1, *Lwoo migrations*. Verona: n.p.

Crazzolara, J. P. 1953. *Zur Gesellschaft und Religion der Nueer.* Studia Instituti Anthropos. Modling bei Wien: Missionsdruckerei St. Gabriel.
Damane, M., and P. B. Sanders. 1974. *Lithoko: Sotho praise-poems.* Oxford: Clarendon Press.
Deng, F. M. 1971. *Tradition and modernization: A challenge for law among the Dinka of the Sudan.* New Haven: Yale University Press.
Deng, F. M. 1972. *The Dinka of the Sudan.* New York: Holt, Rinehart and Winston.
Deng, F. M. 1973. *The Dinka and their songs.* Oxford: Clarendon Press.
De Vaux, R. 1961. *Ancient Israel.* 2 vols. New York: McGraw-Hill.
Dostal, W. 1959. The evolution of Bedouin life. In *L'Antica società Bedouina*, ed. F. Gabrielli. Rome: Centro di Studi Semitici, Instituto di Studi Orientali-Università.
Drake-Brockman, R. E. 1912. *British Somaliland.* London: Hurst and Blackett.
Dumézil, G. 1958. *L'idéologie tripartie des Indo-Européens.* Bruxelles: Latomus.
Dumézil, G. 1968. *Mythe et épopée.* Vol. 1, *L'idéologie des trois fonctions dans les épopées des peuples indo-européens.* Paris: Gallimard.
Dumézil, G. 1970. *The destiny of the warrior.* Trans. A. Hiltebeitel. Chicago: University of Chicago Press.
Dumézil, G. 1971. *Mythe et épopée.* Vol. 2, *Types épiques indo-européens: un héros, un sorcier, un roi.* Paris: Gallimard.
Dumézil, G. 1977. *Les dieux souverains des Indo-Européens.* Paris: Gallimard.
Ehret, C. 1971. *Southern Nilotic history: Linguistic approaches to the study of the past.* Evanston: Northwestern University Press.
Ehret, C. 1974. Patterns of Bantu and Central Sudanic settlement in central and southern Africa (ca. 1000 B.C.–500 A.D.). *Transafrican Journal of History* 4(1):1–71.
Eickelman, D. F. 1976. *Moroccan Islam: Tradition and society in a pilgrimage center.* Austin: University of Texas Press.
Evans-Pritchard, E. E. 1936. The Nuer: Age sets. *Sudan Notes and Records* 19:233–71.
Evans-Pritchard, E. E. 1940. *The Nuer: A description of the modes of livelihood and political institutions of a Nilotic people.* Oxford: Clarendon Press.
Evans-Pritchard, E. E. 1949a. *The Sanusi of Cyrenaica.* Oxford: Clarendon Press.
Evans-Pritchard, E. E. 1949b. The Nuer col wic. *Man* 49:7–9.
Evans-Pritchard, E. E. 1949c. Nuer totemism. *Annali Lateranensi* 13:225–48.
Evans-Pritchard, E. E. 1951a. *Kinship and marriage among the Nuer.* Oxford: Clarendon Press.
Evans-Pritchard, E. E. 1951b. Some features of Nuer religion. *Journal of the Royal Anthropological Institute* 81:1–13.
Evans-Pritchard, E. E. 1953a. The Nuer conception of spirit and its relation to the social order. *American Anthropologist* 55:201–14.
Evans-Pritchard, E. E. 1953b. The Nuer spirits of the air. *Annali Lateranensi* 17:55–82.
Evans-Pritchard, E. E. 1956. *Nuer religion.* Oxford: Clarendon Press.
Finnegan, R. H. 1970. *Oral literature in Africa.* Oxford: Clarendon Press.
Fortes, M., and E. E. Evans-Pritchard, eds. 1940. *African Political Systems.* London: Oxford University Press.

Fortune, G., and A. C. Hodza. 1979. *Shona praise poetry*. Oxford: Clarendon Press.
Gellner, E. A. 1969. *Saints of the Atlas*. London: Weidenfeld and Nicolson.
Glickman, M. 1972. The Nuer and the Dinka: A further note. *Man*, n.s. 7:586–94.
Gluckman, M. 1940. The kingdom of the Zulu of South Africa. In *African political systems*, ed. M. Fortes and E. E. Evans-Pritchard. London: Oxford University Press.
Gonda, J. 1972. *The Vedic god Mitra*. Leiden: E. J. Brill.
Gottwald, N. K. 1979. *The tribes of Yahweh: A sociology of the religion of liberated Israel 1250–1050 B.C.* Maryknoll, N.Y.: Orbis Books.
Gough, K. 1971. Nuer kinship: A reexamination. In *The translation of culture: Essays to E. E. Evans-Pritchard*, ed. T. O. Beidelman. London: Tavistock Publications.
Gourlay, K. A. 1972. The ox and identification. *Man*, n.s. 7:244–54.
Herskovits, M. J. 1926. The cattle complex in East Africa. Parts 1–4. *American Anthropologist* 28:230–72, 361–88, 494–528, 633–64.
Hobley, C. W. 1922. *Bantu beliefs and magic, with particular reference to the Kikuyu and Kamba tribes of Kenya Colony*. London: H. F. & G. Witherby.
Holy, L. 1979a. The segmentary lineage structure and its existential status. In *Segmentary lineage systems reconsidered*, ed. L. Holy. Queen's University Papers in Social Anthropology, no. 4.
Holy, L. 1979b. Nuer politics. In *Segmentary lineage systems reconsidered*, ed. L. Holy. Queen's University Papers in Social Anthropology, no. 4.
Howell, P. P. 1947. On the value of iron among the Nuer. *Man* 47:131–34.
Howell, P. P. 1954. *A manual of Nuer law: Being an account of customary law, its evolution and development in the courts established by the Sudan government*. London: Oxford University Press.
Huffman, R. 1931. *Nuer customs and folk-lore*. London: Oxford University Press.
Huntington, R. 1983. Comment on *Reading "The Nuer"* by Karp & Maynard. *Current Anthropology* 24:494.
Jackson, H. C. 1923. The Nuer of the Upper Nile Province. Part 1. *Sudan Notes and Records* 6:59–107.
Jacobs, A. H. 1977. Maasai inter-tribal relations: Belligerent herdsmen or peaceable pastoralists? In *Warfare among East African herders*, ed. K. Fukui and D. Turton. Osaka: National Museum of Ethnology.
Jardine, D. 1923. *The mad mullah of Somaliland*. London: Herbert Jenkins.
Johnson, D. H. 1981. The fighting Nuer: Primary sources and the origins of a stereotype. *Africa* 51:508–28.
Karp, I., and K. Maynard. 1983. Reading The Nuer. *Current Anthropology* 24:481–503.
Karugire, S. R. 1971. *A history of the kingdom of Nkore in western Uganda to 1896*. Oxford: Clarendon Press.
Kelly, R. C. 1985. *The Nuer conquest: The structure and development of an expansionist system*. Ann Arbor: University of Michigan Press.
Kenyatta, J. 1938. *Facing Mount Kenya: The traditional life of the Gikuyu*. London: Heinemann.
Kesby, J. D. 1977. *The cultural regions of East Africa*. London: Academic Press.

Khazanov, A. M. 1978. Characteristic features of nomadic communities in the Eurasian steppes. In *The nomadic alternative*, ed. W. Weissleder. The Hague: Mouton.

Khazanov, A. M. 1981. Myths and paradoxes of nomadism. *Archives of European Sociology* 22:141–53.

Kiggen, J. 1948. *Nuer-English dictionary*. London: St. Joseph's Society for Foreign Missions.

Kirk, J. W. C. 1905. *A grammar of the Somali language, with examples in prose and verse and an account of the Yibir and Midgan dialects*. Cambridge: Cambridge University Press.

Krige, E. J. 1936. *The social system of the Zulus*. Pietermaritzburg: Shuter & Shuter.

Kuper, A. 1982. Lineage theory: A critical retrospect. *Annual Reviews in Anthropology* 11:71–95.

Laitin, D. 1977. *Politics, language, and thought: The Somali experience*. Chicago: University of Chicago Press.

Lambert, H. E. 1956. *Kikuyu social and political institutions*. London: Oxford University Press.

Leakey, L. S. B. 1977. *The southern Kikuyu before 1903*. 3 vols. London: Academic Press.

Lestrade, G. P. 1937. Traditional literature. In *The Bantu-speaking tribes of South Africa*, ed. I. Schapera. London: Routledge & Kegan Paul.

Lewis, B. A. 1972. *The Murle: Red chiefs and black commoners*. Oxford: Clarendon Press.

Lewis, H. S. 1966. The origins of Galla and Somali. *Journal of African History* 7:27–46.

Lewis, I. M. 1955–56. Sufism in Somaliland: A study of tribal Islam. *Bulletin of the School of Oriental and African Studies* 17:581–602; 18:146–60.

Lewis, I. M. 1960. The Somali conquest of the Horn of Africa. *Journal of African History* 1:213–30.

Lewis, I. M. 1961. *A pastoral democracy: A study of pastoralism and politics among the northern Somali of the Horn of Africa*. London: Oxford University Press.

Lewis, I. M. 1965a. Problems in the comparative study of unilineal descent. In *The relevance of models for social anthropology*, A.S.A. Monographs no. 1. London: Tavistock Publications.

Lewis, I. M. 1965b. Shaikhs and warriors in Somaliland. In *African systems of thought*, ed. M. Fortes and G. Dieterlen. London: Oxford University Press.

Lewis, I. M. 1966. Dualism in Somali notions of power. *Journal of the Royal Anthropological Institute* 93:109–16.

Lienhardt, G. 1958. The western Dinka. In *Tribes without rulers*, ed. J. Middleton and D. Tait. London: Routledge & Kegan Paul.

Lienhardt, G. 1961 *Divinity and experience: The religion of the Dinka*. Oxford: Clarendon Press.

Lincoln, B. 1981. *Priests, warriors, and cattle: A study in the ecology of religions*. Berkeley: University of California Press.

Littleton, C. S. 1973. *The new comparative mythology: An anthropological assess-

ment of the theories of Georges Dumézil. Berkeley: University of California Press.

McLaughlin, J. 1967. Tentative time depths for Nuer, Dinka and Anuak. *Journal of Ethiopian Studies* 5:13-27.

Maquet, J. J. 1961. *The premise of inequality in Ruanda: A study of political relations in a Central African kingdom.* London: Oxford University Press.

Maquet, J. J. 1972. *The civilizations of Black Africa.* Trans. J. Rayfield. London: Oxford University Press.

Marks, S., and R. Gray. 1975. Southern Africa and Madagascar. In *The Cambridge history of Africa, from c. 1600 to c. 1790,* ed. R. Gray. Cambridge: Cambridge University Press.

Meeker, M. E. 1979. *Literature and violence in North Arabia.* Cambridge: Cambridge University Press.

Meeker, M. E. 1988. Heroic poems and anti-heroic stories in North Arabia: Literary genres and the relationship of center and periphery in Arabia. *Edebiyat* n.s. 2:1-40.

Meeker, M. E., K. Barlow, and D. M. Lipset. 1986. Culture, exchange, and gender: Lessons from the Murik. *Cultural Anthropology* 1:6-73.

Merker, M. 1910. *Die Masai: Ethnographische Monographie eines ostafrikanischen Semitenvolkes.* Berlin: Dietrich Reimer.

Morris, H. F. 1964. *The heroic recitations of the Bahima of Ankole.* Oxford: Clarendon Press.

Muriuki, G. 1974. *A history of the Kikuyu 1500-1900.* Nairobi: Oxford University Press.

Nebel, A. 1936. *Dinka dictionary with abridged grammar.* Verona: Missioni Africane.

Newcomer, P. J. 1972. The Nuer are Dinka: An essay on origins and environmental determinism. *Man,* n.s. 7:5-11.

Oberg, K. 1940. The kingdom of Ankole in Uganda. In *African political systems,* ed. M. Fortes and E. E. Evans-Pritchard. London: Oxford University Press.

Ogot, B. A. 1967. *History of the southern Luo.* Vol. 1, *Migration and settlement 1500-1900.* Nairobi: East African Publishing House.

Oliver, R. 1977. The East African interior. In *The Cambridge history of Africa,* vol. 3, ed. J. D. Clark. Cambridge: Cambridge University Press.

Oliver, R. 1978. The emergence of Bantu Africa. In *The Cambridge history of Africa,* vol. 2, ed. J. D. Clark. Cambridge: Cambridge University Press.

Omer-Cooper, J. D. 1976. The Nguni outburst. In *The Cambridge history of Africa,* vol. 5, ed. J. D. Clark. Cambridge: Cambridge University Press.

Paulitschke, P. 1896. *Ethnographie nordost-Afrikas: Die geistige Cultur der Danakil, Galla, und Somâl.* Berlin: Dietrich Reimer.

Peters, E. 1960. The proliferation of segments in the lineage of the Bedouin of Cyrenaica. *Journal of the Royal Anthropological Institute* 90:29-53.

Peters, E. 1967. Some structural aspects of the feud among the camel-herding Bedouin of Cyrenaica. *Africa* 37:261-82.

Pettazzoni, R. 1956. *The all-knowing god: Researches into early religion and culture.* London: Camelot Press.

Pettazzoni, R. 1967. *Essays on the history of religions*. Leiden: E. J. Brill.
Rigby, P. J. 1971. The symbolic role of cattle in Gogo ritual. In *The translation of culture: Essays to E. E. Evans-Pritchard*, ed. T. O. Beidelman. London: Tavistock Publications.
Roscoe, J. 1923. *The Banyankole*. Cambridge: Cambridge University Press.
Routledge, W. S., and K. S. Routledge. 1910. *With a prehistoric people: The Akikuyu of British East Africa*. London: Thomas Nelson.
Sahlins, M. 1961. The segmentary lineage: An organisation of predatory expansion. *American Anthropologist* 63:322–45.
Salzman, P. 1978. Does complementary opposition exist? *American Anthropologist* 80:53–70.
Samatar, S. S. 1982. *Oral poetry and Somali nationalism: The case of Sayyid Mahammad Abdille Hasan*. Cambridge: Cambridge University Press.
Schapera, I. 1940. The political organization of the Ngwato of Bechuanaland Protectorate. In *African political systems*, ed. M. Fortes and E. E. Evans-Pritchard. London: Oxford University Press.
Schapera, I. 1953. *The Tswana*. London: International African Institute.
Schapera, I. 1965. *Praise-poems of the Tswana chiefs*. Oxford: Clarendon Press.
Schmidt, W. 1935. *Der Ursprung der Gottesidee: Eine historisch-kritische und positive Studie*. Vol. 6. Münster: Aschendorffsche Verlagshandlung.
Schneider, H. K. 1979. *Livestock and equality in East Africa: The economic basis for social structure*. Bloomington: Indiana University Press.
Seale, M. S. 1974. *The desert Bible: Nomadic tribal culture and Old Testament interpretation*. New York: St. Martin's Press.
Seddon, D. 1979. Political ideologies and political forms in the eastern Rif of Morocco, 1890–1910. In *Segmentary lineage systems reconsidered*, ed. L. Holy. Queen's University Papers in Social Anthropology, no. 4.
Seligman, C. G., and B. Z. Seligman. 1932. *Pagan tribes of the Nilotic Sudan*. London: Routledge & Kegan Paul.
Southall, A. 1976. Nuer and Dinka are people: Ecology, ethnicity, and logical possibility. *Man*, n.s. 11:463–91.
Stubbs, J. M., and C. G. T. Morison. 1938. Land and agriculture of the western Dinka. *Sudan Notes and Records* 21:251–65.
Weber, M. 1958. *The Protestant ethic and the spirit of capitalism*. New York: Charles Scribner.
Wikander, O. S. 1938. *Der Arische Männerbund: Studien zur indo-iranischen Sprach- und Religionsgeschichte*. Lund: Hakan Ohlsson.

Index

Abuk, 51, 52, 55–57, 66, 99, 167*n1*, 168*n2*
Afar, 134
Afro-Asiatic speakers, 171*n22*
Age of Exploration, 131
Age-sets, 116, 119, 121, 178*n21*; absence among Somali, 142; among Kikuyu, 177*n13*; among Maasai, 123–24; among Nuer, 78, 82–86, 89–90, 169*n11*; Dinka, 14, 15, 21–22, 23, 28, 89, 90, 166–67*n5*; Zulu abandonment of, 179*n29*
Agnation, 78, 141; among Dinka, 57–65; among Nuer, 81, 90, 170*n18*
Agriculturalists: Bantu speakers as, 109, 111, 121, 177*n10*; Hutu as, 109, 113; Iru as, 109; Kikuyu as, 178*n19*; Tiv as, 83
Agriculture, 72, 125, 134
Allah, cult of, 154
Alueeth, 9
Americas, 179*n3*
Ancestral ghosts and spirits. *See* Patriarchal ghosts and spirits
Angels, 49
Anthropomorphism, 43, 44, 46, 49, 51, 52, 53, 93, 99, 101, 166*n5*
Arabia, 134, 142, 152–54, 161, 180*n12*, 180*n13*, 181*n22*, 182*n28*
Aryans, 133, 157

Bantu speakers, xiv, xv, 83, 106, 109–11, 119, 130, 121, 124–30, 166*n2*, 172*n3*, 176*n7*, 177*n10*, 177*n11*, 178*n15*, 179*n24*
Bedouins, 152, 154, 161, 171*n19*, 171*n22*, 180*n12*, 180*n13*, 181*n22*, 181*n26*, 182*n28*, 182*n29*
Berbers, 171*n22*

Black Africa, 133, 172*n3*; religions of, 93
Blessings, 142, 180*n8*
Bloodwealth, 139
Bovine idiom, 138
Brideprice, 113, 120
Bridewealth, 11, 12, 20, 72, 126, 139, 165*n4*, 169*n8*
British, 79, 142, 144, 180*n6*, 181*n17*, 182*n24*
Buk, Nuer version of Abuk, 99, 100
Burundi, 108–9, 118, 177*n10*

Calvin, xvi
Camel herding, 134–43, 152–54, 180*n12*, 181*n22*, 182*n28*
Camel raiding, 138–41, 147, 149–50, 152, 153, 180*n13*
Camel standard, 139
Cameloid idiom, 139
Caste, 108–9, 111, 114, 161, 177*n10*
Cattle. *See* Cattle herding; Cattle raiding
Cattle complex, 118, 125, 134, 138, 166*n8*
Cattle herding, xii, xiv, xv, 4, 14, 15, 29, 71, 107, 118, 131, 133, 146, 155, 160, 182*n1*; among Bantu speakers, 106, 110, 124–25, 166*n2*, 172*n3*, 178*n15*, 179*n24*
Cattle raiding, xiii, xiv, 14, 48, 66, 68, chap. 4 *passim*, 92–98, 105–6, 111, 112, 118–24, 128, 133, 150, 156, 160, 161, 169*nn2–3*, 169*n10*, 170*n11*, 170*n12*, 170*n18*, 172*n24*, 175*n4*, 176*n9*, 177*n10*, 177*n13*, 178*n15*, 178*n19*, 179*n29*, 181*n16*, 182*n1*, 183*n7*. *See also* jaang; naath
Central Africa, 179*n24*
Central Asia, 182*n1*
Ceremony, 94, 97, 111, 142, 145, 160

191

Index

Chiefdoms, 110, 111, 118, 125, 126, 179n29. *See also* Kingdoms
Chiefs, 117, 119, 120, 121, 125, 126, 128–29, 145, 166n3, 178n16, 179n27, 179n29, 179n31
Christianity, 31, 49, 153, 172n3
Cieng, 4–5, 7, 25, 76, 97
Circumcision, 122, 181n19
Clan-divinities, 50, 51, 52, 57–67, 91, 92, 94, 95, 98, 99, 100–106, 168n3
Colwic, 101, 102
Commoners among Nuer, 105, 175n16
Compromise of patriarchal authority, xiv, xv, 57, 73, 91, 94, 96, 104, 106, 117, 135, 137, 154
Cosmic patriarchal spirit, xiii–xv, 117, 124, 130, 134, 142, 143, 150, 152, 153, 160, 173n4, 174n5, 180n7, 181n21. *See also* Divinity, among Dinka; God, among Nuer
Court poetry, 176n6
Creation myths, 33–39, 40, 43, 45
Creativity, 44–45, 46, 47, 66, 168n2
Cuong, 97
Curses. *See* Blessings
Cushitic speakers, 31, 93, 109, 124, 134, 139, 172n3, 173n4, 180n7, 181n21

Deng, 51–56, 66, 99–101, 167n6, 168n2
Dervish, 138
Dheeng, 4–5, 7, 76
Dil: Nuer aristocrats, 80–81, 105
Dinka, xiii, chaps. 1–5 *passim*, 110, 118, 134, 135, 141, 160, 165n6, 172n1, 172n3, 172n24, 172n25, 174n6, 177n10, 182n23
Divinities: Indo-European, 157. *See also* Clan-divinities; Free-divinities; Patriarchal ghosts and spirits
Divinity, among Dinka, xiii, 30–48, 49–60, 65, 66, 91, 92–95, 100–106, 166–67n5, 167n7, 168n5; "oneness" of, xiii, 30, 32, 49, 50, 66, 97; and clan-divinities, 50–51, 59–60; and Deng, 53, 54, 101; and free-divinities, 50–51, 103; and Middle Eastern monotheisms, 92; and patriarchal ghosts and spirits, 49, 50–52; anthropomorphism of, 43, 44, 46, 52, 93, 101, 166n5; as creator, 32–38; qualities of, 44, 46–47, 66, 168n2. *See also* Cosmic patriarchal spirit; God, among Nuer
Dynasties, of Hamitic-speaking pastoralists, 111

Ekirahiro, 114, 128, 176n6
Ekyevugo, 114–15, 128, 176n6
Ethiopia, 29, 134, 181n21
Ethnography, xi, 96, 155; of Cushitic speakers, 181n21; of Dinka, xiii, 10, 16, 32, 36, 43, 47, 50, 52, 56, 60, 74, 76, 92; of Kikuyu, 118, 119, 177n14; of Nguni and Sotho, 125; of Nilotic speakers, 70; of Nuer, 66, 74, 76, 77, 78, 82, 83, 86, 90–91, 92, 96, 102, 170n14, 171n20; of Somali, 143
Europe, 156, 179n3, 182n30, 182n1
Europeans, 131, 154

Female spirits, 51
Fetishes, 105, 135, 160, 174n5, 175n16
Feudalism, 109, 110
Feuds, among Nuer lineages, 89
Fighting spear, 94
Fishing spear, 75
Free-divinities, 50–57, 66, 91, 92, 94, 95, 98, 99–100, 103, 167n1, 168n6, 175n14

Gabay, 146, 147, 150–52
Galla, 134, 166n2, 171n22, 172n3, 173n4, 180n5
Gand, 173n4
Garang, 51–52, 55, 56, 66, 99, 167n1, 168n2
Geeraar, 146, 147, 149, 150
Genies, 49
Ghosts and spirits. *See* Patriarchal ghosts and spirits
Goats, 134–36, 139
God, among Nuer, 91, 92–96, 98, 99, 101–6. *See also* Cosmic patriarchal spirit; Divinity, among Dinka

Hamitic-speakers, 109, 110, 111, 173n4
Hebrews, 131, 133, 154, 166n2, 182n31
Heroic recitations, 113, 114, 116, 117, 119, 123, 128, 129, 130, 175n2, 175n3, 175n4, 176n7. *See also* Poetry
Hierarchy, 109, 177n10. *See also* Spiritual hierarchy; State hierarchy

Hima, 109–19, 130, 161, 176n6, 176n7
Homicide, 77, 90, 172n27
Honor, 76, 86, 96, 97, 130, 138
Horn of Africa, 29, 134, 135, 140, 142, 143, 153, 180n5, 180n12
Horse, xv, 134, 138–43, 146–50, 152, 153, 158, 161, 180n13, 181n20, 181n21, 181n22
Hutu, 109, 110, 113, 117
Hymns, xiii, 16, 32, 39–43, 116, 145, 167nn8–9

India, 156
Individualism, xii–xvi, 6, 8, 35–36, 39, 41, 42, 48, 54, 57, 74, 94, 96, 98, 106, 111, 115, 117, 124, 126, 129, 140, 141, 155, 156, 158, 160–61, 167n1, 170n12
Indo-European speakers, 133, 156–58, 173n4, 182n1, 183n3, 183n5, 183n7
Indra, 159, 160
Inheritance, 12, 54, 65, 72
Initiation rites, 5, 14–16, 21–23, 72, 74, 85, 89, 90, 119, 121–24, 142, 179n29, 181n19
Interlacustrine region, 108–9, 111, 179n24
Iru, 109
Islam, 31, 49, 134, 142, 143, 152, 153, 154, 172n3, 181n19, 181n22
Israel, 154

Jaang, "those who are raided," 68, 70–71, 72, 86, 170n18, 181n16. *See also* Naath
Jerusalem, 154
Judaism, 31, 49, 153
Jur. *See* Fetishes

Kenya, 108, 134
Kikuyu, 118–24, 177n11, 177n13, 177n14, 178n15, 178n16, 178n19, 178n21
Kingdoms of East Africa, xii, xv, xvi, 111
Kingship, xii, xv, xvi, 107, 110, 111, 112, 114, 117, 120, 121, 123, 161, 176n9, 177n10
Kinship and marriage, 84–85
Kuth dwanga. *See* Spirits of the air
Kuth piny. *See* Spirits of the earth
Kwoth nhial. *See* God, among Nuer

Language: Dinka, 70, 169n6; Indo-European, 156; Nuer, 70, 169n6

Legal customs, 90, 174n8
Leopard-skin chiefs, 88, 89, 90, 172n27
Lineages, 71, 73, 76–78, 80–90, 99, 101–5, 117–18, 127, 134–37, 141, 142, 154, 171n19, 181n14, 181n15

Maasai, 118–24, 131, 133, 166n2, 172n3, 173n4, 177n13, 178n19, 178n21
Macardit, 51, 52, 54–55, 56, 99
Man of the cattle, 89–90
Marriage, 11, 37, 114, 177n13
Masculine identity, xii, 8, 20–21, 91, 119, 133, 170n15, 177n14
Master of fishing-spear, 88, 89, 90, 94, 172n26
Mecca, 154
Military organization, xv, 14, 15, 84, 85, 89, 112–13, 161, 175n2, 177n13, 178n19, 178n21, 179n29
Mitra, 159, 160
Monotheism, xvi, 31–32, 48–50, 49, 57, 65, 92, 93–94, 98, 102, 105, 131, 133, 142, 143, 153, 154, 166n2, 173n4, 174n5, 181n21
Mother goddess, 166n1
Mother/child relationship, 34–35, 36, 38, 44–45
Mothers, 56, 60, 63
Mugabe. *See* Kingship
Muhammad, 182n31
Mut. *See* War spear
Myths, xiii, 133, 145, 183n1, 183n3, 183n7; Indo-European, 156–58. *See also* Creation myths

Naath, "those who raid," 70–71, 72, 86, 105–6, 170n18, 171n18, 181n16. *See also* Jaang
Nasatya twins, 159
New World, 179n3
Nguni agriculture, 124–30, 178n15
Nhialic. *See* Divinity, among Dinka
Nilotic speakers, xv, 31, 70, 71, 77, 83, 90, 93, 107, 109, 110, 118, 121, 123, 124, 127, 131, 133, 138, 139, 172n3, 173n4, 176n7, 179n2
Nkore, 109, 111–23, 161, 175n2, 175n4, 177n10
Nomadism, 125, 153, 154, 180n6, 181n14, 182n31

North Africa, 171n19, 181n14
Nuer, chaps. 4-5 passim, xiii, 57, 97, 99, 100, 101, 110, 134, 135, 141, 160, 167n9, 169n6, 172n1, 174n10, 181n17, 182n23

Oedipal conflict, 12, 13, 20
Old Testament, 93, 154, 172n3, 182n32
Old World, xiv, xv, 133, 134, 135, 141, 143, 154, 155, 161, 179n3
Oral tradition, 143, 182n23, 182n32
Oratory, 143-45, 152, 182n24

Pastoral ecology, xii, xiii, xiv, xv, 165n5, 177n10, 179n2, 179n24, 180n4, 180n6, 180n12, 181n21, 181n22, 182n31, 182n32; among Bantu speakers, 106, 108-11; among Dinka, 4, 16, 25, 27, 65, 67, 107, 121-22; among Indo-European speakers, 156, 158, 160-61; among Kikuyu, 118, 121, 124; among Maasai, 178n19; among Nguni and Sotho, 126, 128, 129, 130; among Nuer, 78, 83, 85, 86, 96, 107, 121-22; among Somali, 133-38, 142, 143, 152, 154; in Nkore, 111, 112, 117, 118
Patriarchal ascendants, 29, 91, 99, 180n8
Patriarchal ghosts and spirits, xii, xiii, xv, 29, 31-32, 45, 48, 49, 50-52, 53, 57, 66, 93, 94, 99, 101, 102, 106, 124, 130, 135, 152, 160, 180n8
Patrilineal descent groups, 57, 58, 81-87
Personality ox, 4-9, 16-20, 25, 26, 27, 30, 35, 42, 74, 75, 116, 140, 165n1, 165n2
Plain song, Hima, 175n3
Poetry, xi, 113, 115, 116, 117, 128-29, 143-46, 152, 177n9, 182n25, 182n27, 182n28. See also Praise poetry; Self-representation; Songs
Polytheism, 153, 181n21
Praise poetry, 126-30, 176n7, 178n15, 179n27, 179n31. See also Poetry; Songs
Prayer, 94, 98, 174n6. See also Ceremony
Predestination, xvi
Priest: Dinka, 39, 40, 45, 50, 58, 88-89, 90, 94, 95, 97, 166n3; Indo-Iranian, 133, 156, 158; Nuer, 88-89, 90, 94, 174n6
Priestly clans: Dinka, 58, 168n3; Indo-European, 156

Prophets, xvi, 52, 53, 55, 172n26, 174n6, 181n17
Protestants, xv
Proto-Indo-European, 156

Rang: Nuer version of Garang, 99
Rebellion of Dinka youths, 18, 20, 65, 150
Recitations. See Heroic recitations
Religion: Bantu speakers, xiv, 106, 124; Black Africa, 93, 173n3; Celtic, 156; Cushitic speakers, 31, 93, 173n3, 180n7; Galla, 173nn3, 4; Greek, 156; Hima, 117; Indo-Iranian, 156; Italic, 156; Middle Eastern, 173n3; Nilotic speakers, 31, 88, 93, 179n2; Old Testament, 173n3; pastoralists, xii, 29; pre-Islamic, 180n7; Somali men, 142, 180n8; Somali, xv, 173n3, 173n4
Rhetoric, 139
Rul. See Commoners among Nuer
Rwanda, 108-9, 110, 118, 175n1, 176n8, 176n9, 177n10

Saho, 134
Saint worship, 49, 102, 180n8
Secularism: of Nuer as opposed to Dinka, 88
Secularization, 91, 94, 95, 97, 98, 130, 142, 143, 160
Segmentary lineage theory, 83, 170n16, 171n22, 181n15
Segmentary principle, xiv, xv, 65, 78-91, 105, 106, 118, 124, 135, 141, 142, 152, 170n15, 171n19, 171n22, 172n22, 181n14
Self-representation, xiii, 6, 7, 9, 15, 17-20, 26, 27, 30-48, 46-47, 54, 74, 114-15, 119, 122, 123, 127, 128, 135, 145, 161, 167n8, 167n10, 178n15. See also Poetry; Praise poetry; Songs
Semitic speakers, 173n4
Serfs, 109
Sheep: among Kikuyu, 118; among Somali, 134, 135, 136, 139
Sociability, xiv, 5, 77
Social controls, 3, 4, 6, 7, 10, 11-12, 20, 22
Somali, xv, chap. 7 passim, 161
Songs, xiii, 6-10, 15-28, 30, 37, 39-42, 46, 56, 74, 115, 116, 117, 119, 122,

123, 127, 130, 139, 144, 145, 146, 148–50, 152, 167*n*8, 167*n*9, 170*n*12, 175*n*14, 176*n*7, 178*n*15
Sotho, 124, 125, 126, 128, 130, 176*n*7, 178*n*15, 179*n*29
Spear, 105, 113, 137. See also Fighting spear; Fishing spear
Spirits of the air, 94, 99–105, 174*n*9, 174*n*12, 175*n*13
Spirits of the bush, 173*n*4
Spirits of the earth, 94, 100–104, 174*n*12, 175*n*13
Spiritual hierarchy, 102–5, 174*n*12, 175*n*13
Spiritual power: of Dinka father, xiv, 88; of Dinka Divinity, 50, 52, 56
State, 108–9, 110, 175*n*1, 177*n*10
State hierarchy, 112, 117, 145
Stock keepers. See Cattle herding; Camel herding
Sudan, 29
Sultanates, 134, 142

Tanzania, 108
Tarikats, 142, 154, 181*n*17
Tiv, 83
Totems, 58, 64, 66, 100, 101, 103, 104, 105, 168*n*5, 174*n*5
Trade, 134, 142, 153, 180*n*6
Tripartite ideology, xv, 156–61, 183*n*4
Tsonga: praise poetry of, 127
Tutsi, 108–10, 176*n*6, 176*n*8, 176*n*9

Uganda, 108
Ugro-Finnic speakers, 173*n*4
Ural-Altaic speakers, 173*n*4
Urmonotheismus, 173*n*4

Varuna, 159, 160
Vayu, 159, 160
Venda, 127

War spear, 74, 75, 76
Warfare, 70, 72, 114, 137, 138, 141, 142, 147, 150, 152, 153, 161, 175*n*3, 175*n*4, 177*n*13, 178*n*21, 179*n*29
Warrior clans: Dinka, 58, 168*n*3
Warrior divinities: Indo-European, 158–60, 161
Warrior function: Indo-European, 156, 159
Witchcraft, 172*n*3, 173*n*4
Women, 4, 11–12; among Somali, 135; and Abuk, 52, 57; and agriculture, 125; and clan-divinities, 59, 61; and Macardit, 54–55; and pastoral ecology, 25; and praise poetry, 127; in Hima plain song, 175*n*3; songs, 16, 25–26, 56, 146

Yahweh, 133, 154, 166*n*2, 182*n*31
Yeeth. See Patriarchal ghosts and spirits
Yemenis, 171*n*22

Zulu, 125, 179*n*29